THE WORLD VIEW OF BEROALDE DE VERVILLE

(Expressed through satirical baroque style in *Le moyen de parvenir*)

DE PÉTRARQUE A DESCARTES
Directeur : Pierre MESNARD
XXIII

THE WORLD VIEW OF BEROALDE DE VERVILLE

(Expressed through satirical baroque style in *Le moyen de parvenir*)

By

Janis L. PALLISTER, Ph. D.
Bowling Green State University

PARIS
LIBRAIRIE PHILOSOPHIQUE J. VRIN
6, Place de la Sorbonne Ve
—
1971

Printed in France

Je te veux enseigner un autre poinct notable :
Pour ce que de la court l'eschole c'est la table,
Si tu veux promptement en honneur parvenir,
C'est où plus sagement il te fault maintenir.
Il fault avoir tousjours le petit mot pour rire,
Il fault des lieux communs, qu'à tous propos on tire,
Passer ce qu'on ne sçait et se monstrer sçavant
En ce que l'on a leu deux ou trois soirs devant.

DU BELLAY : *Le poète courtisan.*

To : Professor Armand A. Renaud,
with my gratitude.

INTRODUCTION

The primary intention of this study is to examine particular features of Béroalde de Verville's *Le Moyen de Parvenir* with the object of disengaging the baroque world view of the author and of arriving at a new evaluation of this late sixteenth or early seventeenth century « novel ». It is true that problems such as the exact dating and authorship of this work exist, and it is one of the aims of this study to assist in at least one of these, the authorship. To this end, certain works known to be Béroalde de Verville's will be brought forth and juxtaposed to *Le Moyen de Parvenir* as extra-textual and consequently non-conclusive but nonetheless convincing evidence of his authorship of *Le Moyen de Parvenir.*

However, always with the objective of gaining insight into Béroalde's world view, the true procedure of this monograph will be to examine certain topographical and textual features of *Le Moyen de Parvenir* and to underline and explore the apparent theological and philosophical points of departure as well as the satirical focuses of the book. In so doing, it will be necessary to bear in mind constantly the fact that *Le Moyen de Parvenir* presents the kind of multiplicity which is characteristic of baroque sensibility and style. For this reason, I have reserved a final chapter for considerations on the style of *Le Moyen de Parvenir,* intending to outline there the stylistic features which we may term *baroque satyrique* — a form of baroque involving the grotesque and the erotic — which in turn unfold into a broader stylistic channel which it seems proper to call *baroque satirique,* or satirical baroque. Through an analysis of the style I also expect to strengthen and reconstruct my earlier demonstrations of the book's baroque character and of the author's baroque world view. At times it will therefore be necessary in the very discussion of a philosophical question to consider, at least in passing, and at that given moment, the style. I have therefore neither thought it profitable nor wise to set controls on this study which would bring about total and absolute separation of the satirical focuses from the style, the style from theological and philosophical points of departure, and the like.

This should not lead one to think, however, that I propose to subject the reader to a completely disorganized discussion of *Le Moyen de Parvenir.* Prolonged examination of the text has led me to hold it in too great respect to indulge in any more chaotic exigesis of these theories than I can prevent. *Le Moyen de Parvenir,* a « novel » largely in dialogue form, is an exceptionally difficult and disorderly book — for a purpose — and orderly discussion of it presents a challenge.

Furthermore, even the editions we presently have pose special problems, for if we are to use the Paul Lacroix edition [1], we are probably confronted with a good many textual errors and certainly with a number of mercurial and unreliable footnotes and commentaries on the text and on the interlocutors. On the other hand, if we use the Royer edition [2], we are confronted with outdated typography, scanty annotations, confusions arising from the end-to-end dialogues, the whimsical punctuation, etc. Of the some thirty-two editions of the novel, I have chosen that of Royer as the most scholarly to date, and in the spirit of a work of this genre, I have decided to adhere closely to the original text, but it is obvious that the work would profit from a careful critical edition. It is, in fact, my ambition to prepare this sorely needed text one day. For the time being, however, let us confine ourselves to the directions that this particular study will take, despite the text, and despite the disorderly nature of the work itself.

As a prefatory remark, I should like to indicate that biographical sketches of Béroalde may be found in the *notice* of Royer at the beginning of his edition of *Le Moyen de Parvenir* (I, x-xxx), in the *notice* preceding Paul Lacroix's edition of *Le Moyen de Parvenir* [3], in Niceron's *Memoires* [4], and especially in Saulnier's *Etude* [5], so that the details of the

1. François Béroalde de Verville, *Le Moyen de Parvenir,* ed. Paul Jacob, i.e., Paul Lacroix (Paris, 1889). Hereafter cited in the footnotes as Paul Lacroix.

2. François Béroalde de Verville, *Le Moyen de Parvenir,* ed. Charles Royer (Paris, 1896). Hereafter cited in the body of the text by volume and page number.

3. Paul Lacroix, pp. xv-xxiv.

4. R.P. Niceron, *Mémoires pour servir à l'histoire des Hommes illustres dans la république des lettres* (Paris, 1736), tome XXXIV, pp. 224-238.

5. V.-L. Saulnier, « Étude sur Béroalde de Verville », *Revue d'Humanisme et Renaissance,* V (1944), pp. 210-239.

author's life need not be repeated here. Furthermore, lists of works known to be Béroalde's are found in most of these same references, so that it is superfluous to reproduce that material here.

It is, however, essential that we stop at this juncture to describe this curious work. Béroalde de Verville's *Le Moyen de Parvenir,* dated at about 1610[6], is a « novel » in dialogue form with a framework in which a narrator, whom we shall have reason to discuss in some detail, tells of the circumstances which have brought together a group of three hundred distinguished guests, almost all with names of real people both living and dead, at a huge symposium which takes place at the home of the amphitryon, the mysterious Bonhomme Se puisse tuer.[7] The group, convoked by Madame Sophie, and presided over by La Bonne Intention, indulges in prodigious drinking and eating, and proceeds to tell one another stories of an exceptionally ribald nature. As a consequence we have a collection of tales in the genre of *The Canterbury Tales,* the *Decameron, Les Cent Nouvelles Nouvelles,* Marguerite de Navarre's *Heptaméron,* Bouchet's *Les Serrées* and in the tone of any of these or of Rabelais, though perhaps even racier.

Of *Le Moyen de Parvenir* Paul Lacroix writes:

> L'idée générale du *Moyen de Parvenir* est assez bien rendue dans ces lignes de La Monnoye : « L'auteur y suppose une espèce de festin général, où, sans conséquence pour les rangs, il introduit des gens de toute condition et de tout siècle, savants la plupart, qui, n'étant là que pour se divertir, causent de tout en liberté, et, par des liaisons imperceptibles, passant d'une matière à une autre, font des contes à perte de vue... Cet ouvrage est une représentation naïve des conversations ordinaires : que trois ou quatre personnes s'entretiennent familièrement, elles parleront insensiblement de mille choses différentes, sans s'apercevoir de la différence des sujets. » Mais La Monnoye n'a pas soupçonné que Béroalde n'avait admis

6. The date of *Le Moyen de Parvenir* is a separate problem which I shall not deal with in this study. See on this subject Saulnier, *ibid.,* p. 284, and also E.-H. Clouzot, « La Date du *Moyen de parvenir* », *Revue des Etudes Rabelésiennes,* IX (1911), pp. 141-143.

7. Compare in Régnier's Satire X (« Le Souper ridicule ») the presence of the amphitryon or unidentified host designated as « Monsieur ».

> au *sympose* du *Moyen de Parvenir* que des philosophes qui s'étaient distingués dans l'étude des sciences métaphysiques, physiques ou morales, et qui pouvaient être à divers titres les convives de la *Sophie* ou de la *Sagesse;* il n'a pas deviné davantage que Béroalde avait caché ses contemporains, et sans doute ses amis, sous les noms des hommes illustres anciens, avec lesquels ils offraient quelque analogie de travaux, de caractère ou d'idées.[8]

There may, of course, be some truth in what Paul Lacroix says of the identity of the interlocutors, and yet, due to the fact that there is no relationship between the tale told and the person doing the telling, due to occasional distortions in the spelling of names, due to anagrams (e.g., Aillol = Loyola?), due to abbreviations of names and the use of initials, in short due to many factors, almost anything one can say about the interlocutors must remain in the realm of speculation. As it would not be of any great advantage to us to explore this aspect of *Le Moyen de Parvenir* in an effort to disengage the world view reflected in its pages, we shall content ourselves with saying from the outstart that while the names ascribed to the interlocutors do reflect possible theological, scientific and philosophical satire, and while these names afford anachronistic and satirical effects that contribute to the over-all humor of the book, no case shall be specifically built around them, since almost every theory one can evolve concerning them is rather easily exploded by some contradiction or conflicting theory. This is perhaps their very secret. In any event, Saulnier has aptly written of this matter:

> Comme dans la *Turba,* les noms des convives sont distribués au petit bonheur. Quant à chercher l'identité de *Madame* et du *Bon homme,* c'est perdre son temps. Qu'on dise si l'on veut que le Bonhomme est Béroalde et Madame la philosophie : on n'en sera pas beaucoup plus avancé. Les mots même dont on a vu Béroalde désigner Madame sont bien faits pour piquer la curiosité du lecteur, l'engager à telle recherche. Mais dans ce roman d'humour, plus on nous engage sur une piste, plus nous devons mesurer nos pas (que l'on songe plutôt à *Jacques le Fataliste,* de Diderot). Au surplus, dans la mesure où

8. Paul Lacroix, pp. xxv-xxvi.

> ces personnages du Bonhomme et de Madame dépasseraient la supercherie pour représenter des symboles, il devient d'autant plus inutile de leur quérir une identité : de même que pour le *Grand Courbe* du *Peer Gynt* d'Ibsen ou la *Bouche d'Ombre* de Hugo; le symbole est ici le contraire de l'allégorie.[9]

Be this as it may, *Le Moyen de Parvenir* has been very little studied over the centuries, not so much because of the obscurities of text, but partly because of its scatalogical content, and, in some measure, because of its shocking disregard of the laws and doctrines of the church, both of which give to the totality of the work a libertine flavor. Nevertheless, *Le Moyen de Parvenir,* though a *livre de haute graisse,* is a masterpiece of baroque literature and deserving of our attention for the insights it affords us into a baroque world view, the baroque mentality, so to speak, and into satirical baroque style, a field relatively unexplored. It is this mentality as it unfolds in the content and form of the novel which I propose to examine in these pages.

Now although the biography of Béroalde along with a listing of his works is superfluous to this end, and although the precise date of *Le Moyen de Parvenir* and a detailed analysis of the names of its interlocutors will not contribute substantially to this objective, an examination of certain of Béroalde's other works will afford us something of the same world view to be found in *Le Moyen de Parvenir.* In his *Dialogue de la Vertu,* for instance, we find the nascent *raconteur* Béroalde will become; we find his urbanity, also to be detected elsewhere. And in some of Béroalde's poems we can discover a marked raciness which announces *Le Moyen de Parvenir.* Of course, the end result of such an examination is a non-conclusive but, even so, convincing argument for Béroalde as the author of *Le Moyen de Parvenir,* a matter which has off and on been disputed.

Immediately upon turning to the title page of *Le Moyen de Parvenir* proper, however, we find innumerable factors which, especially when related to the text, tell us a great deal about the *Weltanschauung* of the author. The time motifs, of baroque inspiration, and, to some extent, the eroticism to be found in the novel are already present on the title page, and hints of the religious satire rampant in the book can be detected. All

9. Saulnier, p. 296.

in all, the parody of religious and erudite practices is underway.

Similarly, a minute analysis of the title, accompanied by pertinent passages in the text and serving as a prelude to the study of the major themes of time and mutability, provides us with ample evidence of Béroalde's intentions and with new insights into the attitudes of this complex mind. In this lengthy analysis of the title, whose main objective is, through internal evidence, to seek out the title's meaning, the reader's patience is enlisted; for while it may seem a long and arduous examination, each thought presented may help us to unravel the mysteries of the book and lead us to an appreciation of the richness of the text. For example, through such an analysis, we can infer still more about the religious satire of *Le Moyen de Parvenir*, and can conclude that the title is integrally tied to this satire. Furthermore, the themes of time, mutability, and death are grounded in the title, all of them recurrent themes in the novel.

Next, in our effort to disengage from *Le Moyen de Parvenir* the world view of its author, we will undertake a close analysis in a modified *explication de texte* manner of the opening quatrain and of the first and last chapters of the novel. Here again, dominating the scene, we find the themes of time, mutability and death, so characteristic of baroque literature. We also find again religious satire, satire of manners, and we discover, especially through the final chapter, to what an extent the novel belongs to the genre of irrational literature, a thing suggested already by the title.

After an examination of the title page, the title proper, the first and last chapters, we move to the second and the succeeding chapters of *Le Moyen de Parvenir* to inspect above all the chapter titles, always with the aim of arriving at an assessment of the author's baroque mentality. Here our efforts are especially rewarding, for the chapter titles present a complexity and an ambiguity especially associated with baroque art. They perform a range of tasks from ornament to ligature, and from emphasizing to reiterating theme and satirical intention. Though many things considered in connection with them are of a stylistic order, I have preferred to treat their stylistic and thematic functions in one unit, so that one might more readily see the entire gamut of services which they perform. Considerations on the chapter titles are adjacent to considerations on the style because of their close connection with it. Yet their thematic implications make of them a separate problem.

In a sense, the chapter titles are a link between theme and style, content and form.

Love of language and verbal somersault abound in *Le Moyen de Parvenir.* This is a characteristic which Béroalde shares with one of his indisputable masters, Rabelais, whose presence is empirically felt in *Le Moyen de Parvenir* and whose influence on certain tales has been established by Herbert Reiche in his *Le Moyen de parvenir von Béroalde de Verville mit besonderer Berücksichtigung der Quellen- und Verfasserfrage.* In our study on the style of *Le Moyen de Parvenir,* however, we will want to establish what in the novel particularly gives it a baroque stamp, and what in the style contributes to a specifically baroque world view. To accomplish this, I have chosen to set *Le Moyen de Parvenir* against the categories of the baroque designated by Buffum in his *Studies in the Baroque from Montaigne to Rotrou.* We shall move through these categories to a statement on what, ultimately, constitutes the unity of the novel, despite its rich complexity; and, finally, we shall see how, despite its apparent cynicism and its thoroughgoing satire in almost every domain, *Le Moyen de Parvenir* preaches a doctrine of laughter and, in general, an acceptance of life.

CHAPTER I

AUTHORSHIP

Although some writers have sought to deny Béroalde's authorship of *Le Moyen de Parvenir,* saying that it is nothing like his other works, which are, according to them, boring and tedious [1], I personally do not feel, from what I have been able to obtain and to read, that the *Weltanschauung* of *Le Moyen de Parvenir* is at great variance with Béroalde's poetry and other prose. It is true that the latter is by and large sober in tone, but it will compare in various ways with *Le Moyen de Parvenir,* both in content and in spirit. Besides, such other work as I have read of Béroalde seems to show him to be in the main an accomplished writer.

For example, the nascent *raconteur* which Béroalde turns out to be in *Le Moyen de Parvenir* is certainly seen in the *historiette* which, vaguely lascivious in the final analysis, is tagged onto his *Dialogue de la Vertu.* [2] The story is intended to serve, as the lady in the dialogue states, as a type of *exemplum.* After much long and rather turgid discussion of the true nature of virtue, Béroalde has his lady, who carries the burden of the conversation (to use the word « conversation » loosely), tell a tale designed to illustrate the difference between virtue and vice. The latter, she feels, emanates from the assertion of human will.

> Il n'y a pas long temps qu'en la maison d'un prince françois, où la courtoisie s'observait avec autant de diligence qu'en lieu du monde, fréquentoit une dame du pais, laquelle tant pour sa beauté que ses vertus, aquit

1. V.-L. Saulnier, « Etude sur Béroalde de Verville », *Bibliothèque d'Humanisme et Renaissance,* V (1944), pp. 210 and 240.
2. François Béroalde de Verville, *Dialogue de la Vertu* (à Paris, pour Timothee Jouan), pp. 1-24 v°.

la bonne grace & le courage de chascun qui la voyait : en mesme lieu & saison hantoit aussi un chevalier tres honneste entre ceux qui font profession d'estre un peu plus que le vulgaire des gentilshommes, qui ne tient conte de se polir, cetuy-cy combien que jeune, avoit le cœur assis en si bon lieu, qu'il n'avoit autre deliberation que si d'aventure il s'affectionnoit de quelque chose, il asserroit son amitié en tel lieu qu'il auroit occasion de se trouver contant, au moins en ses desirs en quelque façon qu'ils puissent reussir : & pourtant la fortune se presentant qu'un jour il entretint cette dame, de laquelle les discours ne tendoient qu'a la vertu, il sentit en soy quelque emotion non accoustumee, qui le faisoit souhaiter pour l'amour d'elle je ne sçay quoy qui ne se peut exprimer, autre toutesfois que le feu, qui allumant le cœur de desirs impudiques ou tendans à une fin commune, ne suit que le contentement passable, en cette pensee s'estans retiré ainsi que l'honnesteté le veut, recherchant à parsoy la cause de ce qu'il sentoit, cognut à peu pres ce que s'en estoit, & partant deslors resolut de servir non cette vaine beauté, non ce discours artificiel, non cette grace, non cette douceur aparente qui a pouvoir sur tous : mais cette image de vertu dont l'idee avoit esté imprimee en son cœur & ce qu'il avoit veu d'excellent en cette dame, à laquelle une fois ainsi qu'ils devisoient de l'amitié, il fit protestation de demeurer eternel serviteur. Elle qui estoit sage, ne desirant ceste commune practique courtisanne qui n'a rien que du fard, voulut sçavoir le but de ses intentions, pource qu'il ne luy venoit point à dedain d'estre servie, aymee et honnoree d'un gentilhomme tant accompli (aussi les Dames n'ont pour tout bien en ce monde que l'honneur & l'amitié qu'on leur porte) & ainsi le mettant en ce discours recognut que la seule vertu, selon que les sujets la practiquent, estoit son intention & esperance, ce qu'estimoit à bon droit le premier entre tous, si ce n'estoit que je veux passer en bref, pource que les umbres de la nuict commencent a empescher nos yeux de voir la lumiere, je dirois les arrests de leur loix d'amitié fondees sur la vertu, & fidelité, cymant des affections veritables, maisme contentant de vous raconter l'histoire simple, je passeray outre, cependant l'un et l'autre satisfais de leur affection mutuelle, se donnoyent du plaisir en leur parti-

> culiers contentements, tant qu'une fois la fortune leur donna quelque ennuy par d'autres qui seuls en fin en partirent, portant le faix de leur impieté. Un conte fort adroit ayant toute sa vie practiqué l'amour & s'en estant contenté s'adressa à ceste dame qui de premier front voyant l'ouvertture de ses propos tomber sur la vertu, comme ordinairement il se void mesmes entre les plus impudiques, ne le rejetta du tout : mais finalement voyant que ce qu'il desiroit estoit contre la vertu, apres luy avoir permis sa frequentation plus d'un an, conservant estroitement l'amitié du premier, l'estrangea d'elle, luy remonstrant qu'il ne faut pas qu'un amy demande de celle qui luy fait part de sa bonne grace, ce que la vertu deffent, & par le moyen de quoy le donnant se monstrat infidele à soy mesme, & par raison sans fidelité à celluy auquel elle se monsteroit trop prodigue : cet eslognement fut effectué avec beaucoup de propos fascheux, cause que le miserable gentil-homme qui en aymoit un autre dont il avoit eu bonne part, se retira non sans luy faire paroistre, ce qui fut cause de son malheur : car elle indignee se voyant trompee par celuy qui, avec mille protestations, l'avoit acquise, se saisit de douleur, & de fortune, pource qu'elle estoit grosse, s'estant tourmentee sentir les dernieres douleurs qui la contraignant se laisser aller aux efforts de la mort, terminerent les miseres de sa vie, donnant à son amy occasion de se retirer pour comblé de malheur se lamenter avec mille amers regrets, sans que jamais l'espoir de mieux l'ait peu alleger. Ainsi achevant ses miserables jours, fable de chascun, fut un exemple d'un abandonné à ses volontez vicieuses, au contraire que les deux autres vescurent contans en leurs ames, tant que le ciel favorisant à leurs chastes desseins, sentirent en fin la juste recompense de leurs vertus (pp. 22 v° - 24 v°).

Even leaving aside the story element as such, we note that the lady telling the story is, as we might expect from the title, « sage », that the *exemplum* is merely a tag to a long dialogue in which are expressed many notions concerning the need to stifle the will and to exercise the reason, or else to fail to undertake that which is « séant », or which helps us onto the right road to virtue. For this we have need of divine providence (p. 15). It will suit our purposes to observe that the *historiette* is couched in a dialogue form; that it has, in other words, a frame; that the story itself is swift, and that it is reminiscent of the type of sentimental tale described by Reynier as being in the taste of the times.[3] Stylistically, it is not utterly out of keeping with *Le Moyen de Parvenir.* Note, for example, the use of hyperbole, just above in the sentence: « ...jamais l'espoir de mieux l'ait peu alleger. » The dialogue contains a very striking baroque image, too, which is advantageously quoted. The question of *prudence* is at hand: « ...bref elle fait que tousiours semblables à nous mesmes nous persistions en la belle egalité que le monde, & sur tout les plus equitables, prisent à bon droit le plus, rendant de nous un tesmoignage selon la verité sans fraude : aussi repousse elle tellement le vice, qu'il s'escoulle devant elle comme une eau qui n'a autre source qu'un petit amas de nege, qui fonde en s'esvanouissant aux premieres ardeurs d'un esté qui la surprennent » (p. 16 v°).

Other examples of hyperbole and baroque imagery can be found (e.g. pp. 19 r° and 21 v°), but what seems to me even more important in this « Dialogue » is the frequent use of the words « moyen » and « parvenir »: it is a question in the dialogue of how one may succeed in attaining virtue, and of the right way (« moyen »). One can, of course, as in the *exemplum,* make mistakes. The point of departure and the *exemplum,* with this concept of the « moyen de parvenir », make one think of the « carte du tendre ». The expression « & par le moyen de quoy... » found towards the end of the text of the *historiette* is noteworthy, as is the following selection in which I have underlined two particularly striking features:

> Or il n'y a rien de tel que la vertu, & l'esprit, parquoy l'esprit doit chercher son bien en la vertu, affin que satisfait en soy mesme, il jouisse du bien de son attente. Voila donc ce qu'il se faut proposer : Mais *pour y pouvoir parvenir* avec plus de facilité, il convient sçavoir que cest que la vertu ses parties ou ce que l'on nomme ainsi en elle pour ces differens effaits & grandeur, & ce qu'elle peut, afin que l'entendant on s'i joigne non à

3. Gustave Reynier, *Le Roman sentimental avant l'Astrée* (Paris, 1908). It would be difficult to give an exact page reference for this statement. Reynier's whole discussion of the sentimental novel, especially its platonic development into which the insistence upon chaste love enters, is involved here.

> la volee, car possible au lieu du vray *le faux* se rencontreroit (pp. 5 v° - 6).

One may pause on the word « faux », since wherever one turns in Béroalde's work, I am convinced he will find under attack false values, be they affectations or mannerisms. It seems to me that this attitude is at the very core of *Le Moyen de Parvenir.* I also bring to bear the following quote from the same dialogue:

> Chascun voulant imiter la verité de nos pensees despeintes par vos beaux discours, proteste ordinairement telles choses, *mais on n'a pas le moyen de parvenir à l'effait apres la cognoissance,* qui fait que plein de perpetuels desirs je deplore la misere qui nous ayant attains nous oppresse miserablement, si que la seule apparence est nostre bonheur, & possible qu'il en est autant tousjours, & que la vertu tant prisee n'est que comme un air delicatement esmeu, qui par la juste proportion des accords heureusement assemblez se conduit à quelque grace, & donne plaisir pour le moment qu'il occupe, puis s'eslevant aussi soudain qu'il cesse, emporte le contentement qu'il causoit sans toucher autrement l'ame (p. 7 r°).

The underscored passage in the above text is as striking as the one following, taken from page 8 v°, where the function of the will is being discussed: « *...la volonté suffit, pour parvenir à la vertu,* estant d'une mesme nature, & suivant semblable but. »

Once more we come across this terminology on page 9 v°, when the gentlemen says, in response to the lady's argument that virtue is a thing we strive for, and that desire for virtue is the prime virtue: « S'il le faut prendre exactement comme vous le voulez, *ie pense qu'il n'est pas possible de parvenir à la moindre partie de cette perfection,* tant desiree de ceux qui pour tendre à la vertu se disent vertueux, & *qu'il est impossible d'y parvenir.* » Again I have underscored the important vocabulary, as in the following pronouncement of the Gentilhomme, taken from p. 13: « Ordinairement on appelle entendus ceux qui alors font que leurs desirs succedent, & que par une dexterité dont ils sçavent user, ils tirent à fin ce qu'ils ont en deliberation : ce qui se cognoist autant au vicieux qu'au vertueux, *car celuy qui par une longue deliberation excogitera le moyen de parvenir au but de ses desseins, se poussera continuellement à l'execution d'iceux,* & s'il avient qu'il jouisse de ses desirs, il sera estimé entendu. » All these underscored passages and concepts of that which is « séant » and the role of reason should, I believe, be set against the title and the sub-title of *Le Moyen de Parvenir.* They should also be related, to my way of thinking, to Hatzfeld's idea that a baroque piece of literature is deeply concerned with Aristotelian ethics [4]; but the relationship of *Le Moyen de Parvenir* to Mr. Hatzfeld's theories is more complex and possibly moot. In any case, the moral point of view of *Le Moyen de Parvenir* will be dealt with later.

The last comment I wish to make on the *Dialogue de la Vertu* is that it is eminently urbane in its tone, so much so that one cannot help but think of the dialogues of Fontenelle, in which the same type of weighty conversation between lady and gentleman takes place beneath a starry sky, all in the name of « science ».

Now it is not only in the *Dialogue de la Vertu* that we find this urbane tone, supporting Béroalde as the author of *Le Moyen de Parvenir.* Humor and content in the licentious vein, as well as urbanity, are to be found in several other works. Indeed, to follow Reynier, this latter is the order of the day; for, despite or perhaps because of the unstable political situation of the period, the salon life was well underway, and Béroalde was fully in its midst:

> Un texte peu connu de Béroalde de Verville nous montre que même en 1583 (c'est la date de son Dialogue de la Bonne Grace), c'est-à-dire au lendemain de la septième guerre de religion, il y a encore des assemblées de gentilshommes et de dames. Il en décrit une qui s'est tenu récemment dans un château, « l'importunité de l'hyver s'estant retiree » : « Or comme ordinairement ès compagnies où la modestie regne, ceux et celles qui aiment la vertu, au lieu de s'amuser à passer le temps aux plus mondaines vanitez, se delectent à recognoistre ce qui est plus propre à la personne qui suit l'honnesteté, les uns se mirent à jouer selon que le temps le permettoit, les autres tant Gentilshommes que Damoiselles entrerent en

4. Helmut Hatzfeld, « A Clarification of the Baroque Problem in the Romance Literatures », *Comparative Literature,* I (1949), pp. 113-139.

devis de tout ce qui coustumierement se dit en tels lieux par familiers discours. »[5]

Reynier again comes to our assistance to testify the importance of salon life in Béroalde's time, and, further, in his own mind: « Béroalde de Verville écrit dès 1596 : Il n'y aura pas de plaisir si parfait que d'estre en bonne compaignie..., où la modestie regne et les Dames aiment la vertu, avec lesquelles il y a plus de contentement qu'entre celles qui passent leur temps au plus mondaines vanités. »[6]

This urbanity, the salon tendencies, and the like, are, it is obvious, connected with the rising influence of women; and the penetration into literature of neoplatonic theories is certainly allied. No doubt it was because of the ladies of the nobility that the course of neo-platonism was not interrupted entirely by the civil wars, even in the time of the Ligue: so reasons Reynier.

The whole « querelle des femmes » is doubtless involved here, and I shall later have reason to refer to its role in *Le Moyen de Parvenir.* In the meanwhile, the following quote from Reynier rapidly reviews the history and the contemporary state of these complicated affairs for us:

> On sait combien sont lointaines les origines de cette querelle des femmes qui est presque devenue en France — comme en Italie — un genre littéraire. Nous n'avons pas à en suivre l'histoire, depuis *le Roman de la Rose,* dont les deux parties, sur ce point comme sur tant d'autres s'opposent, depuis le livre de Matheolus ou depuis les *XV Joies de Mariage.* Rappelons que jusqu'aux environs de 1540 entre les deux partis dont l'un représente la tradition courtoise, l'autre le réalisme bourgeois, c'est le second qui paraît garder l'avantage : l'ouvrage qui semble clore cette période, c'est la copieuse et véhémente satire de Gratian du Pont, seigneur de Drusac, *Les Controverses des sexes masculin et féminin.*[7]

Béroalde's connection with the neo-platonic camp of this quarrel is also discussed by Reynier, who cites in footnote 2 on pages 211-212 of his *Roman sentimental avant l'Astrée* a list

5. Reynier, p. 156, footnote 5, running to p. 157.
6. *Ibid.*, p. 171, footnote 2.
7. *Ibid.*, p. 212.

of books which show « une reprise assez nette du mouvement platonicien » and in which he includes Béroalde de Verville's *Dialogue de l'Honneste Amour,* dating it at the first of November, 1583.

From all appearances, Béroalde is, then, very closely linked with the *saloniste* movements of the day, and if epigram is a characteristic of the baroque style, it is equally true that the *maximes* of La Rochefoucauld and others represent the genre contribution of the *précieux* style coming out of the literary and social salons of the time. Although I believe the two things to be connected from the standpoint of sensibility, I do not think the *maximes* to be so much an offbranching of the classical Senecan epigram found in abundance in the plays of, say, Montchrestien, but rather an outgrowth of sophisticated salon chit-chat. In all sophisticated circles the clipped, the cryptic, the urbane have ever been appreciated, and I believe the following citation of Saulnier from the *Cabinet de Minerve* shows Béroalde to be a past master at the witty, the urbane statement, if this has not been adequately proven by my own quotes from the *Dialogue de la Vertu :*

> « Je vous dirai mon intention : je suis en peine de savoir qui est *ON*. Car s'il se fait ou dit ou pratique quelque nouveauté ou ancienneté, cela est rapporté à cet *ON*. Il va à la chambre du Roi, en celle des Dames, il devise de tout; si quelqu'un fait quelque chose, c'est *ON*, et je ne sais s'il est mâle ou femelle, car les hommes prennent de leur part, et aussi les Dames. Si une Damoiselle a une robe nouvelle, c'est comme *ON* les porte aujourd'hui; si elle est d'autre sorte, c'est comme *ON* les portait le temps passé. Et *ON* fait tout ou pis ou mieux ou de même. Il est le but de la perfection et le but du défaut, il est véritable, il est menteur, il cause, il se tait, il est sain, il est malade, bref tout passe par ses mains. *ON* fait bonne chère, *ON* jeûne, *ON* fait bien, *ON* fait mal. *ON* fait d'un en un pays et d'autre en l'autre pays, ainsi c'est lui qui gouverne et perd, parquoi si vous me l'alléguez, je ne pourrai que vous dire. » [8]

8. Saulnier, p. 215.

The above passage illustrates, in addition, the love of language play found in such abundance in *Le Moyen de Parvenir*, which, says Reiche, even Rabelais could scarcely have equalled.[9]

But can Béroalde, the austere scholar, seriously be confused with the author of *Le Moyen de Parvenir?* There is a difference in character, to be sure, and yet the period knew many similar splits, such as Ronsard, Malherbe, d'Aubigné.

Let us seek evidence within the works recognized by all as Béroalde's, not merely of wittiness, not merely of urbanity, but more tellingly of a marked raciness hitherto denied him by many commentators who were, in the final analysis, unacquainted with his other works.

At the end of Béroalde's beautiful *Soupirs amoureux* are three extremely suggestive poems[10], at least two of which have glaring connections with *Le Moyen de Parvenir.* For example, against the opening paragraph of the novel:

> Car est il, que ce fut au temps, au siecle, en l'indiction, en l'Aere, en l'Hegire, en l'hebdomade, au lustre, en l'Olimpiade, en l'an, au terme, au mois, en la sepmaine, au iour, à l'heure, à la minute, & iustement à l'instant, que par l'auis & progrez du Daimon des spheres les esteufs descheurent de credit, & qu'au lieu d'eux furent auancees les molles balles, au preiudice de la noble antiquité, qui se jouoit si joliment. Confuz soient ces inuenteurs de nouueautez, qui gastent la jeunesse, & contre les bonnes coustumes, troublent nos jeux... Mais qu'est ce que jouer ? C'est se delecter sans penser en mal. Beaucoup de maux sont auenus à cause de ce changement, qui troublera l'intelligence des histoires, & gauchira toute la mappemonde (I, 3-4).

should be set the same use of ball games found in the poem entitled « Le Pallemail », which Saulnier has quoted from *Les Soupirs amoureux* in his *Anthologie*[11]:

9. Herbert Reiche, *Le Moyen de parvenir von Béroalde de Verville mit besonderer Berücksichtigung der Quellen-und Verfasserfrage* (Coburg, 1913), p. 55 : « Das Wortspiel ist das Feld Bs. Selbst Rab. kommt ihm darin nicht gleich. »

10. The explanation for their presence at the end of this serious work is surely a baffling problem. It would seem at present all we can say is that this would be in keeping with the comprehensive view — the erupting and ever-changing nature of the baroque mentality.

11. V.-L. Saulnier, *Anthologie poétique de Béroalde de Verville* (Paris, 1945). See Randle Cotgrave, *A Dictionarie of the French and English Tongues* (London,

Nous sommes trois passants qui demandons logis,
Au moins pour une nuit, chez vous mesdemoiselles,
Et quand nous nous serons quelque peu rafraîchis,
Du lieu d'où nous venons vous dirons des nouvelles.

Nous venons d'un pays où nous avons appris
Du jeu du Pallemail l'exercice agréable,
Dans les beaux promenoirs de la belle Cypris,
Environnés de fleurs et tout couverts de sable.[12]

Not only is this a revelation of one aspect of Béroalde, but it is an important aspect, for, as we see, he returns even to the same wording, to the same preoccupations, in the same way in his sonnet « Le May », also quoted by Saulnier from *Les Soupirs amoureux* in his *Anthologie:*

Maintenant que l'Amour renaît heureusement
Et qu'à ce beau printemps il commande qu'on plante
D'un Mai long et dressé la désirable plante
Il faut suivre l'arrêt de son commandement.[13]

In his *Anthologie* Saulnier remarks that reference to May in Béroalde is « Toujours plus ou moins avec une arrière-pensée gaillarde[14] ». That is a masterpiece of understatement, for the sonnet in question does not depend upon an *arrière-pensée* so much as upon a pun built on the words *Mai* and *mail,* at the time rather close in sound, although distant in meaning.

Another of the « pièces facétieuses » from *Les Soupirs amoureux,* quoted by Saulnier in his *Anthologie,* is « L'Alchémiste » whose first four stanzas follow:

On dit qu'en ce pays les dames ont envie
D'entendre les secrets de la philosophie,
Et pourtant moi je veux leur être serviteur,
Pour ce que, les sachant, des hommes n'ai que faire,
Aux dames seulement je veux dire l'affaire,
Leur montrant par effet de l'œuvre la douceur.

1611), under *Palemaille :* « A game, wherein a round box bowle is with a mallet struck through a big arch of yron (standing at either end of an alley one), which he that can do at the fewest blowes or at the number agreed on, winnes. »

12. Saulnier, *Anthologie poétique.* See my Appendix A for the entire poem and page references.

13. Saulnier, *Anthologie poétique.* See my Appendix B for the entire poem and page references.

14. *Ibid.,* p. 138.

En infinis endroits la matière peut être
Qu'il faut diligemment en facultés connaître;
Car animale elle est végétant doucement;
Aussi pour subsister sa force est métallique,
Par quoi triple par soi, sa vertu harmonique
Fait une liaison d'un juste assemblement.

Cette matière encore est et mâle et femelle
Et si n'est rien des deux; mais comme naturelle
Aux deux sexes elle est, avecques son vaisseau.
Son alembic aussi est en une partie,
Sa curcurbite en l'autre, et le cyment qui lie,
Pour rien n'évaporer, par le col, le vaisseau.

Pour la bien préparer, par une flamme douce
Naturelle de soi il faut qu'elle se pousse,
Pour son autre chercher, comme le fer l'aimant :
Les pareils naturels il faut conjoindre ensemble
Par un lien d'amour qui les choses assemble
De nature excitant le formel mouvement.[15]

This poem, witty, lascivious, satirical, drawing as it does on the pseudo-scientific terminology of the alchemist, and in the third strophe reflecting in a humorous fashion the concept of the androgyne, combines two preoccupations of Béroalde — alchemy and a play on images, language and substance. It is related to many passages in *Le Moyen de Parvenir,* but the following quote, having to do with the « pierre philosophale » will be sufficient to illustrate the connections:

> GUIDO. — Je pensois que vous voulussiez donner jusques à sainct Denys, & parler de frere Jerosme qui cherchoit la pierre à casser les œufs.
>
> ALAIN. — Qu'est-ce à dire ?
>
> VIVES. — Vous le sçaurez tantost. Ce moine, pour le dire plus gayement, cherchoit la pierre philosophale, & estoit Parisien; & de fait, j'ay esté en beaucoup de lieux & plages du monde habitable philosophic, & ie ne vis jamais en aucun endroit tant de Parisiens qu'à Paris. Et bien que durant le grand Iubilé ie visse beaucoup de

15. Saulnier, *Anthologie poétique.* See my Appendix C for the entire poem and the page references.

> Bretons à Rome, si n'en ay-je tant veu onques en vn monceau qu'en Bretaigne. Ne fou desplaise, — o gros Theuet, beste de bon esprit, que tu estois sot quand tu me dis qu'il n'y auoit point de contree où il y eut plus de vingt-quatre heures de jour, & que tu estimois que Payennerie fut nationneté, comme tu dis en ton liure des Grecs, Latins & Payens...
>
> Thevet... Or frere Ierosme cherchant la pierre philosophale, que sans doute on trouuera ici, & ce que ie vous dis est vray, & s'il n'est vray, je puisse mourir deuant toute la compagnie... (I, 73-74).

The chapter following this, entitled « Mappe-Monde » (I, 76-78) contains further allusion to frere Ierosme and the « pierre philosophale », which must be construed both literally and as an erotic word-play.

One could further quote the sonnet « A Son Verre », taken from *Floride*[16], but I think that the point of Béroalde's dual nature, wittiness and eroticism, independent of *Le Moyen de Parvenir,* has been made with the quoting of the above three poems. I do feel, however, that in treating this licentious verse, we must bear in mind that so was the climate of the times. We must not forget, either, that this was the world-view of the so-called « libertine » poets of the following generation, for example Théophile de Viau. For these reasons, we should not be surprised to find such raciness in the poetry of Béroalde. In fact, the early seventeenth century poets of this type may have learned more from *fin de siècle* writers like Béroalde than we had previously suspected.

Thus we may learn much about the authorship of *Le Moyen de Parvenir* from some of Béroalde's recognized works, and, as we study the title in an extensive fashion, we will see, among other things, that still more about authorship of *Le Moyen de Parvenir* is to be discovered from the titles and subtitles of other works whose author is recognized to be Béroalde.

16. Saulnier, *Anthologie poétique,* p. 132, quoted from *Floride,* II, p. 90.

CHAPTER II

THE TITLE PAGE

No ascertainable *editio princeps* of *Le Moyen de Parvenir* exists. The first published edition is without date, but is described by Royer[1] as bearing the « reliure du temps ». He has compared it with another early undated version of the same number of pages, and found variance in the titles. The title of the first is as follows:

> *Le | Moyen de | paruenir. | Oeuure contenant la | raison de tout ce qui | a esté, est, sera : | Auec demonstrations certaines ne- | cessaires, selon la rencontre des | effects de Vertu. | Et aduiendra que ceux qui auront nez à | portrr* (sic) *lunettes s'en seruiront; ainsi qu'il | est escrit au Dictionnaire à dormir en tout- tes langues S.* Recensuit Sapiens ab A, ad Z. | *Nune* (sic) ipsa vocat res, Hac inter (sic) est. | Æneid. IX. 310. (Fleuron). | Imprimé ceste anée.

The edition he compares this to, though the same edition, has certain variations in the title as well as in the text, leading to the conclusion that it is a second printing. The title is as follows:

> *Le Moyen | de paruenir. | Oeuure contenant la | raison de tout ce qui a esté, est, & sera. | Auec demonstrations certaines & | necessaires, selon la rencontre | des efects de Vertu. | Et aduiendra que ceux qui auront nez à | porter lunettes s'en seruiront, ainsi qu'il | est escrit au Dictionnaire à dormir en tout- | tes langues S. |* Reueu corrigé & augmenté par le | mesme Autheur.

1. See Royer, pp. liii-lxii for a complete discussion of editions up to the date of publication of his own edition of 1879.

Recensuit Sapiens ab A, ad Z. | Nunc ipsa vocat res. Hac iter est. | Æneid. IX. 320. | (Fleuron autre que le précédent.) | Imprimé ceste Anee.

Obviously the most salient difference is the addition of the words « Reueu corrigé & augmenté... » which Royer points out, and which nonetheless leads Royer to the conclusion that « Ce livre n'en est pas moins l'édition princeps ».

The most interesting statement this distinguished editor makes concerning the second text, outside of pointing out the high error count of this edition, is that « ...l'interprétation fausse et ordurière du troisième vers est imputable à l'ouvrier imprimeur qui, n'entendant rien au jeu de mots, le transcrit en terme brutal »[2]. It is understandable that Royer would construe this as an error, in view of the many others he points out. However, since the publication of the Royer edition, the appearance of a new manuscript dated at the beginning of the 17th century has been described by Ed. Champion. In his *compte rendu* of the « Vente Ed. Moura » (3-8 décembre 1923), Champion writes:

> Précieux manuscrit des premières années du XVIIe siècle, offrant donc les meilleures leçons de ce recueil de facéties.
>
> Le troisième vers du quatrain final, qui, d'après beaucoup de commentateurs, doit se lire ainsi :
>
> *Apportez quatre gros ès trons* (pièces de monnaie) se trouve ici seulement composé de quatre mots, les deux derniers n'en faisant plus qu'un seul très ordurier.
>
> De plus, un quatrain scatologique, sans doute inédit, figure au verso du titre.[3]

Royer feels there can have been no edition printed before 1612, because of the reference to *Le Moyen de Parvenir* found in Béroalde's *Le Palais des Curieux,* which has a *privilège* for November 5, 1611.[4] He maintains that the reference in *Le Palais des Curieux* plainly states that it was a manuscript

2. See Royer, p. lvii.

3. Champion, « Compte rendu », *Revue d'Histoire littéraire de la France,* 31e année (1924), p. 141. This compte rendu contains a description of a new manuscript of the 17th century. A « scatalogical » quatrain appears opposite the title in the Royer edition, for example, as well as in the Garnier edition (s.d.) and in the Jean Fort edition of 1921, but not in the Lacroix edition. The omission of this opening quatrain in earlier editions is pointed out by Royer, p. lvi.

4. Royer, p. xxxi.

that was in question. However, it does not seem to me that Béroalde would be unduly concerned about someone else's reworking of a manuscript of his, unless he were aware of a distribution of the work, and Royer does not leave us enough time for enough *manuscripts* to be circulated. It would seem therefore that Béroalde is indeed referring to a printing of the work.

Be this as it may, the above two editions of *Le Moyen de Parvenir* cannot be exactly dated, for, as Royer points out, none of the older editions have a date, editor, or place, and all are anonymous. The scholar must therefore resort to more tenuous dating processes, such as the typography, ornamentation, references within the work, etc. Naturally, the fact that these early editions are anonymous makes the establishment of authorship, which has already been discussed, even more difficult. In fact, the first edition of *Le Moyen de Parvenir* to bear the name of Béroalde did not appear until 1757. It is listed by Royer as follows:

> *Le Moyen de parvenir.* Nouvelle édition. A * * * * * *. 1000070057. In-12. Deux tomes. I, 2ff. pour le frontispice par Martinet et le titre sans le quatrain, lxxvj pp. pour la *Dissertation,* le *Sommaire des chapitres,* et les *Contes tirés du Moyen de parvenir,* et 335 pp.; t. II, lf. pour le titre, lij pp. pour le *Sommaire...* et les *Contes...* et 330 pp. — Le nom Beroalde de Verville paraît ici pour la première fois en tête du *Moyen de parvenir;* il est inscrit au frontispice dans la bordure du cadre qui entoure son portrait (?) la tête en bas. Le frontispice a pour légende : *Charites inter jocosve regnat Moria.* Le titre est pour la quatrième fois modifié.[5]

Of special interest among editions of the late seventeenth century, however, is the appearance of an identical edition of *Le Moyen de Parvenir* under two different titles. Following is Royer's description:

> *Le Coupecu de la melancolie, ou Venus en belle humeur.* A Parme. Chez Iaques Le Gaillard. M. DC. XCVIII. In-12 de 348 pages. La bibliothèque de Reims possède un

5. Royer, p. lxi.

exemplaire (n° 1740) annoté par Jamet, dont nous avons reproduit quelques notes dans le Glossaire. — V. 9°.

Le Salmigondis, ou le Manège du Genre Humain. A Liège, chez Louis Refort. M. DC. XCVIII. In-12 de 348 pp. — V. 9° et 10°.[6]

The first title is noteworthy because, while it would lead a potential reader away from the realization that *Le Moyen de Parvenir* was at stake, it suggests the idea of a game (therefore relating it to one of the central themes of the novel) and boldly announces the erotic nature of the book, which is barely suggested by previous titles. Of this there is little doubt, because at the end of a previous edition of *Le Moyen de Parvenir,* both titles are advertised in a « Liste de quelques liures galands qui se vendent en Hollande », and the first is announced as « Le Coupe-cu ». An internal suggestion of this title (there are many) can be seen in the following indignant remark made at the end of a chapter, and terminating an *historiette* by Pindare: « ...Va, la gorge te coupe le cou » (I, 89). The word melancholy (also found in the text) refers to the « humours », of course, and so this particular title seems to imply how to extinguish the tyrant melancholy (Stoicism?) and, so, set up the « usurper » (Epicureanism?).

The second spurious title is of even more interest, for it adds another dimension to the interpretation of *Le Moyen de Parvenir* as a baroque work, the word « salmigondis » implying, as it does, *a potpourri,* in other words, a little bit of everything, or refusal to compose. The American literature student will perhaps find here a new lesson in the work of Washington Irving and his collaborators entitled *Salmagundi,* especially if he keeps in mind the editors' resolution that they are « ...clearly of opinion that wisdom, true wisdom, is a plump, jolly dame, who sits in her arm-chair, laughs right merrily at the farce of life — and takes the world as it goes »[7].

In all, Royer lists 28 separate editions prior to his own, and to these Saulnier adds those which are available, including, in addition to Royer's edition, and the manuscript already discussed, the three twentieth century editions:

6. Royer, p. lix.

7. Henry August Pochmann and G. W. Allen, *Masters of American Literature* (New York, 1949), pp. 338-347. See especially footnotes 7 and 8, p. 338.

Le Moyen de Parvenir... nouv. éd. collationnée sur les textes anciens avec notes, notices, sommaire analytique et index alphabétique. Paris, 1911, in-12, xiv-436 pp.

— édition illustrée par Martin van Maële (8 eaux-fortes et 65 illustrations dans le texte); introd. de Pierre Dufay. Paris, Jean Fort, 73 faubourg Poissonnière, 1921, in-8°.

— édition de Henri Leduc, illustrée d'aquarelles et dessins originaux d'Uzelac. Paris, aux éditions de la Belle Etoile, 1937, in-8°. 125 F.[8]

Saulnier puts the number of editions at 38[9], thus indicating the good fortune of *Le Moyen de Parvenir* as far as a reading public has been concerned.[10]

Hints at the title of *Le Moyen de Parvenir* and its subtitles have been pointed out by Paul Lacroix[11] and others as substantiation of Béroalde's authorship. It has not been suggested that the opposite might well be the case, and that if *Le Moyen de Parvenir* was pirated, the titles could quite likely have been placed there to mimic this man[12] of whom Colletet has said: « 'Iamais homme n'eut apparemment dans tout ce qu'il fit plus d'inclination pour la vertu, dont le nom luy couloit incessament de la plume.' »[13] This is merely a possibility, of course, or a counter-argument, which leaves us no further ahead on the question of authorship. An examination of the other titles and descriptive subtitles of Béroalde are nonetheless interesting in either of the two cases. Already

8. V.-L. Saulnier, « Etude sur Béroalde de Verville », *Revue d'Humanisme et Renaissance*, V (1944), p. 319.

9. *Ibid.*, p. 319.

10. There is no mention anywhere of translations, and I have not discovered whether *Le Moyen de Parvenir* has been translated into any other languages than English. Students of English literature will surely find interesting the fact that a translation of *Le Moyen de Parvenir* was made by Arthur Machen (see bibliography) during the Victorian period, thus fitting into the period's counter-current, along with Oscar Wilde, etc.

11. Paul Lacroix, pp. xvii-xxi.

12. The notion is not without some substantiation, for the following quatrain, written in ridicule of Béroalde's « Histoire des vers qui filent la soye », had, in part, brought forth the publication of *Les Muses incognues* :

« ' *Que dit on du sieur de Veruille,*
Et de son ouvrage nouveau ?
Vn chacun dit parmy la ville
Que son ver procedde d'vn Veau.' » (See Royer, p. lii.)

13. Royer, p. xlix.

in 1579, the subtitle of the second work (the first was a study of mathematics), suggests the title of the masterwork:

> *Le Blason des Armoiries, | Auquel est monstrée la maniere de la- | quelle les Anciens & Modernes | ont vsé en icelles. | Traicté contenant plusieurs Escus differens, par le moyen | desquels on peut discerner les autres & dresser | ou blasonner les Armoiries.* | A Lyon...[14]

Note especially the words « contenant » and « moyen ».

A similar promise of didacticism is revealed in a scientific work of 1583 (incorrectly dated M.D. XXLIII):

> *Recherches de la Pierre Philosophale, & du moyen qu'il y faut tenir, si elle existe ou peut exister : auec une preface contre les soufleurs imposteurs & sophistes, & quelques sentances contenans tout l'art. Par F. B. de Veruille.*[15]

In addition to the words « moyen » and « contenans » which again appear, the presence of the anti-sophist subjunction is revealing in connection with the « Sapiens » of the frontispiece of *Le Moyen de Parvenir*, and the general nature of the gathered assembly of the novel. This connection has not been pointed out before, to my knowledge, although Paul Lacroix approaches it in his « Notice ».[16]

The year following we again have a title containing the promise of instruction, this time leading toward « bonnes meurs »:

> *L'Idee de la Republique de François de Béroalde Sieur de Veruille. En ce poeme est discouru du deuoir de chasqu'vn, de ce qui conserue la police en son entier, parfait l'estat, & monstre à tous selon leur qualité & condition le moyen de bien & heureusement viure en la societé humaine, & se façonner aux bonnes meurs.* A Monsieur Du Gast. A Paris. Pour Thimothée Ioüan...[17]

14. Royer, p. xxxiii.
15. *Ibid.*, p. xl.
16. Paul Lacroix, p. xvi. « Il avait sans doute, dans sa jeunesse, poursuivi avec passion la chimère du Grand-Œuvre, car en beaucoup d'endroits de ses écrits il se moque des *souffleurs*, comme un homme qui regrette d'avoir partagé leur folie et d'y avoir perdu son temps ainsi que son argent. Lorsqu'il n'était pas encore tout à fait désabusé de ses illusions hermétiques, il composa ses *Recherches de la Pierre-philosophale...* »
17. Royer, p. xlii.

It comes as no surprise to see the word « vertu » appear over and over again in subsequent titles, given the nature of the above. In the same year, occasionally bound with *L'Idee de la Republique* and *Les Souspirs amoureux,* the following work appears:

> « '*Dialogue de la Vertu. Par François de Béroalde Sieur de Veruille.* A Paris. Pour Timothee Iouan...' »[18]

Internal evidence of the title of *Le Moyen de Parvenir* has already been seen in the above *Dialogue,* as the reader will recall. In relation to this, consider the following quotation, which will require no explanation:

> *De la Sagesse, liure premier. Auquel il est traicté du Moyen de paruenir au parfaict estat de bien viure, remedier aux afflictions, embrasser la Confiance, & trouuer l'entier contentement selon l'institution Diuine. Par Béroalde de Veruille.* A Tours, chez Iamet Mettayer...[19]

Of the five parts of the *Auantures de Floride* which follow *De la Sagesse,* four contain elements that are noteworthy, especially the insistence on the word « vertu ». The third is less interesting in vocabulary, but the thought is in the same general direction as the other four. Bellow is a list of the titles:

> *Premiere partie des Auantures de Floride. En ceste Histoire Françoise on peut voir les differens euenemens d'Amour, de Fortune & d'Honneur, & combien sont en fin agreables les fruits de la Vertu.* Reueuë...[20]
>
> *Seconde partie des Auantures de Floride. En laquelle, outre la suitte de l'Histoire, se rencontrent diuers succez Vertueux.* A Rouen, Chez Thomas Mallard...[21]
>
> *Troisieme partie des Auantures de Floride. En laquelle on recognoist par euenements diuers les punitions de ceux qui ont voulu contreuenir à l'honneur.* A Rouen, Chez Thomas Mallard...[22]

18. Royer, p. xliii.
19. *Ibid.*
20. *Ibid.*, p. xliv. Though not the first edition, no other is known.
21. *Ibid.*, p. xliv-xlv.
22. *Ibid.*, p. xlv.

> *Quatriesme partie des Auantures de Floride, qui est l'Infante determinee. Où se voyent plusieurs trophees de la Vertu triomphante du Vice. De l'inuention de Béroalde de Veruille.* Reueu, corrigé...[23]
>
> *Cinquiesme partie des Auantures de Floride, qui est le Cabinet de Minerue. Auquel sont plusieurs singularitez. Figures. Tableaux. Antiques. Recherches saintes. Remarques serieuses. Où se voyent plusieurs trophees de la Vertu triomphante du Vice. De l'inuention de Béroalde de Veruille.* A Rouen, Chez Theodore Reinsart deuant...[24]

In a later edition of *Le Cabinet de Minerue,* essentially the same wording appears, except that the word « deuoir » comes up, and more particularly, the word « sage » which, in a certain sense, leads us to the word « Sapiens » (cf. *De la Sagesse*), but is of greater interest in respect to the interior of *Le Moyen de Parvenir:*

> *Le Cabinet de Minerue. Auquel sont plusieurs Singularités... serieuses. Observations amoureuses. Subtilités agreables. Rencontres joyeuses & quelques histoires meslées ès auantures de la Sage Fenisse patron du Deuoir. Par Béroalde de Veruille.* A Tours, chés Sebastien Molin...[25]

Two subsequent novels bear within them reference to virtue. The first is dated 1598 (although the « privilège » is dated 14 septembre 1597) and the second is dated 1597:

> *Les Amours d'Aesionne, Où se voyent les hazards des armes, les ialousies, desespoirs, esperances, changemens & passions, que les succez balancent par la vertu. De l'inuention de Béroalde de Ver-uille* (sic, ainsi qu'au privilège). A Paris, Chez Matthieu Guillemot...[26]

The other title is substantially the same as the above; the principal change comes in the capitalization of the word « Vertu »:

> *Le Restablissement de Troye, auec lequel parmy les hazards des armes, se voyent les amours d'Aesionne, ses*

23. Royer, *ibid.*
24. *Ibid.*, p. xlvi.
25. *Ibid.*, p. xlvii.
26. *Ibid.*, p. xlviii.

> *ialousies, desespoirs, esperances, changemens & passions que les succes balancent par la Vertu. De l'inuention de Béroalde de Veruille.* A Tours. Par Sebastien Molin...[27]

These last two titles should be noted in connection with the quotation from the *Æneid* on the title-page of *Le Moyen de Parvenir,* which I shall shortly discuss. Also notable is the expression « ...les hazards des armes... » to which I shall be returning.

Other titles, which I shall not quote, contain the idea of virtue, chastity, and the like, but are not applicable here, since the vocabulary does not relate to the title and title page of *Le Moyen de Parvenir.* One might loosely relate, for example, *La Pucelle d'Orleans...* or *L'Histoire d'Herodias...* from the standpoint of virtue rewarded and vice punished; one might also relate the *Tableau des riches inuentions,* in which we find *Le Songe de Poliphile,* etc., to the words « Dictionnaire à dormir » found on the frontispiece of *Le Moyen de Parvenir.* Finally, we could set the title of a work published in 1611 against the stress on knowledge hinted at on the title-page and recurring throughout the text of *Le Moyen de Parvenir:*

> *Le Palais des Curieux. Auquel sont assemblées plusieurs diuersitez pour le plaisir des Doctes, & le bien de ceux qui desirent sçauoir.* A Paris, chez la Veufue M. Guillemot, & S. Thiboust...[28]

Any theories about authorship based on the titles of Béroalde's other works, however convincing the argument, cannot, however, be conclusive. There is always the chance that if he is *not* satirizing his own work, or if some other author is not, he is satirizing a title formula which was current. A mere glance through the recent bibliography of Cioranescu and Saulnier, for example, turns up the following work of Guillaume Postel (1510-1581): « Les raisons de la monarchie et quels moyens sont nécessaires pour y parvenir; là où sont compris les tres admirables privileges et droicts, tant divins, celestes comme humains, de la gent gallique et des princes par icelle esleuz et approuvez, par *G. P. P.*, 1551, 8°, 48 p. »[29]

27. Royer, *ibid.*
28. *Ibid.*, p. liii.
29. Alexandre Cioranesco and V.-L. Saulnier, *Bibliographie de la Littérature française du seizième siècle* (Paris, 1959), *Item* 17825, p. 567.

It will perhaps be noticed that there is hesitation on the part of scholars concerning the punctuation of the word « p » of « Parvenir ». Early editions show a small « p », and Royer uses the small « p », in accordance with these editions, and with Colletet. The same practice is followed, for example, by Reiche, and by the editor of the Jean Fort edition of 1921, as well as by Clouzot. Although Paul Lacroix uses a capital « p », I would not base my argument for this usage upon his practice, as opposed to the majority who do not use the capital. However, I support the use of the capital by three arguments. The first is that V.-L. Saulnier who has studied Béroalde extensively does this. The second, a more sophistic argument, is that the word « Parvenir » seems to me to be as weighty in the title as the word « Moyen ». But the best argument of all, it seems to me, is that Béroalde de Verville himself seems to have capitalized it, for it is with a capital that the word « Parvenir » appears in the famous passage from *Le Palais des Curieux:* « Je vous avise que comme icy je donne des atteintes à plusieurs fautes, que j'ay fait un œuvre lequel est une satyre universelle où je reprends les vices de chacun. Je pensois vous le faire voir sous un tiltre qui est tel *Le Moyen de Parvenir,* mais on me l'a vollé, si que pour en avoir le plaisir, vous attendrez encor. » [30]

⁂

Following is the title page of *Le Moyen de Parvenir,* as it appears in the Royer edition, which he has based on a reprinting of the second edition he lists. Royer's publisher has used a facsimile print which is duplicated here.

30. Saulnier, « Etude sur B. de V. », pp. 284-285, cited from p. 461 of *Le Palais des Curieux.*

LE
MOYEN DE
PARVENIR.

Oeuure contenant la raiſon de tout ce qui a eſté, eſt, & ſera : auec demonſtrations certaines & neceſſaires, ſelon la rencontre des effects de VERTV.

Et aduiẽdra que ceux qui auront nez à porter lunettes s'en ſeruirõt : ainſi qu'il eſt eſcrit au Dictionnaire à dormir en toutes langues. S.

Recenſuit Sapiens ab A, ad Z.

Nunc ipſa vocat res.

Hac iter eſt.

Æneid. IX. 320.

IMPRIME CETTE ANNEE.

1. 1

Now, the title *Le Moyen de Parvenir,* which calls for lengthy analysis, is at once evocative and ambiguous. It is vague. It is also sensual. Of it Bernard de la Monnaye has said, « Le titre seul excitait la curiosité ».[31] In and of itself, the title, by its very vagueness, reveals that the book will be mystifying. It has the ring of a « how-to-do-it » book, and yet we are not just sure what it is we are being instructed in. Analysis of the title page shows that virtually all the dominant themes of the novel are prefigured by the title and its constituent parts. Taken with its subtitle, « Oeuure contenant la raison de tout ce qui a esté, est & sera : auec demonstrations certaines & necessaires, selon la rencontre des effects de VERTV", the title suggests a type of catechism for arriving at a state of *VERTV.* Yet, one of the major ambiguities lies in this last word, which raises the question as to whether *VERTV* has the larger sense of Christian "virtue" or whether it implies the exclusion of women and concentrates on the art of "being manly". The second interpretation would simultaneously foreshadow the misogynic traits found in the novel as well as its partiality for "being manly" — i.e., the "manly" arts of war, philosophy, drinking, eating, carousing in general.

Furthermore, this interpretation finds reinforcement in the seemingly irrelevant quote from the *Æneid:*

Nunc ipsa vocat res.

Hac iter est.

Æneid. IX. 320.

The presence of this quotation and of its source reminds us that the great epic is, in the true nature of the epic, a man's story. Its conventional opening, « Arma virumque cano... »[32] is more than likely intended to be evoked, admittedly in mock grandiose style, by the presence of the title *Æneid.* The quotation from the *Æneid* « Hac iter est », or « here is the way » echoes Béroalde's title: *Le Moyen de Parvenir* — i.e., « here is the way ».[33]

The passage quoted from the *Æneid* not only reflects Béroalde's principal title but also serves to call forth one of

31. Béroalde de Verville, *Le Moyen de Parvenir,* ed. Jean Fort (Paris, 1921), p. xl. — Hereafter cited as Fort.

32. Virgil, *Æneid,* ed. H. Rushton Fairclough (London, 1954), vol. I, p. 240.

33. Lines 157-8 of Régnier's Satire X (« Le Souper ridicule ») allude to the « hac itur » which was comically applied to the drunkard's blotches, a fact which has definite bearing on the text at hand.

the bloody battles of the *Æneid,* and to prepare us for possible statements on war, or at least on the manly art of bearing arms. We may note, also, that the time for undertaking this adventure, and for picking up this manual is *now:* « nunc ipsa vocat res ». It is necessary to add to the quotation from the *Æneid,* in order to see what bearing certain surrounding lines may have upon our understanding of the title and the title-page of *Le Moyen de Parvenir.*

In the passage in question, Nisus, the son of Hyrtacides is speaking to Euryalus, at a point when both men seek to warn and to summon Æneas; for Rutulian strategy threatens to undo the Trojans:

> Egressi superant fossas noctisque per umbram
> castra inimica petunt, multis tamen ante futuri
> exitio. passim somno vinoque per herbam
> corpora fusa vient, arrectos litore currus,
> inter lora rotasque viros, simul arma iacere,
> vina simul. prior Hyrtacides sic ore locutus:
> « Euryale, audendum dextra; nunc ipsa vocat res.
> hac iter est. tu, ne qua manus se attollere nobis
> a tergo possit, custodi et consule longe;
> haec ego vasta dabo et lato te limite ducam. »
> si memorat vocemque premit; simul ense superbum
> Rhamnetem adgreditur, qui forte tapetibus altis
> exstructus toto proflabat pectore somnum,
> rex idem et regi Turno gratissimus augur;
> sed non augurio potuit depellere pestem.
> tris iuxta famulos temere inter tela iacentis
> armigerumque Remi premit aurigamque sub ipsis
> nactus equis ferroque secat pendentia colla;
> tum caput ipsi aufert domino truncumque relinquit
> sanguine singultantem; atro tepefacta cruore
> terra torique madent, nec non Lamyrumque Lamunque
> et iuvenem Serranum, illa qui plurima nocte
> luserat, insignis facie, multoque iacebat
> membra deo victus; felix, si protinus illum
> aequasset nocti ludum in lucemque tulisset.
> impastus ceu plena leo per ovilia turbans
> (suadet enim vesana fames) manditque trahitque
> molle pecus mutumque metu, fremit ore cruento.
> nec minor Euryali caedes; incensus et ipse
> perfurit ac multam in medio sine nomine plebem...[34]

34. Virgil, *Æneid,* vol. II, p. 132 and p. 134.

The lines surrounding the quotation from the *Æneid,* would, it is to be expected, have those erotic overtones always sought after by the author of *Le Moyen de Parvenir.* However, by use of these two particular lines of the *Æneid,* Béroalde manages to evoke for the Renaissance reader — thoroughly familiar with virtually every line of the Latin epic — the accompanying admonishment of Nisus to Euryalus that the latter should be his own reconnaissance and rear-guard, that he should look carefully ahead and carefully behind. This warning, in its turn, seems to me to announce, and very subtly, too, the theological satire rampant in *Le Moyen de Parvenir.* There is frequent appearance in the novel of the phrase « devant & derriere », as, for example: « ...ce que ie desire me resectionner d'vn peu de viande & de liqueur, est que ie crains de perdre le deuant & le derriere, comme ceste abstinente de Consolant; ie m'en rapporte aux Medecins » (I, 145), or: « Ie suis tout esmeu d'esprit prophetique & cognois deuant & derriere qu'ici se resoudront toutes les questions du monde... » (I, 216). I suspect that the phrase « devant et derriere » is used to suggest the proverb that one cannot trust a woman from the front, a mule from the rear, or a clergyman from any side. Des Periers brings this proverb to play in one of his *Contes*[35]; and the phrase itself, no doubt also reflecting the proverb, is used by Viret to attack Antoine Catelan (Antoine du Val) along with other papists. Viret puns on du Val's name when he writes in his *Satyres Chrestiẽnes de la Cuisine Papale:*

> Monsieur le singe PASSAVANT
> Asne derriere, asne deuant,
> Autrement Antoine du Val,
> Grand asne faisant du cheual.
> Il faut bien dire, o piteux cas !
> Qu'il y a faute d'aduocas
> Pour telle cause maintenir,
> Quand il faut pour la soustenir,
> Que des Asnes la Kyrielle
> Portent le fais de la querelle.[36]

35. Bonaventure des Periers, *Contes ou Nouvelles Récréations et Joyeux Devis suivis du Cymbalum Mundi,* ed. Paul Jacob (Paris, 1872), p. 142.

36. Pierre Viret, *Satyres Chrestiẽnes de la Cuisine Papale.* Imprimé par Conrad Badius (1560), p. 46.

In view of these observations, can the phrase « devant & derriere » as it is used in *Le Moyen de Parvenir,* be tied to this quotation from the *Æneid?* Is it meant to call forth the proverb? Does the phrase refer to du Val specifically? It is possible, for many other names are buried in puns in *Le Moyen de Parvenir.* Besides, could one not bring to bear upon the argument that it is specifically du Val who is being alluded to the fact that the interlocutor « Toni » or « Thoni » has not yet been satisfactorily identified, and might well be du Val?

But whether the quote from the *Æneid* and the phrase are meant to refer to a specific person, or to be general in nature, it is certain that the quotation on the title-page is not present as a mere satire on pedantic title-page glosses, nor even as a simple statement of virility, as it applies in war. The quote is not there, with its evocation of the surrounding lines, wherein Euryalus is told to look ahead and look behind, merely for licentious purposes. Like all the other facets of the title-page — including the title itself, the announcement that all knowledge from « a » to « z » is to be found here, the statement that this is a « dictionnaire à dormir » — the quotation from the *Æneid,* as well as the evocation of the lines surrounding it and the proverb I have mentioned, clearly announce theological satire. The quotation, and the passage from which it is taken, set against the proverb, appear to state that the « way to get where you are going » is not only to carry along an authoritative guide such as *Le Moyen de Parvenir* but also to « be on your guard » against women, against the clergy, even against the Pope, the « mule ». All three of these, it would appear, encumber you in your progress toward certain goals, especially, I think, in your efforts to attain self-sanctification (perfection, as it is stated in the text) and to inherit the kingdom of heaven.

In addition, the quotation bespeaks the theological order of the satire by its unmistakeable reference to Aeneas Sylvius — Pope Pius II — an interlocutor of *Le Moyen de Parvenir,* referred to twice in the text (chapter CX, « Ordonnance » and Chapter XXXIII, « Remonstrance »). This pope, Lucas tells us, early in his life wrote a novel called *Lucretia and Euryalus,* a work as salacious as that of Boccaccio, but one which, having become pope, Sylvius regretted.[37] Consequently, Béroalde is

37. Henry S. Lucas, *The Renaissance and the Reformation* (New York, 1934), pp. 273-274.

making specific reference to changes of heart in the clergy and to the peccadillos of the Holy Fathers.

Equally important in the passage from the *Æneid* is Nisus' insistence that Euryalus, the younger of the two (and for this reason in a position to have Nisus point out « the way » to him) keep keen-eyed and cautious guard over the rear, in order that no force be allowed to spring up and attack them from behind. Just a bit later he again emphasizes the fact that he knows the road as well as the ropes, for he promises him that he will take care of all who are present, and that he will then lead him onward down a clear, wide lane. Hence, the words « Hac iter est », are reinforced by the « haec ego vasta dabo et lato te limite ducam ».

Now the fact that Nisus insists upon keen-eyed and cautious guard recalls a portion of the sentence on the title-page just above the quote from the *Æneid:* « ...ceux qui auront nez à porter lunettes s'en servirõt... » The author of *Le Moyen de Parvenir* is half-jokingly, half-seriously implying that one must be able to « see clearly » his intention. There is, of course, a licentious implication here, without any doubt. Perhaps it is unnecessary to say that the size of the nose is related since time immemorial to the degree of virility, and so the phrase echoes the ambiguous word *vertu* of the subtitle. For a contemporary treatment of this relationship, one might refer to the end of Viret's *Satyres.*[38] The word *nez* in most cases also includes a pun on *né (natus),* so that the question of nobility in connection with the *homme bien fait,* the man versed in the « art of war », etc., is involved. On the other hand, the relation of spectacles to the novel in general, as to its prismatic themes, is not to be minimized. In several ways then, Béroalde is already — on the title page — riding the idea that one must « read between the lines » if one is going to understand the true purpose of the book.

Continuing with the second half of the same sentence, following the reference to eyeglasses, we find: « ...ainsi qu'il est escrit au Dictionnaire à dormir en toutes langues ». Here Béroalde is making reference to the polyglot editions of the time, and, perhaps, particularly to the polyglot dictionary of Ambroise Calepino, properly called dà Calepio. It is noteworthy that « Calepin » turns out to be one of the interlocutors in the dialogues of *Le Moyen de Parvenir,* and is identified by

38. Viret, pp. 119-124.

Paul Lacroix as this particular lexicographer.[39] According to Lacroix, Calepino had published his dictionary in 1502, and died in 1511 while still working on the dictionary. That Calepino was well-known around the time of the appearance of *Le Moyen de Parvenir* is shown by the very startling coining of a word from the name Calepino by the author of *La Pícara Justina,* Lopez de Ubeda, who speaks of a « calepina machorra », which Valbuena y Prat explains in a footnote as meaning a sterile woman, or « la mujer metida a estudios, ciencia y aficiones propios de hombres ».[40] In that same novel, Calepino is again referred to, for we find there: « '...y como porcedente del sequndo al bachillerejo pretencioso que en virtud de ciertos cursos interpolados que había tenido en dichas escuelas, lleuaua un pujo de dezir necedades como si vuiera tomado alguna purga confecionada con ojas de Calepino de ocho lenguas...' »[41]

I have already noted that the title *Le Moyen de Parvenir* suggests a Bible, so that the word polyglot suggests not simply a dictionary, Béroalde's cover, but could be understood to suggest the polyglot Bible. Thus the religious satire of the book is alluded to not only by the title, but also through the hazy use of the word *VERTV*[42] and the duplicity of the phrase « Dictionnaire à dormir en toutes langues ». Special attention is called to the fact that the word « Dictionnaire » is capitalized, which may not be a mere whim on the part of the author.

On the other hand, the « à dormir », seems to establish a paradox contradicting the first half of the sentence, « et adviẽdra que ceux qui auront nez à porter lunettes s'en servirõt ».[43] To the extent that Béroalde intends the polyglot

39. Paul Lacroix, p. 441.

40. Angel Valbuena y Prat, *La Novela Picaresca Española* (Madrid, 1946), p. 716, footnote 1.

41. Francisco Lopez de Ubeda, *La Pícara Justina,* ed. Julio Puyol (Madrid, 1912), vol. 3, p. 73.

42. The complex connections of « vertu » and the Republic as later set forth by Montesquieu perhaps have some place here, when we take into consideration the fact that Béroalde is the author of « L'Idée de la République ». If so, then the title also has political dimensions.

43. Compare in *La Pícara Justina,* Valbuena y Prat, p. 720:

> Y en parte no se engañará quien pensare de mi aquesto. Porque yo en el discurso de este mi libro no quiero engañar como sirena, ni adormecer como Cándida, ni transformar como Circe o Medea, ni entontecer como Cecrope, ni deslumbrar como Silvia. Que si esto pretendiera, no pusiera las redes en la plaza del mundo, ni las marañas por escrito y de molde. Quiero despertar amodorridos ignorantes, amonestar y enseñar los simples,

dictionary as a symbol, in reality, for a polyglot Bible, the « Dictionnaire à dormir » will have to mean a Bible, or at least a missal, leading us along the right paths and preparing us for our final « sleep ». In this way, the relationship between the themes of time and death are presented on the title page. The connection between sleep and death is scarcely original with Béroalde and really needs no support, though one can find ample proof of the bearing the one is thought to have on the other. The satirical connections are less obvious, however.

Having bearing on this « Dictionnaire à dormir en toutes langues » is the following passage from chapter XCI of *Le Moyen de Parvenir* entitled « Doctrine »:

> MELVIN. — Il a raison, d'autant que tous ces memoires, dictons, discours, sentences & paroles, sont prises du dictionnaire à dormir en toutes langues, de l'institution à lire sans poincts, sans lettres, sans caracteres, sans accens, sans figures, sans notes : aussi bien les notes font faillir, ainsi que le prouuoit frere Ambroise, qui disoit qu'il eust bien chanté, mais la notte empeschoit. Aussi sans chifres, & telles choses, a esté fait ce liure par le fils du dernier homme : Item de l'Epitome des Bibliotheques de S. Germain & autres, du Grand Luminaire des sots, tous liures extraits de cestui ci, auquel si chacun auoit remis ce qu'il y a pris, il n'y auroit plus qu'vn liure au monde.
>
> SVIDAS. — Tu és bien sot de nous conter ceci, afin que tout le monde le sçache, & on le vouloit celer (II, 170-171).

Paul Lacroix suggests that the titles in Melvin's speech are imaginary, but, he adds, « on peut croire que Béroalde, à l'instar de Rabelais dans le Catalogue de la Bibliothèque de Saint Victor, avait en vue quelques ouvrages contemporains. Celui-ci peut donc être : *Val. Schindleri Lexicon pentaglotton hebraïcum, chaldaïcum, syriacum, talmudicorabbinicum et arabicum.* Hanov., 1612, in-folio. On doit se rappeler aussi, à propos du titre de *Dictionnaire à dormir,* que Rabelais fait étudier à Gargantua

para que sepan huir de lo mismo que al parecer persuado. No hablo con los necios que, para ser oidores de mi sala, a los tales cuéntolos por sordos y aun ternia a gran merced si para en caso de leer fuesen ciegos, que de esta suerte pensaría que, siéndolo, me serían más aceptas las oraciones que me rezasen a cierra ojos, que con ellos.

le *Dormi secure,* recueil de sermons latins d'un cordelier allemand, imprimés au quinzième siècle. »[44] The hermetic nature of the work, implied by the list of things it is without, as well as by the retort of Svidas, recalls the subtitle of Béroalde's *Voyage des Princes fortunez, Oeuure steganographique, receuilli par Béroalde.*[45] Again Paul Lacroix observes with point: « Béroalde a l'air de se moquer ici du fameux traité stéganographique de l'abbé Trithème, traduit en français par Gabriel de Collange vers le milieu du seizième siècle, mais publié en latin pour la première fois au commencement du dix-septième : *Steganographia, hoc est ars per occultam scripturam animi sui volum...* [lacuna] *absentibus aperiendi certa.* Francof., 1606, in-4°. Le titre de la traduction a plus d'analogie encore avec celui cité par Béroalde. »[46] This note is, of course, reinforced by the fact that Tritheim or Thrithemius, the fifteenth century hermetic philosopher, is one of the philosophers participating in the dialogues.[47]

The following passage from « Proposition » has great bearing upon the above:

> — Et bien Coüillaut, que dis tu de cecy ?
> — Ie dy que ceux qui s'amusent à nos folies, sont comme les Medecins qui regardent & espluchent les ejections des autres, qui sont aussi fous que nous, si mieux n'aiment estre dit fous d'Inde, ou fous de Ludonnois. Dieu sauue les beaux coqs, poules & poulets, amen. Et contez diligemment les jours, parce que d'icy à deux cents trois ans, dix mois, sept jours, dixneuf heures, quarante minutes & trois secondes justement, le grand Steganographique fera vne nouuelle translation de ce liure, à cause du changement de religion (I, 21).

Furthermore, lest we doubt our narrator's Renaissance-like concern with being gifted in many tongues, let us look, for additional evidence, at the following passage, taken from an early chapter entitled « Coqalasne »: « ...j'ay pensé le nommer par son droit nom, bien le pouuois-je, dautant que je sçay plusieurs langues, mais il me faut icy parler François... » (I, 33).

44. Paul Lacroix, p. 337.
45. Royer, p. li.
46. Paul Lacroix, p. 337.
47. *Ibid.*, p. 498.

A quite similar attitude is reflected in the following passage, where intention to evoke the polyglot Bible is apparent:

> GONTERI. — I'attendois que vous parleriez de ce petit ruisseau que nous passames auec ceste compagnie-là, quand nous y fusmes pour les affaires des Vbiquitaires; ie me souuiens qu'ayant passé le pont de beurre, Curion nostre hoste de Basle nous fit baisser pour voir ce ruisseau tant celebre. Le Seigneur Cheualier, grand Hebreu, & si sçauant qu'il en estoit bossu, a mis l'histoire dans le Talmud, qu'il a reueu quand nous le faisions imprimer à Basle; ie le vous diray, aussi bien il n'y a personne qui ne le sçache, & c'est pour vous monstrer que j'ay de l'esprit, & que ie m'entens à l'Hebreu comme vne pie à estendre du beurre frais du pain : quand i'en faisois leçon cela alloit à la balance, comme vn chat qui pese des doublons en vne bouteille; mesmes s'il vous souuient ie le vous diray en nostre langue, pour suruenir à ceux qui n'entendent pas le chrestien. Vn iour pour faire le mignon i'auois à l'eglise mon psautier en Hebreu, où ie lisois ne plus ne moins qu'vn singe qui épluche des noisettes vertes; ie deuois dire la leçon, ie laisse mon liure & m'en vois au letrain : si tost que ie fus descendu de ma chaire, nostre ami Chastin prit mon liure, & l'ouurit, mais aussi tost il le laissa & se retira de là, allant se plaindre aux autre Chanoines que ie tenois des liures meschans, que i'estois magicien & que ie ne portois à l'Eglise que des liures prophanes, comme vne Bible, & autres de telle farine. Par despit, ie diray mon histoire en langage que tout le monde entendra, s'il s'y cognoit; ie la dirois bien autrement, mais ie n'y entens que le haut Alemand; il est trop froid, cela ne seroit iamais fait (I, 177-178).

Although Paul Lacroix seems only to see the reference to polyglot dictionaires, Saulnier is, of course, quite aware of the connection between the *Dictionnaire à dormir* and the polyglot Bibles. He writes:

> « La plaisanterie sur les lunettes est évidemment une lapalissade; on la rapporte au *Dictionnaire à dormir en toutes langues*, c'est-à-dire, selon nous, la Bible : la mode des Bibles polyglottes (même avant celle de Walton) est répandue au XVIe siècle : Plantin à Anvers en publie une en 1569-1572, en 8 volumes in-folio; une autre est publiée,

ex officina Sanctandreana, 1587, 2 vol. in-folio, etc. Comparer les livres de facéties à la Bible, c'est une plaisanterie de Rabelais dans la préface de Pantagruel : la Bible présentée implicitement comme le modèle des livres célèbres et ennuyeux, par opposition avec les livres de haute graisse. »[48]

Of other elements of the subtitle, Mr. Saulnier says:

> « Le reste du titre parodie la présentation des livres savants; la citation et la référence à l'Enéide sont exactes. 'Imprimé cette année' est une nouvelle lapalissade. Quant au quatrain, Béroalde est dans l'usage d'en disposer un de même cadence au début et à la fin des Princes fortunés, etc.
>
> » Au total, le procédé de la farce consiste à entourer d'un appareil d'érudition une série de naïvetés, et à leur donner un ton doctoral. Le tout en parodiant, dans le tracé général, les traités savants en cours, et, dans le détail, des habitudes de Béroalde. »[49]

Hence, where Mr. Saulnier does not see parody of the Bible, he sees parody of the techniques of learned treatises, and mimicry of pedantry, and all of this is indeed present.

One of the most interesting passages concerning language is the following, in which a satirical intention against polyglot ideals of the Renaissance will be noted, and in which the mocking themes of prophetic and hermetic intent, of mutability, of « truth », of the « dictionnaire à dormir », the « querelle des Anciens et des Modernes » (the relative merits of French over other modern and over ancient languages or of the New over the Old Testament) and the polyglot Bibles converge:

> « Il est vrai que i'ay regret pour l'amour des ignorans de mettre cecy en la plus magnifique langue du monde, tesmoin Charles le Quint qui disoit que les Espagnols parloient en glorieux, les Alemans en chartiers, les Italiens en charlatans, les Anglois en niais appriuoisez, mais les François en Princes; & de fait il n'y a que ce liure & les belles tragedies ou graues histoires, qui ayent graces en ce langage, toute badinerie & conte de iougleur n'y

48. Saulnier, « Etude sur B. de V. », pp. 292-293.
49. *Ibid.*, p. 293.

parroissent point : voila pourquoi ayant tant de maiesté en ceci, lui en donnant dauantage, i'ay grand peur que ceci ne soit si difficile, que chacun le cachera, de peur aussi que les secrets ne soient diuulguez, en quoi ie crains vn notable accident pour le pauure peuple, si les destinees n'y ont preuenu & prouueu. Or est il, & ie le senz à la disposition de ma fressure, que les bons destins m'ont contraint de faire ce que ie fay pour honorer le monde; aussi i'eusse mis ce liure en autre langue, mais tout à son tour; si ce n'eust esté de peur de faire dormir la ieunesse, ie l'eusse mis en langue de veau; mais quoi! la vicissitude des choses l'a emporté; i'eusse bien dit des chouses, sans que ie sçay comment il faut parler, dautant qu'il n'y a gueres de femmes qui escriuent ce mot de chose sans y faillir. Ignorez vous pourquoi le vulgaire en Grece ne parle plus grec, en Iudee hebreu, en Italie latin : & la cause pour laquelle ces bons langages ne sont plus vulgaires ? oyez ceste verité que ie prononce; c'est pour ce que les sciences y sont traictees, & sur tout la doctrine de maquerellage, en latin, & que l'on n'a pas voulu que les disciplines fussent communes au peuple; partant on a caché les langues, pour auec leur secret ne les communiquer qu'aux gens de bien & d'honneur, ainsi que langues de beuf à la cheminee, qui ne sont pas pour les gueux, au moins par deliberation, si que le menu peuple n'y peut toucher; & ma crainte qui sans doute aura occasion de durer, dautant qu'il est euident que ce que ie crain aduiendra, c'est que ce liure venant à estre gousté, sauouré & digeré, on taschera d'abolir le François & oster de la bouche du peuple ce beau langage, de crainte que ces bonnes & meilleures doctrines ne viennent à tomber entre les mains du populaire, qui aduenant tel cas seroit aussi aisement la pierre philosophale que les doctes, qui sans faute la trouueront es rencontres où nous parlons plus finement & disons des choses que les blasphemateurs prendroient en vn autre sens, & pource il les faut bien & diligemment peser. Il y a encor vn autre danger de bien grand mal, c'est que si i'euuse fait ce liure en grec, la medecine fut perie; si en latin, les loix eussent esté abolies; & ne s'en est gueres fallu que ie ne l'aye mis en Hebreu pour faire plaisir aux Theologiens, qui seuls eussent eu tout ce labeur, qui est la quinte essence du

> Coras, des Talmuds, du Seserholam, du Zoar, & tels liures faits ou à faire, ce que ie n'ay garde, & n'en seray rien par depit d'vn moine huguenot qui disoit que ceux qui estoient en colere, & ne iuroient point, estoient heretiques » (I, 275-277).

The extreme length of the passage just quoted seems to me to be justified for the amount of themes it brings together, some of which I have indicated. The last few sentences, however, are especially notable for their Protestant cast. It seems evident that Béroalde is poking fun at the idea that a people's religion should be presented to them in a language with which they are unfamiliar, almost as if the idea in so doing were to keep them from understanding too much. Had he presented his « bible », *Le Moyen de Parvenir,* in an obscure, dead language, he suggests, he would have presented to the scholars something to labor over and to decipher. There is the implication that these learned gentlemen might then have thought they had found the philosopher's stone (the Bible, in other words, as in *Cymbalum Mundi*), or might have established themselves as sorcerers distilling the « quinte essence » of this rare and secret alembic which *Le Moyen de Parvenir* might have been, written in any other language than French. The passage appears to me to stand as indictment of non-democratic procedures, and as we progress in our examination of *Le Moyen de Parvenir* we discover that that is probably what it is, and that it is no more Protestant of a necessity than it is mockery of the mania for analysis of Biblical texts which learned Protestants and Catholics share. Similarly, the Querelle des Anciens et des Modernes may not be the only or even the *real* issue here, but, rather, the disputes of Protestants and Catholics concerning the relative didactic and dogmatic purport of the Old and New Testaments.

As for the initial « S. » following this portion of the title page, I have arrived at no entirely satisfactory answer for it. We may postulate Joseph-Juste Scaliger[50], an interlocutor in the novel, to whom early in the text we find the following

50. Paul Lacroix (pp. 3-4) in his note on Scaliger tries to date *Le Moyen de Parvenir* before 1609, the date of the latter's death. Lacroix argues that the author depicts Scaliger as still living, and that this constitutes proof that the composition of the novel took place prior to 1609. I personally cannot consider this as ample proof, since the author also depicts Mahomet, etc., *ad infinitum,* as still living.

reference: « Cheut ! ie vous prie si vous allez à l'écolle enseignez ce mot de grammaire à Lipsius & à Scaliger, afin que l'on die cy apres promettre & effectuer... » (I, 7). Yet another possibility is the Florentine Salvino Degli Armati, who, around 1284, invented the eyeglasses. More probably, it stands for the family of printers, the Estiennes, who all signed under the Latin name Stephanus. This family of printers, scholars, polyglots, philologists, compiled works in several languages, and was mixed up in religious and satirical questions of the period; and, rather convincingly, it was Robert Stephanus, son-in-lw of the editor Badius, who, in 1514, gave a Parisian edition of Calepin's dictionary. Still another though more whimsical theory is that the « S. » stands for « Dame Sophie » or « La Sagesse », the key figure of the novel, around whom all other characters and themes revolve. If I am right in this conjecture, then we are easily led to the following line of the title page: « Recensuit Sapiens ab A, ad Z. » The reader cannot fail to take note of the capitalization of the word « Sapiens », and if he has not yet been made aware that he will be presented with a group of philosophers, he is now promised that the whole spectrum will be in the offing. Just how « wise » these « wise-ones » are, in comparison or contrast with their hostess, « La Sagesse », remains to be seen; but certainly the word « Sapiens », taken in the light of the words *Raison* and *Demonstration*, announces the scientific attentions of the book.[51] I take the words « ab A, ad Z » to mean not only the living and the dead, but also to hint, once again, at religious teminology, this time the Alpha and Omega.

It is surely not unreasonable to suspect, too, that the *S.* stands for « Saint », *S.* being a common abbreviation for the word « Saint » during the Renaissance. If this is true, the author gains additional undercover religious satire, of course,

51. In his *Etude sur Béroalde de Verville*, p. 242, Saulnier establishes Béroalde's concept of alchemy. He says: « Par *alchimie*, Béroalde entend l'analyse pratique des corps, antidote des savoirs livresques. » The quotation which Saulnier gives us from Béroalde's *Palais des Curieux* is in the spirit of Francis Bacon, a late contemporary of Béroalde. Béroalde writes: « ...je vouldrois que la science et la practique fussent bien unies ensemble. » Is it not reasonable to relate the word « Demonstration » used facetiously in the subtile of *Le Moyen de Parvenir* to this notion ? Compare Francis Bacon, *Essays, Advancement of Learning, New Atlantis, and Other Pieces*, ed. Richard Foster Jones (New York, 1937), p. 200: « Here therefore [is] the first distemper of learning, when men study words and not matter... » (Not my brackets.)

and takes another stab at pedantry, what is more. In conjunction with this we might compare Des Periers' dedication of *Cymbalum Mundi,* from which Béroalde doubtless derived more than one ingredient for *Le Moyen de Parvenir.* Des Periers, at the beginning of *Cymbalum Mundi* writes: « Thomas du Clevier, à son amy Pierre Tryocan S. », the name Clevier representing « incrédule » and Tyrocan « croyant », with the « S » standing for « Salut ».[52]

Several times in the discussion of the title of the novel and its frontispiece I have alluded to time, and to religious satire already present at this point. Going directly to the subtitle, « Oeuure contenant la raison de tout ce qui a esté, est & sera : auec demonstrations certaines & necessaires, selon la rencontre des effects de VERTV ». Within this fragment one may easily see one of the dominant baroque themes of the novel: time and mutability.[53] Nowhere in the entire novel, in fact, is there greater eruption than that produced by the shifting tenses of no less than the verb *être,* which in and of itself should imply something static. Yet it does not seem to be enough to say simply « la raison de tout ce qui est ». We must also have gradations of time. For this reason, other words in the frontispiece underline the temporal concept and the related theme of mutability. I have already stressed the word « nunc » from the *Æneid.* To this I would add the very word « parvenir » implying, as it does, motion from one place to another, or at least change of position. Nor can one omit the word « effects », which gives us outward motion or growth, is resultant. The word « rencontre » (like the later « Recensuit »)

52. Des Periers, p. 299.

53. Jean Rousset, *La Littérature de l'âge baroque en France* (Paris, 1954), p. 121:

> « Quelles que soient les traditions assez diverses : stoïcienne, platonicienne, biblique ou philosophie de la nature, qui s'amalgament alors en combinaisons variables chez chacun, ce que tous en retiennent, l'amplifiant et le répétant sous toutes les formes, c'est le refrain du *Tout change.* Il retentit partout, avec des résonances diverses selon l'éclairage, de Béroalde de Verville, qui acquiesce à la ' durée par succession ' de Du Vair parce qu'elle fait passer l'homme du mal au bien et du bien au mieux :
> » Tout ce qui est ça bas n'est rien que changement,
> » Tout est naissance et mort, car éternellement
> » Comme un estat se perd, un autre prend sa forme...
> » Nous partons d'un endroit pour aller en un autre... »

The lines are taken from Béroalde's « Stances de la Mort et de la Vie ». See Rousset, p. 273, note 2 to Chapitre V.

gives this feeling to a lesser degree; but we could not possibly overlook the verb « aduiẽdra », closely related to « parvenir », the future tenses subsequent to it, nor, for that matter, the temporal charge of the words « Alpha and Omega » implied by « ab A. ad Z. », which I have already proposed as having religious overtones.

The religious implications of the subtitle « Oeuure, etc. », containing the phrase « ...la raison de tout ce qui a esté, est & sera... » are immediately perceived, of course. They are very likely meant to echo the French version of the Gloria Patri or lesser doxology.

Thus the hermetic qualities of the title are linked by internal characteristics and passages, more of which I shall shortly deal with, to the dominant characteristics of the book proper, its textual obscurity, its themes of time and mutability, as well as its penchant for satire of religious change or difference, of the professions such as medicine and law, of pedantry, of laborious literature, and so forth. But religion, and its themes of time and mutability, especially as they are linked with the baroque sensibility, are definitely in the ascendancy.

Finally, the « Imprimé cette année » at the bottom of the title-page, which Saulnier says « ...est une nouvelle lapalissade » [54] is another treatment of time. The perpetuity of the book is guaranteed by it; the time element « année » loses all force when used with the ultimately meaningless demonstrative. Time itself becomes timeless.

In summary, the major themes of *Le Moyen de Parvenir* are subtly presented in the frontispiece, through both the title and the subtitle, as well as the glosses, be these latter synthetic or authentic. One knows that it is going to be a « man's world » that is portrayed to us, and, at that, more than likely the world of the philosopher (though this will need some modification as we go along). It is probable, too, that in this context we will find allusion to war, or at least to the art of war; that there will perhaps be a touch of misogyny resulting from this special clustering of ideas. There is little question that the title and other features of the frontispiece involve the implication that our book is to be some kind of catechism, and that satire of the Christian faith, and even of other faiths

54. Saulnier, *Etude sur B. de V.*, p. 293.

as they are sifted through the human mind and used for purposes of self-advancement or celebration of the ego will be present. We may even anticipate anti-clericism in this almost exclusively « male » book. In addition, allusion to the polyglot dictionary may forecast some literary satire.

The erotic nature of *Le Moyen de Parvenir* is, however, only obliquely inferred. One will have to linger on the word « VERTV », take into consideration the twisted reading Béroalde might have found in the lines surrounding the quotation from the *Æneid*, and even stop to realize that in the final analysis, we are not really told just what it is we will get to by reading the book. Still there is little doubt that religious satire and the related themes of time and mutability are present with certain immediacy. If there is ambiguity in the title, this is for one thing characteristic of the baroque mind, so that the style itself is, in a sense, predicted. What is more, this very ambiguity has a definite purpose: it constitutes a protective device. Similarly, the presence of the word « VERTV » might well have averted possible censure [55] of the kind to which Bruno and Vanini were almost contemporaneously subjected. From 1610 on Parlement will be very severe, and the assassination of Henri IV will not dispose it to benevolence. We are reminded,

55. See Paul Lacroix, p. xxi, where certain remarks of his suggested this idea to me.

> « C'est à peu près vers la même époque (1610) que *le Moyen de Parvenir* vit le jour, et l'on a lieu de supposer que les éditions se multiplièrent secrètement, sans l'aveu de l'auteur et sans la sauvegarde d'un privilège du roi : on en connaît quatre ou cinq qui ont été imprimées évidemment à Tours, ou à Rouen, ou à Lyon dans les vingt premières années du dix-septième siècle. On ne voit nulle part que la censure théologique se soit exercée contre ce livre impie et obscène : on pourrait affirmer que le Parlement de Paris n'a pas arrêté la vente ni poursuivi le libraire, soit oubli, soit indifférence. Il est vrai que Béroalde avait, selon son habitude, fait figurer la *vertu* sur le frontispice de son scandaleux ouvrage, qui est intitulé ainsi dans l'édition que le père Niceron regarde comme la première et croit sortie des presses elzeviriennes. »

That which scandalizes in our day — and in the nineteenth century — did not necessarily scandalize our ancestors, at least not in the same way. The words which modern dictionaries classify under « trivial » were current, and still enjoy robust health in the country and in certain popular milieus, and one spoke rather boldly in certain connections.

In short it is not obscenity (especially not our kind) which excited the anger of the « Puissances publiques et religieuses », but the aberrations which smacked of heresy or blasphemy (e.g. making fun of holy things, infringing on the laws of the Church, priding oneself on one's libertinage, etc.).

furthermore, of the censure *Le Parnasse Satyrique* underwent some years after the composition of *Le Moyen de Parvenir.* As we analyse the novel proper, we will see that our suspicions are verified, and that the intentions of Béroalde de Verville are, despite the baffling character of the title — the meaning of which we will now study — and despite certain baffling passages in the text, quite unmistakeable.

CHAPTER III

THE MEANING OF THE TITLE

Over and over again the words of the title recur in the text proper of *Le Moyen de Parvenir.* They are like the recurrent theme in a symphony, and each time they appear, from the beginning clear to the end of the novel, they shed new light on the interpretations we may lend to the title, many of which I have already proposed. If, on the one hand, one cannot reason forward from the title and the title page — which is no doubt inevitably a *post hoc* proposition —, one can certainly reason back from the text. The *mot d'ordre* of this assembled company is to keep one's word *(promettre et effectuer),* Béroalde tells us. The implication is that that is the substantial ingredient in the « perfection » of *bienséance,* to which he frequently refers for one purpose or another. Right in the second chapter of the book (a chapter entitled « Poinct »), we are confronted with a variation on the title. Béroalde is scorning the idea of splitting hairs over the meanings of *promettre,* and, says he: « I'ay ouy dire à ce propos que les docteurs de ce temps ont défoncé les pippes de leurs sciences, pour trouuer vne glu qui peust congeler les parolles & les faire tenir. Ie pense qu'ils y paruiendront, moyennant qu'ils sachent ce volume... » (I, 7).

This is the first clue, then, in the actual text, that the book is to be regarded as a handbook, or a kind of mock bible, and that the knowledge of it will lead one wherever one wishes to go. The quotation ends: « ...& que par ceste doctrine qui leur sera infuse comme vne poignée de bon vin, ils ayent cognoissance de la glaire concentrique de l'emolument naturel, qui peut produire ce dont ils ont affaire » (I, 7). With this book and the appropriate amount of wine, then, one has the « Cognoissances nécessaires » !

Yet, behind this bogus language, with its obvious erotic

evocation of the opening quatrain (especially in the word *emolument*), and its additional sensualities, lurks a concept which is never far from the author's mind. He is ever concerned with that which is central, centrifugal, concentric, and internal.[1] This can be noted, of course, in the words « la glaire concentrique », but it is elsewhere present in conjunction with the author's own commentary on the book. While the sexual implications and the humorous aspects of the imagery are obvious, one should take note that the sphere is referred to here and in other parts of the novel, no doubt in connection with internal-external relationships, so that geometric patterns, as well as problems of the macrocosm-microcosm, and of the heliocentric and geocentric theories of the universe are complexly involved, probably with satirical intent. We should ever be aware, however, of the mathematical, as well as the scientific, philosophical, and theological workings of this incredibly rich mind, which is, literally and figuratively, at play before us. Present at all times and in direct focus, of course, are the sensual and artistic sides of the author's nature. To this I should add that the foregoing compound of sensuality and artistry is, to my mind, a true baroque characteristic, while the additional ingredients of the man's outlook, his satirical and pessimistic views, lead me to the more specific terms *baroque satyrique* and *baroque satirique,* two interrelated categories, the sensual leading into and applicable to the broad, universal lines of the satire.

In the meanwhile, lest doubt be cast on the claims I have

1. Here we might make note of Béroalde's intense and personal utterance in *Les Cognoissances nécessaires:* « ' Je recherche de tout la forme intérieure. ' » This is quoted by V.-L. Saulnier in his « Etude sur Béroalde de Verville », *Revue d'Humanisme et Renaissance,* V (1944), p. 253. The reader might well call to mind for sake of comparison with such passages from the novel another sensual and partly satirical piece containing its own libertine arguments. I allude to Andrew Marvell's « To his coy mistress », and especially to the following lines: « Let us roll all our strength and all/Our sweetness up into one ball... » — Quoted from J. William Hebel and Hoyt H. Hudson, *Poetry of the English Renaissance* (New York, 1941), p. 867.

In addition, the spherical images noted in these earlier passages recur in a much later chapter, entitled « Section », perhaps in reference to the title, perhaps merely by coincidence. One of the interlocutors, apparently Mécénas, speaking of a particular act, makes the following analogy: « ...comme quand on perce le noyau moyen ou bouton d'vne rouë... » (I, 262). It should be noted that Paul Lacroix gives the following footnote in his edition (p. 178): « On dirait maintenant moyeu. »

already made concerning the various meanings of the title as they appear in the text, I should like to submit and to examine certain other important passages. Still near the beginning of the novel, in a chapter entitled « Circoncision », Béroalde writes of the « perfection » of « bienséance »:

> De mesme cecy doit estre meslé en vostre ceruelle, il le vous faut bailler tout meslé; le personnage qui vous produit en tout honneur ces saincts memoires de perfection, a pensé que le texte ne valloit pas mieux que le commentaire, parquoy il les a fait aller ensemble. Donques soit que vous lisiez ou non, ou que vous commenciez icy ou là, n'importe, ce liure est par tout plein de fidelles instructions & sens parfait, tellement que c'est tout vn par où vous lisiez. Il est vn globe d'infinie doctrine, il y a autant à apprendre en vn lieu qu'en l'autre, en ceste sorte-cy qu'en celle-là, il n'y a ligne, endroit, verset ou passage... qui ne soit tout farcy de science mystigorique & concluante (I, 36-37).

The above passage lends weight to the argument that the book is a bible, and adds to this suggestion the further one that the text and the glosses are interwoven, so that we can read our moral instruction anywhere in the book. What's more, we will be able to make perfect sense of the book, which is, I take special pains to point out, « vn globe d'infinie doctrine », and we will not be in any trouble, for every aspect of it is a « science mistigorique et concluante ». Hence, we are able to add two more dimensions to our understanding of the nature of the book: it is, we learn, secret, or ambiguous, and the ideas are, the author confesses, tossed at us pell-mell. Two more baroque features could not be found in a work, were one to set out to track them down intentionally; and yet the author unabashedly confesses to the random style of his « novel ». Here, as in another passage we shall look at, Béroalde quite clearly admits his refusal to compose, another truly baroque characteristic. That he has gone so far as to say just above this passage:

> Ie vous asseure que ce liure estoit simple & net, beau comme le jour, ainsi qu'il est encores, bien qu'il soit pesle-mesle de notes & considerations à la façon du bon homme Guoy, qui à l'âge de cent ans se mit à viure capuchinement; il auoit esté page de chez le Roy, puis

> il estudia, fut à la guerre, se fit Cordelier, s'en retira pour estre huguenot, se fit sçauant, deuint Ministre, mangea tout, puis se mit à demander sa vie : on luy donnoit de tout ce qu'il luy falloit, qu'il mettoit en son escuelle, pain, chair, souppe, potage, vin, sert, dessert ensemble; & on luy disoit, « Pourquoy ne mangez-vous & boiuez d'ordre & à part ? — Ha ha, disoit-il, lourdaut mon amy puis qu'ils se doiuent mesler au ventre, il n'y a point de danger de luy enuoyer tout desia meslé » (I, 36).

only further proves the point, and, what is more, clarifies one of the spurious titles of the novel, « Le Salmigondis... », which has already been discussed.

In addition, Béroalde rather boastfully insists here on the book's hermetic qualities — and for him they are indeed *qualities* which are both necessary and distinctive. This, amongst other things, is pinpointed in the following passage, which follows hard on the foregoing, and offers new variations on the themes already set forth: « Ie le diray doncques l'vn, & celuy d'aupres ie le nommeray l'autre... ainsi ie disposeray les secrets afin qu'ils ne soient entendus que de ceux qui ont bon nez, lesquels par ce moyen soubs ceste plaisante escorce chercheront le noyau qui est caché en l'vn & en l'autre » (I, 39).

Thus, the need to seek out the meaning of the book is insisted upon, and it would appear that only those who are correctly appointed (« qui ont bon nez »), only the wellborn, the correctly instructed, by extension, only the initiate, will fathom this book. The secondary subtitle, « *Et aduiēdra que ceux qui auront nez à porter lunettes s'en seruirōt...* », is, of course, to be recalled. If one sets aside the blatant sexual connotations of the passage, one can again note here the internal *(noyau)* and the external *(escorce)* spherical images, which should fall into our large symbolic cluster, a cluster which is at once a symbol of the sexual organs and of a universal system. The two are, to say the least, quite inter-related themes.

After all this, can we be surprised to find in the following chapter, entitled « Pause Derniere », that Béroalde is instructing his reader to bring honor to these « saincts memoires » (I, 36) — these *Vies de saints,* if you will —, and to have these « precieuses reliques » held in reverence (I, 42)? He writes:

> Or commençons de conclure, & soyez auertis, vous qui verrez ces precieuses reliques des richesses du monde,

> que vous deuez porter honneur à cet ouurage, que si vous n'estes assez forts pour luy en porter assez, trainez-le, ou luy enuoyez, ou le roulez, ou luy faites tenir en reuerence, & prenez garde à ce que cet honneur soit distribué honnestement aux scientifiques personnes & discrettes qui sont en ce banquet... (I, 42).

As to the activities of the group, which are many and colorful, one is not too surprised either to find them crowned with the most supreme of all activities (whatever *that* is, and about that, too, there is at least room for a theory). Let us transcribe the catalogue:

> On parla, on mangea, on beut, on fit st, on se teut, on fit du bruit, on protesta, on rencontra, on rit, on baailla, on entendit, on disputa, on cracha, on moucha, on s'estonna, on s'esbahit, on admira, on gaussa, on raporta, on entendit, on broüilla, on s'esclaircit, on debattit, on s'accorda, on trinca l'vn à l'autre, on fit carroux, on remarqua, on tremoussa, on s'accouda, on cria tout bas, on se teut tout haut, on se mocqua, on murmura, on s'auisa, on se reprit, on se contenta, on passa le temps, on douta, on redouta, on s'assagit, on deuint, on paruint (I, 43).[2]

Among these activities, some contradictory and irrational, some pertaining to the heretical, and some to the administration of the sacrements, we should linger for a moment in this long list on the words « on passa le temps ». Going back to my previous statement that the central-most theme of the book is to my mind that of time and mutability, I feel that the position of this phrase in the list is very important, coming as it does near the end. I note too that out of this particular activity come the really *important* things, such as doubt, fear, gaining wisdom, becoming and (« arriving »). There appears to be a stratification of activities in the list, and yet we are left to wonder what, exactly, is meant by the verb *parvenir*, once given its sexual and social connotations... and even these are never openly stated.

2. Paul Lacroix explains « fit carroux » as « *carrousse, bonne chère* », p. 26; and Royer, in his glossary (vol. II), is in agreement with this meaning. Is there not, too, the suggestion of a game here?

Directly following this long list of verbs comes Béroalde's overt statement that the book, whose title now appears in the text for the first time, and in capital letters, is a « breuiare ». Calling back into play the verb of his secondary subtitle, « Et aduiẽdra que ceux... », he asks, « Qu'en auint-il ? », and he continues:

> Il en auint ce docte monument, ce precieux memorial, ce joyeux repertoire de perfection, cet antidote contre tout malheur, ceste affiloire de bonnes graces, CE MOYEN DE PARVENIR, vnique breuiaire de resolutions vniuerselles, & particulieres : à quoy on ne peut contredire, ny opposer d'hyperboles, ny le redarguer de fausselé; & dittes que vous en auez, captieuses tignes, qui voulez tout reformer & refondre; mais vous sectateurs des vrayes vertus Cardinales, gens haïs de l'oisiueté, qui aimez mieux vous amuser à boire, que penser à mal, ou perdre le temps inutilement, considerez ceci, empoignez ce volume, volume dit à cause de la verité qu'il contient, comme vn beau verre plein de bon vin. Verre & volume sont equiuoques, le verre est vn volume, il est vray que c'est le petit, c'est l'epitome, d'autant que le gros volume est le poinçon bienheureux : qui ont belles & amples bibliotheques remplies de tels volumes, ils sont capables de rendre victus tout le monde tant docte soit-il (I, 43-44).

That the book is no *vade mecum* or *breuiaire*, strictly speaking, we know from the earlier commands that we drag it or roll it (!), if necessary. Still, this is a small matter, for the fact is that our author has finally told us quite plainly that he intends the book as a mock prayerbook, a missal, at the very least; and insofar as he claims it to be full of « resolutions uniuerselles » [3], it is my feeling that we may go so far as to say that it is a question of the Bible itself. I also underline the fact that the « Verre et volume sont equiuoques », thus recalling my discussion of the topsy-turvy nature of the book, and the fact that it is composed in such a way that, like a glossed Bible, one can open it at any spot and read and understand (?). Naturally I am not unaware of the sexual

3. Here I feel an analogy exists with the description of *Le Moyen de Parvenir* as a « satyre universelle », to be found in *Le Palais des Curieux* and quoted by Saulnier, « Etude sur B. de V. », pp. 284-285.

interpretations of the passage, above all in view of the tale about the curate and his « breuiaire » which directly follows, in a chapter whose title is, significantly enough, « Vidimus ». Nonetheless, here, as always, there is a deeper meaning than the purely sexual one at stake.

It is in that next chapter, « Vidimus », that full elaboration of the nature, size and portent of the book is given. Béroalde lingers on the concept of the book as a *breuiaire,* and even goes so far as to call it « le Livre », capitalizing the « l », and thus alluding almost directly to the Bible. All is to be found in this book, says he, so that,

> ...afin d'auoir le credit de se chausser au beau feu d'intelligence, entendez, vous qui auez enui de paruenir, que nous vous faisons part de ce fin recueil de mysteres autentiques, vous proposant deuant les yeux les symboles de chacun, comme ils ont esté proferez; si tost que quelqu'vn ouuroit la bouche pour prononcer sa goulee, aussi tost les secretaires le mettoient par estat, & colligeoient les paroles & propos, comme belles & bonnes perles és riues d'Asie, dont ce volume a esté compilé, & lequel de tout le temps a esté & sera, à cause de son excellence, pour son merite, & à iamais, par ceux qui ont de l'entendement en grosse lettre dit & nommé le Liure, ne dictes pas sans queuë, d'autant qu'il aduiendra ainsi qu'il est aduenu plusieurs fois, & que les grands, au detriment des plus foibles, le trouuant, & craignant qu'il soit veu du petit & bon monde, le seelleront comme Chanceliers à simple queuë, ou à double, ou telle que le temps admettra. Ie vous prie bonnes personnes de ne dire rien de cecy, & n'alleguer ce mot que nous n'auons pas mis au tiltre, d'autant que s'il y estoit on le reco gnoistroit tout aussi tost, & il en aduiendroit trop de malheur, le plaisir des gens de bien seroit perdu; ces meschans escommuniez qui font tant mettre de daces & imposts sur le peuple au desceu du Roy, le pauure homme qui ne l'entend pas, ces malheureux là viendroient & prendroient ce liure, & le vous vendroient vn escu pour lettre au meilleur marché, ioint qu'à tel on vendroit la lettre cinquante escus, & ainsi se seroient tout d'or comme Simon Magus & son chien, & les ministres quand ils seront affriandez aux lettres d'enuoy comme en Angleterre (I, 47-48).

Again, then, the mysterious verb « aduenir » is brought to bear; the secret formulae of the book are insisted upon; the hint at religion is ever present, as in the expression « recueil de mysteres » — suggesting the mystery play or religious mysteries. Also, the time dimension is now given full-bodied statement; for, Béroalde, recalling passages in which he has said « on passa le temps » or has sharply chastized those who can « perdre le temps inutilement », now states that his book, because of its excellence, for its merit, throughout all time « a esté & sera... à iamais... le Liure... ». In this way, we are reminded of the first subtitle of *Le Moyen de Parvenir,* « Œuvre contenant la raison de tout ce qui a esté, est, & sera... ». Notice, too, that this book is great in part for its pearls gathered from the Orient. For a book to have such a reputation, it must have truth, and this is indeed one of the things we are commanded to realize of the book. « Ne le redarguer de fausseté... » he has already told us, for the book is full of « vrayes vertus » (see next to last quotation [I, 43-44]); and we are not to put it to doubt. We are again warned about appropriate treatment of this precious document, for Béroalde continues:

> Iouyssez amis de cet œuure sans le prophaner, & sçachez que par le rapport des sçauans il est tel, que les plus gens de bien racontent & afferment par tout qu'il contient tout ce que chacun sçait, a sçeu, & sçaura, ou doit sçauoir & entendre; il embrasse les mysteres approuuez de toutes sciences, pour autant qu'il est la iuste, solide & naïue interpretation de la pure cabale de valeur non imaginaire. Ne parlez plus de clauicules ou clauifesses, n'y d'arts apperitifs, canons & artillerie qui sont engins grandement ouurans, puis que vous auez ces cayers de verité : ce bon volume qui est la grosse clef d'ordonnance, à laquelle pend le trousseau de toutes clefs (I, 48).

Not only have we the truth, but we have in our hand the depository of all human knowledge accrued through the ages, as will be noted again, in the temporal phrase: « que chacun sait, a sçeu, & sçaura, ou doit sçauoir & entendre ». We must, therefore not profane (!) this book. And though it is in essence the « cayers de verité », it has deep mysteries. In other words, Béroalde enlists the reader as the sharer of his secret, as his confidant. He even goes as far as to give as counterpoise to the interlocutor « Moy » another interlocutor designated as

« Vovs ». Probably mocking the mystics who write in the tradition of Dionysius the Areopagite, he implies that the reader (were he to understand) is getting true, first-hand information, which he must impart to no one. Béroalde uses the technique of bringing the reader « in on the act », through what might be labelled as flattery — though once we have seen the true flavor of this satire, the flattery is diminished. In a previous passage, he has addressed his audience as « bonnes personnes » whom he entreats to say nothing of the book, so that speculation with it will not take place; further on, he addresses his readers as « amis », begging them not to profane the book. Should they mistreat it, then they are « captieuses tignes » (teignes): « ...& dittes que vous en auez, captieuses tignes, qui voulez tout reformer & refondre », he says, involving his reader in much the same way that the author of *La Pícara Justina* does with the recurrent « hermano lector » or that Baudelaire has done in the opening poem of *Les Fleurs du Mal,* with its famous line, « Hypocrite lecteur, — mon semblable, — mon frère ! »[4]

Béroalde, returning to his theme of eternity, with its shifting times and tenses, says to his reader:

> Receuez donc ce present, ce passé, ce futur, beaux & fidelles esprits, vous y trouuerez vn insigne profit, attendu que tous les liures qui furent iamais faits, ou seront faits par hommes ou femmes, filles ou garçons, ou neutres, sont signez, ou marquez, ou paraphrasez, ou predictions de cestuy-cy tant naïf, clair & euident, lequel est la fin finale & intelligible de tous; & ainsi tous ne sont & ne seront que interpretations des secrets icy exposez, & qui ne se trouuent que par dessein en ce beau petit abondant moule de perfection exemplaire. Quiconque le sçaura capable de toutes sciences, & n'ignorera que ce qu'il ne sçaura pas, d'autant que tout est icy au petit pied en parfaict Idee, clarifiant tout autant qu'il est possible. Que si quelques mauuais opiniastres, incredules, heretiques, stupides, conscientieux, faussonniers, ou autre ribaudaille ne me veut croire, ie parle à vous qui estes de telle qualité; & vous dy que si vous ne me croyez, que ie veux & desire qu'en guise de personne demy-saincte, chacun pour soy, vous puissiez receuoir vne bonne secouade d'estrapade, qui vous dure vne semaine, redoublant tousiours pour

4. Charles Baudelaire, *Les Fleurs du Mal* (Paris, 1941), p. 7.

> mignarder vostre constance, ou vne gesne de rage de fondement, ou vne cuisson de carnosité intollerable, ou vn chatouillement de fines gouttes, ou passion colique, voire tout ensemble auec toutes autres sortes d'incommoditez à la sauce d'Allemagne, tant qu'à vostre requeste ie vous donne remede, & ne vous scandalisez si en l'excez de mes charitez, ie vous souhaite auec si bonne & saincte affection, tel & si grand bien; asseurez vous que ce n'est sans cause, d'autant que ie sçay qu'il vous en aduiendra vn merueilleux emolument, à cause que chatouillez de telles friandises de maux & troubles de l'aise cruel que vous en sentirez, aurez cognoissance de vostre faute, & ne serez plus iuges ingrats d'autruy, qui peut estre vaut mieux que vous. Ainsi ce mal vous reussira en bien, à cause que vous souuenant de ce liure en vos rigueurs, vous y aurez recours, & vous vous en trouuerez ou de mesme, ou de mieux, ou pis, au grand aduantage du salut de vostre ame, si vous en sçauez bien vser, & comme bons peres de famille qui traictent bien leurs hostes & entretiennent les toits de leurs maisons de peur d'estre incommodez (I, 54-55).

Thus, we are under moral obligation to seek out the truth which is presented to us, and though Béroalde confesses that the secret is well hidden, it is not impossible to come to understand the book; for, says he, there is a key to this « Bible », the Author of which is doubtful! We can, with effort, then, or given a certain type of initiation, penetrate its meaning. Doubtless, the idea is to ridicule concordances, glosses, polyglot editions of the Bible, learned commentaries on the Bible, and the like. The key, a sexual symbol as well as a literary term, was come by in a curious way, through a cure worked by « le père Rabelais, le docte » for the Cardinal du Belay. Of Rabelais Béroalde says: « & je le mets icy en auant, pour ce que les substances de ce present ouurage, memoires & enseignemens de ce Liure, furent trouuees entre les menues besognes de la fille de l'Autheur » (I, 49).

I can give little credence to the conjectures made by Paul Lacroix in his introduction that Béroalde had indeed touched up any manuscript of Rabelais[5], as he seems to think

5. Paul Lacroix, p. xiv.

that Béroalde is implying in the passage just above. It is on the basis of this obviously farcical passage that Paul Lacroix has based his argument of Rabelais as the original author of *Le Moyen de Parvenir.* This and many other things have been conjectured concerning the authorship of *Le Moyen de Parvenir.*[6] But is it not to miss the whole point of the passage, and to forget that these « textes & memoires meslees de toute sapience, moyens, elemens & enseignemens à bien viure, les meslanges que vous trouuerez sont suruenus à cause de l'antiquité de ce volume, & des annotations, apostilles, & interpretations qui y estoient mise... » (I, 35)?

A conjecture which has never been advanced is the possible debt to Erasmus' *Praise of Folly,* here, as in other dominant features of *Le Moyen de Parvenir.* Erasmus, in his *Praise of Folly,* says:

> « Nor will it be amiss also to imitate the rhetoricians of our times, who think themselves in a manner gods if like horse leeches they can but appear to be double-tongued, and believe they have done a mighty act if in their Latin orations they can but shuffle in some ends of Greek like mosaic work, though altogether by head and shoulders and less to the purpose. And if they want hard words, they run over some worm-eaten manuscript and pick out half a dozen of the most old and obsolete to confound their reader, believing, no doubt, that they that understand their meaning will like it the better, and they that do not will admire it the more by how much the less they understand it. Nor is this way of ours of admiring what seems most foreign without its particular grace; for if there happen to be any more ambitious than others, they may give their applause with a smile, and, like the ass, shake their ears, that they may be thought to understand more than the rest of their neighbors. »[7]

There is some possibility that Béroalde had such a passage from Erasmus in mind, and that he is mimicking those whom Erasmus is attacking, by suggesting that he has a very *old*

6. See my earlier discussion of authorship, where by bringing to bear texts known to be Béroalde's I aim at establishing him as the author of *Le Moyen de Parvenir.*

7. Desiderius Erasmus, *The Praise of Folly,* trans. John Wilson (Ann Arbor, 1958), pp. 11-12.

manuscript, and by vaunting the obscurity of his text. In quite another light, further evidence can be brought to support the theory that the *Praise of Folly* is very likely in the mind of Béroalde as he sets down his great satire, his « satyre universelle » as he calls it, reminding one of Erasmus' dedicatory epistle, in which he says: « ...he that spares no sort of men cannot be said to be angry with anyone in particular, but the vices of all. »[8] When we undertake to analyze the social structure of the book, the interlocutors, etc., we have much greater cause to turn to Erasmus' *Praise of Folly*, and to consider to what an extent this witty piece was likely to have been in the mind of Béroalde in the composition of *Le Moyen de Parvenir*. If *Le Moyen de Parvenir* is « le Livre », and if CE LIVRE EST LE CENTRE DE TOVS LES LIVRES, as we are told in the middle of the chapter entitled « Circoncision » (I, 51), it is then the Bible, it is the *central* reference, in which all things are found and all things are explained to the seeker. The authorship of the vast portion of such a book would, then, be unknown, or an amalgamation of the work of many people, but the writings themselves would be the product of a central intelligence, of a god, who, consequently, is « l'Auteur » — printed, we must point out, like « le Livre », with a capital letter! The explanation further on that the book is the combined writings of « ...cestuy-cy, tant naïf, clair et euident, lequel est la fin finale & intelligible de tous... » (I, 54) has bearing on the argument. The role of Rabelais in *Le Moyen de Parvenir* is admittedly complex, but consider the fact that everything else that has been said about the « Book » including its antiquity is said with tongue in cheek. Why then, should we take this seriously? Is it not better to suppose that Rabelais here is pictured as « le père », as a priest, and as a doctor, administering the kind of cure only he might have qualified for in a book like *Le Moyen de Parvenir*, being, as he was, both a *sage* and a *bon buveur?* Books (including the Bible) are subject to *remaniement*, to pirated editions, to falsification through interpretation, says Béroalde shortly thereafter, so that the reader, be he Béroalde's contemporary or a reader of the future, is commanded as follows:

> Apres l'exhibition de ces apozemes ie pense que ceste preuue est de merite; auisez doncques bien & diligemment

8. Erasmus, pp. 4-5.

> espluchez, & voyez auec curieuse conference tous les autres pretendus liures, cayers, volumes, tomes, œuures, liurets, opuscules, libelles, fragmens, epitomes, registres, inuentaires, copies, brouillars, originaux, exemplaires, manuscrits, imprimez, esgratignez; bref les pancartes des bibliotheques, soit de ce qui a esté, ou est, ou qui iamais encore fut, ou ne sera, sont icy en lumiere profetisez ou restituez. De perdus sont retrouuez & recouurez, & s'il y a bien dauantage, si quelqu'vn a desrobé vn œuure il sera icy decouuert, comme il se presume en verité, par vne bonne reuisitation de textes, paraphrases, commentaires, metaphrases, homelies, annotations, recensions, notes, aduersaires lectures, leçons, & autres telles negoces & inuentions de gloses & interlignes pedentines, & les calculez, vous les trouuerez icy, sans qu'il soit plus besoin de tant de liures, romans, poesies, prosnes & bauarderies, qui occupent les esprits mal à propos, & lesquels apres que l'on les sçait, ne laissent pas l'industrie d'auoir vn paillard escu... (I, 49-50).

All truth, all human knowledge, can be discovered here in this book, all things are either reconstructed or prophesied so that to spend time with others is to wind up having « desplaisir & regret au temps qui se perd en la lecture de tant de liures de fadaises, de surcroist emplis de douleur & obscurité » (I, 50). Indeed our narrator tells us:

> ...ie vous diray le secret des secrets : mais ie vous prie afin qu'il soit secret, de vous embeguiner le museau du cadenac de taciturnité & escoutez, CE LIVRE EST LE CENTRE DE TOVS LES LIVRES : voilà la parole secrette qui doit estre descouuerte au temps d'Helie, artiste, ains que disent les Alquemistes; tenez le fort caché & vous gardez des pates pelues de ces enfarinez, qui gourmandent la science & l'emplissent d'abbus : estrangez vous de ces pifres presomptueux, qui voyans les bonnes personnes desireuses de se calfeutrer le cerueau d'vn peu de bonne lecture & profitable s'en scandalisent : chassez ces escorcheurs de latin, ces escarteleux de sentences, ces maquereaux de passages poëtiques qu'ils produisent & prostituent à tous venans; gardez-vous de ces entrelardeurs de Theologie alegorique, de ces effondreux d'argumens, & de tous ceux qui aiguisent les remonstrances sur la meule

> d'hypocrisie; fuyez telles bestes, & ne leur communiquez point ce rare thresor, ains le commettez à gens de bien, comme gens de bien ont pris la peine de le vous donner, non pour en abuser, dautant que ce seroit vn peché plus que contre nature, parce qu'il n'est ny masle ny femelle; ie m'en rapporte à ces sages & prudens Prestres, qui nomment leur breuiaire leur femme, ô quelle impieté rouge comme sang ! Ceux qui parlent d'abuser de ce qui peut seruir ne l'entendent pas, ie les renuoye au Principal du college de Geneue, i'en atteste la pantoufle du Pape que ie dis vray (I, 51-2).

As Béroalde says, « commençons de conclure », at least as far as our initial discussion of the meaning of the title is concerned, the while realizing that to understand in some measure the title is to understand in some measure the book itself. Throughout the book the title recurs, in various circumstances. Two chapters after the above passage, in a chapter entitled « Correlaire », we find the following:

> « Mais je ne t'ay pas laissé, ho maistre sophiste, perdu de la vanité de tes imaginations, ame desloyalle qui ne peus comprendre le legitime moyen de paruenir, auquel tu pretends d'arriuer par sottise ou fraude ordinaire; entens, vestaudier, que nous ne parlons icy que des liures d'humanité, & t'en faire penser à mon barbier, il te donnera pour te faire Docteur vne éponide ou espauliere, d'vn coup de barre de fer sur le collet en guise de chausse d'hypocras, ou de hallebarde de drap » (I, 58).

The participants in the dialogues frequently use the formula of the title in response to some tale told by one of the guests, and it is particularly here that one can agree with Reiche when he says that the title of the novel can only be true if we take it in the reverse: how not to (behave), or else if we apply some motto such as *Castigat ridendo mores.*[9] The following exchange of dialogue between L'Avtre and Lycvrgvs in the chapter entitled « Parlement » is of special interest in this connection:

9. Herbert Reiche, *Le Moyen de parvenir von Béroalde de Verville mit besonderer Berücksichtigung der Quellen-und Verfasserfrage* (Coburg, 1913), pp. 16-17.

> I'AVTRE. — Ie me suis tant amusé à vos fadaises de sagesse estant jeune, que i'ay laissé passer les oiseaux. Par mon serment, si iamais la paix est faite j'iray à la guerre aussi bien que les autres, & croyez que si j'eusse sceu ce que ie sçay maintenant, ie fusse dedans; & à ceste heure que ie sçay le secret, on se défie de moy. Que male foire embrenne le nez de ceux qui m'ont fait perdre le temps, que cent coups de cornes au cul leur dessirent le fondement, que puissent-ils deuenir coquus apres le trespas de leurs femmes de bien ! Ie gage que vous ne sçauez ce que ie veux dire; 'Ni moy aussi' dit Chipon quand il perdit le manteau de son maistre. 'Ie gage, dit ce Seigneur, que ce coquin a perdu mon manteau. — Gagez, monsieur, vous gaignerez'; le paillard l'auoit destourné pour s'en approprier.
>
> LYCVRGVS. — Ce fut vn moyen de paruenir. Voila, il y en a qui paruiennent diuersement, les vns sans y penser, les autres par artifice, aucuns par danger, quelques vns rencontrans d'vn cherchant d'autre, aucuns courans comme ils attrapent, quelques autres en despit d'eux, & s'en faut raporter aux exemples, ainsi qu'vne truye qui auorte.
>
> BODIN. — Voila de belles maximes, & desquelles ie pourrois tirer beaucoup de sciences, i'esplucherons en passant que de ceux qui paruiennent (I, 167-168).

This same chapter has begun with a tirade on the superiority of man over woman, supposedly delivered by the same speaker (L'Avtre), and carried over from the previous chapter (« Notice »), although Royer and Paul Lacroix do not attribute the speech to the same speaker. In the Paul Lacroix edition, the entire final speech of the chapter preceding is given to L'Avtre, but in the Royer edition, it is split between (1) L'Avtre and (2) Paracelse, so that according to the Royer edition, Paracelse would be the one who says, at the beginning of the chapter entitled « Parlement »:

> Dieu fit la fille, & l'homme l'a faite femme. He bien, voila pas les hommes qui sont bien choses plus accomplies ? Ainsi est-il du monde de piperie, plus joli, plus accord, plus parfait, plus delicat & mieux sentant son bien que le premier. Et qui a-t'il en cet Vniuers cogneu des sages ? qu'y a-t'il de remarquable ? vne quinte essence celeste, direz-vous; vrayement vous auez raison, vostre asne pette;

> & au nostre qu'y a-t'il ? quoy, qué qué ? vne quinte essence plus profitable, plus penetrante, plus glorieuse, plus intelligible, & plus viuificante; les sages & les paruenans l'ont recogneuë, & l'ont apprise à plusieurs. Ceux qui ont esté plus subtils, & ont recogneu les quatre elemens de piperie, extraits ainsi de la supposition Ecclesiastique, iudicaire, medicinale & trafiquante ont tasché à y entrer pour paruenir. Aussi n'y a-t'il point d'autres moyens à cest effet, outre ceux ci, qu'vn, qui est la vraye quinte essence, selon laquelle plus aisements, & auec moins de peine, on gaigne dauantage, ayant plus de loisir & plus grand profit; & c'est ceci qui se remarque en tous ordres, où le moyen de paruenir est proposé, auquel comme en toutes vacations ceux qui font le plus de bruit, ont le plus de soin & de peine, s'auanceant en plus de trauail gaignent le moins, & par consequent ceux qui sont les plus accomodez ont moins de sollicitude, & auec moins de difficultez emportent le plus de profit. Ceci obserué de siecle en siecle (pource que les vignerons ne boiuent pas le bon vin, les miniers ne possedent gueres d'or, encor qu'ils le serrent en grands labeurs, sans que pour le preparer il leur en demeure és mains) il n'y a que maquereaux pour estre aisez, dautant qu'ils entendent aussi les matieres. Le grand Alexandre n'auança jamais qu'vn voleur, vn maquereau & vn traistre (I, 164-165).

In a chapter shortly before this entitled « Genealogie », the same discrepancy as to speaker appears, Lacroix giving the « C'est le moyen de parvenir » only once to Paracelse, and the second use of the title to Celsus, Royer giving it both times to Paracelse, as follows:

> PETRARQVE. — Voila qui est bon, mais ie demande que c'est que les affaires du monde.
>
> PARACELSE. — C'est le moyen de paruenir.
>
> CELSVS. — Vous nous l'obscurcirez tout, comme vous auez fait la Medecine, en vous vantant, & n'y disant que des ventositez. Ie vous prie, amusez vous à boire.
>
> PARACELSE. — Ie vous prie, ne vous faschez point, ie vous diray de belles choses & douces, & auec facilité : le moyen de paruenir comprend tout, & est composé des quatre elements de piperie auec leur quinte essence.

ERASTE. — C'est vne nouuelle philosophie, voire si nouuelle que l'on ne la cognoist pas.

PARACELSE. — C'est à ce coup que vous estes trompé, d'autant qu'il y en a qui la sçauent bien, & qui se moquent de nous, qui nous amusons à voir des vrines & soufler du charbon, & les autres attrapent les commoditez. Or ie vous diray comment, & ronfleray en axiomes merueilleux. Ca, que ie trenche des sentences toutes pleines d'abondance mystigorique, que ie vous en donne non Ecclesiastiquement, ny chichement, ny Iustinianiaisement, mais liberalement & philosophiquement en charité (I, 155).

Although Paul Lacroix identifies for us Paracelsus, the stormy petrel of medecine whose bombastic nature is reflected in Celsvs' speech, and tells us that Celsvs is no doubt « le philosophe épicurien Celsus, qui vivait au deuxième siècle et qui écrivit contre les chrétiens, en opposant à leur religion la philosophie naturelle » [10], he misses the happy arrangement of speakers, as a result of which Celsus and Paracelsus, in their repartee, as well as by their names, form an amusing bit of point and counterpoint. It should be noted, too, that Béroalde has it be Paracelsus who uses the term « le moyen de parvenir », and, in the light of Paracelsus' own nature, as well as in view of the element of nihilism which I find present in the book, this is of some significance. Also, by the last two passages quoted, the reader may clearly see how the title makes its ghost-like appearance from time to time in the dialogues proper. He will not be unaware, either, of the title's almost perpetual relation to time, as is especially noticeable in the next to last quotation, in the speech of L'Autre, who shows his irritation with « ...ceux qui m'ont fait perdre le temps », and in turn passes upon those people a curse which, from a temporal standpoint, is highly improbable. Other features which I have already enlarged upon will be readily perceived, such as the scientific, philosophical and religious terminology, as well as the suggestion of alchemy, most of which appear, along with their relationship to the title, in the speeches of Paracelsus. This is true, for example, of such words as « Ecclesiastique », « quinte essence », « iudiciaire », « medicinale », etc.

In fact, the whole sequence in this section of the book

10. Paul Lacroix, p. 44.

is of great interest, and may profitably be reconstructed. In the chapter entitled « Genealogie » (I, 153-7), Paracelsus, Celsus and Eraste are speaking, and Paracelsus volunteers to explain the term « le moyen de paruenir ». In the following chapter, entitled « Notice » (I, 158-163), we have a tirade by Paracelsus [11] in which the explanation (!?!) of the « quatre elements de piperie auec leur quinte essence » is given, the four elements having been « formez d'vne mesme matiere » (I, 159). The concept of the microcosm and the macrocosm again appears here: « Tout ainsi que le monde est beaucoup de fois plus grand que l'homme qui est le petit monde, & le monde le grand animal corporel... » (I, 159). Paracelsus, recalling for all the world a supposedly indignant Béroalde in *Le Palais des Curieux,* is upset over the theft of his manual, but avoids criticism for fear of being called a heretic. He goes on record, however, as being opposed to thieves, (though some are in the company) and as hating thieves who have taken elements of the Antechrist's doctrine. Here reflecting the first subtitle of the novel, Paracelsus says, « ...vous sçaurez tantost que c'est, & iugerez que ie ne passe point les limites de raison... » (I, 160). This false « essence » was counteracted by « les plus sages », who, to protect themselves, concocted a new essence (piperie) and arrived at « L'œuure parfaict de benoiste extraction » (I, 161). The rapport with the subtitle will once more be noted, as well as the religious parody intended by the word « benoiste ». Paracelsus claims that by too much mixing (social intercourse) the four elements became one (as with the Apostles, « vn symbole »). Our historian goes on to tell that people « ont trouué la cinquiesme essence necessaire, dont il est tant fait d'estat entre ceux qui veulent paruenir » (I, 161). (The word *necessaire* should also be related to the subtitle, of course.)

Thus, in the following chapter, called « Parlement » (I, 164-168), Paracelsus properly explains what the four elements which have melted together are, and what the *quinte essence* is: « ...les sages et les paruenans l'ont recogneuë... Ceux qui ont esté plus subtils, & ont recogneu les quatre elemens de piperie, extraits ainsi de la supposition Ecclesiastique, iudiciaire, medicinale & trafiquante ont tasché à y entrer pour paruenir » (I, 164-5). Hence, says Paracelsus, there is only one way — and that way is through the « vraye quinte essence » (I, 165). As

11. Paul Lacroix, p. 109. See footnote.

Paracelsus likes to keep his audience guessing, he goes on to say « c'est ceci qui se remarque en tous ordres, où le moyen de paruenir est proposé... » (I, 165). Ultimately, he gets to the point: « ...& de fait ils l'ont trouuée », says he, « à sçauoir és finances, où se pratique, non pas transpiration imperceptible, ains par emplissement naturel, le plus sainct, magnifique & commode secret d'amasser » (I, 166). The suggestion of the strait gate and of the attainment of paradise is rather more than less present, it seems to me. However, at the end of this chapter, we are left, like Lycvrgvs to conclude that « ...il y en a qui paruiennent diuersement, les vns sans y penser, les autres par artifice, aucuns par danger, quelques vns rencontrans d'vn cherchant d'autre, aucuns courans comme ils attrapent, quelques autres en despit d'eux, & s'en faut raporter aux exemples, ainsi qu'vne truye qui auorte » (I, 168).

In a chapter entitled « Livre de Raison », well preceding the jocular story of Paracelsus, we find a curious use of the title proper of the novel. It is as unquestionably linked to the title of the chapter, as the word « raison » is to the subtitle of the novel. Its curious and macabre nature makes its presence most baffling, and should give us reason to pause:

> Rvfin. — Laissez à part ces remonstrances, nous sommes ici en liberté, nul ne parle ceans pour scandaliser ains pour edifier & corriger s'il est besoin : & de fait ces preceptes tant beaux, & ces enseignemens si iustes feront plus de gens de bien, que tous les sermons ensemble de ces fagoteux d'eloquence, qui sous ombre d'estre humble aualent la gloire, comme vn Alemand qui par humilité fait carroux contre deux Suisses.
>
> Macrobe. — Or là auant n'espargnons personne, aussi bien tous ont failli, les Prestres ont accusé Iesus Christ, les gens de iustice l'ont condamné, les Ministres l'ont foüetté, le peuple l'a iniurié, les passans se sont mocqué de lui, les gens-d'armes l'ont crucifié, il n'y a que les pauures femmes qui l'ont pleuré, & ainsi ont trouué le moyen de paruenir, sans quoy elles seroient trop deuergondees; pour mieux faire laissons tels sophistes au Diable, aussi bien il y a de nouueaux imposteurs qui disent que Ministre signifie bourreau, ainsi il n'y aura que le Pape qui ne soit bourreau, à cause que comme il est en nos heures, celui qui respond à la Messe est dit Ministre, par là il n'y auroit Euesque, Prestre, ny Clerc, qui ne fut de ce beau mestier (I, 111).

To the word *ministre* Paul Lacroix attaches the footnote: « *Minister* en latin signifie souvent exécuteur. On a dit en français : *ministre de justice* et *maître* ou *ministre des hautes-œuvres.* »[12]

We can note, for one thing, how Macrobe says « Or là auant n'espargnons personne, aussi bien tous ont failli... », which foreshadows the statement of Q.P., « ...& que cependant nostre satire soit perpetuelle, pour decouurir l'abomination des affaires du mauuais monde » (I, 154). The stratification of activities from « accusé » to « pleuré » is probably no more a coincidence than the one seen in the activities of the people assembled at the banquet, terminating « ...on passa le temps, on douta, on redouta, on s'assagit, on deuint, on paruint » (I, 43).

I am tempted to conclude, in terms of these violent accusations of society, and in view of the dramatic finale given the list of activities of our gathering, that *Le Moyen de Parvenir* has as its point of departure a serious and *not* comic view of life. For this reason, I should find it difficult to agree entirely with Reiche's statement that Béroalde's sole purpose is « um Gelächter zu stiften ».[13] That would be, I feel, to oversimplify the author's intent, which has been hinted at again and again in the book. Rather, *Le Moyen de Parvenir* is a cynical attack on society, similar to that found in the picaresque novel. It is also a mocking handbook — a kind of Bible — with whose help those who read closely may attain: but attain what? I have just suggested that this may ironically be a « paradise », — something comparable to the « Champs Elysées » in Pierre Faifeu — and realize that in so doing, I run the risk of reading in too much. As a counter-argument to this potential criticism, however, I propose that if some kind of paradise more or less Lucianic in nature is not implied, one cannot easily explain away the fear, the doubt, the growing wise, which follow hard on the passing of time, and directly precede the attainment. Then too, how else shall we explain Lycurgus' statement, « ...il y en a qui paruiennent diuersement, les uns sans y penser, les autres par artifice, aucuns par danger,

12. Paul Lacroix, p. 72.

13. Reiche, p. 49. However, Reiche seems to deny that Béroalde's only purpose was « to stimulate laughter » when on pp. 55-56 he suggests that there is a certain morality in *Le Moyen de Parvenir*, whose message, then, would appear to be « les parfaits sont aux Cieux ». Furthermore on p. 57 Reiche recognizes the thorough-going nature of this satire of vices.

quelques vns rencontrans d'vn cherchant d'autre, aucuns courans comme ils attrapent, quelques autres en despit d'eux... » (I, 168)? In Lycurgus' list I believe special attention should be paid to the expression « par danger » which is perhaps connected with the assertion that in the home of the host, the « father », « se puisse tuer ». The word « danger » may well be read in the root meaning, « to fall under the dominion of », thus giving cross-reference to a general symbolic cluster which, under the arbitrary heading « father », would include the concept of God, or the Pope, a priest, or some other spiritual leader of this group, which, *generally speaking,* is non-hierarchical. Also, if some such an implication as « paradise » is not involved, how can one explain the fact that the women found their « moyen de parvenir » through tears shed at the death of Jesus Christ? (When, incidentally, by a rather misogynistic affirmation, they would not otherwise have been able to do so!)

Naturally, in a book such as *Le Moyen de Parvenir,* where the general tone is ribald, earthy, and gay, it is easy to overlook the serious substructure upon which the frolic and the comic ornaments are heaped. In point of fact, these ornaments, put in proper perspective, become altogether functional, and so they are better defined as complimentary ironies than as « comic effects ». It is also equally easy to overstate the seriousness of that substructure, which, at best, is not what we call « high seriousness », but, more accurately, a seriousness emanating from cynicism or pessimism, and evolving into wry, sometimes distorted, usually coarse, and often irrational forms of humor. For a similar argument, we might bring to bear the following statement of Professor Lambert C. Porter, who is speaking of the two related genres, *la fatrasie* and *le fatras:* « A côté de ces deux aspects de la littérature, il existait, toujours inébranable, la veine un peu pessimiste — et cynique — qui a mis au jour la plupart des genres légers et irréguliers. »[14] This opinion is, I think, a rather widely-accepted and certainly a solid one. Of particular interest to us is the fact that behind such a world view and such a sense of humor lies a certain attitude towards death, and towards the quite obviously related themes of time, mutability, epicureanism, and so forth. In other words, behind the coarse humor and even the more refined humor (the latter

14. Lambert C. Porter, *La Fatrasie et le fatras* (Genève, 1960), p. 70.

derived from the realms of wit and satire) lies that peculiar brand of mysticism discussed by Porter. He, of course, is concerned with its appearance in *la fatrasie* et *le fatras;* but these two genres, in their obscenity, in their themes and in their irrational character, have marked ressemblances to *Le Moyen de Parvenir,* so that his statements on the subject of mysticism in this type of literature have definite bearing on our discussion. Porter realizes that to find mysticism in these genres is to push them even further than the poet probably intended, and that the poet would no doubt laugh at such an idea. This, I suspect, is equally true of Béroalde, but I justify my hypothesis concerning the profundities of *Le Moyen de Parvenir* in terms of the not uncommon duality of great art (the mixture of the tragic and the comic, or, at least, the ability on the part of the artist to be inspired by either muse). There is little question that a man of Béroalde de Verville's sensibility and versatility would have been subject to such a duality. If such a justification is not sufficient, then consider the following quotation from Porter, in which he supports a similar treatment of poems ordinarily taken at face value, as being comic or nonsense verse:

> Nous sommes au XIIIe siècle. Déjà au cours d'au moins quatre croisades des milliers de Français ont connu le Proche-Orient et certains d'entre eux ont subi à des degrés divers l'influence de sa science et de sa philosophie. Nous n'allons pas dire que la Fatrasie s'est inspirée directement du mysticisme islamique; ce serait sans doute présenter de façon assez inexacte les faits. Mais il est certain que c'est pendant la période de l'infiltration, si légère fût-elle, de ce mysticisme qu'est né ce genre, et il y a, à la vérité, chez l'auteur des *Fatrasies d'Arras,* un je ne sais quoi de mystérieux qui rappelle de temps à autre l'esprit subtil et évasif d'un Omar Kheyyam. Il semble parfois que la clef, introuvable, de l'inconnu, le secret des âges, le hante — et se dérobe. Les signes de sa quête n'apparaissent, malheureusement, qu'en de courts passages, où ils jaillissent du bizarre, comme l'éclair des nuages, brillent pendant un instant et disparaissent soudain derrière le rideau du grotesque ou du ridicule.[15]

15. Lambert C. Porter, p. 53.

There is little that Porter says in this passage that is not applicable to *Le Moyen de Parvenir,* including the presence of Oriental touches which are immediately noticeable in the novel. It is this strain of mysticism running through *Le Moyen de Parvenir* which I wisch to develop, and which will push my discussion of the internal evidence of the title and of the author's intentions to its conclusion. It is of utmost consequence that Porter continues his discussion of the potential mystic reading of *fatrasie* and *fatras* by saying that

> Ces manifestations pouvaient prendre bien des formes, mais dans les *Fatrasies d'Arras* elles se donnent jour le plus souvent dans des références au sujet du Temps. Il semble que les unités de temps aient surtout intéressé le poète; il s'agit tantôt d'un jour, tantôt d'un siècle, mais la période dont il parle est toujours bien délimitée. Rien ne rappelle ici le concept populaire d'une durée indéfinie que nous associons volontiers au sujet.[16]

At this period, and in these particular genres, however, time is notably fixed, Porter tells us. Quite the contrary is true of *Le Moyen de Parvenir,* where time explodes, erupts, is perpetually out of focus, and where mutability is portrayed in every conceivable fashion.

Now, the connection of time with death is inevitable: time, as Mr. Porter says, « seul ennemi invincible de l'homme ».[17] However, the variation in treatment of death comes again through a difference in period, bringing about a more macabre or grotesque and at times burlesque view of death in *Le Moyen de Parvenir* than had been possible during the medieval period (as Porter points out), for the genres he is studying are previous to the development of the *danse macabre,* the devastating plague, the unwinding of the Renaissance with its bloody civil wars, its violent cruelties, etc. Since this whole question of the treatment of death in the Middle Ages and at the close of that era is amply discussed by Huizinga, and, with special reference to the « irrational » comic genres of *fatrasie* and *fatras,* by Porter, there is no need to dwell upon its treatment in works other than *Le Moyen de Parvenir.* It should be remembered, nevertheless, that the treatment of time

16. Porter, p. 53.
17. *Ibid.*, p. 54.

and death in *Le Moyen de Parvenir* is clearly distinct from the more static medieval treatment, and from the more rational, ordered treatment of the earlier Renaissance where the problems of death and time often seem to be purposely introduced for little other reason than to expand an Epicurean argument. In *Le Moyen de Parvenir,* time and death are organic to the work; but both are constantly falling away from our everyday, rational understanding of them. They defy definition; they slip out of focus incessantly. Given the fact that the author views these questions of perennial human concern in the particular way in which he does, their treatment should properly be described as baroque.

With these considerations in mind, let us now revert to the possible reading of « parvenir » as attainment of the « au-delà », recalling as we go the two passages in which a series of activities terminate with an attainment, one of them following the *passing of time,* the other following the spilling of tears for the crucified Christ. In the second passage, we should also take note of the grim pun, doubly involving the inescapable theme of religion — this time at the expense of the clergy — and the theme of death, present in the play on the words *bourreau* and *ministre* (i.e., *exécutant*): « ...Ministre signifie bourreau, ainsi il n'y aura que le Pape qui ne soit bourreau... » (I, 111).

Leaving aside the fact that death is all too obviously a theme, insofar as *Le Moyen de Parvenir* is, descriptively speaking, a collection of dialogues of the dead (and of the living), the mysterious phrase, « se puisse tuer », which is used in connection with the host of the banquet, occurs very early in the novel, and has some connection (though at this point vague) with the above reference to the Pope. Be this as it may, we cannot overlook the fact that self-inflicted death is perhaps implied by the phrase. In the event that this is the sense of the phrase, and it is not supposed to receive a passive reading (get killed), nor be an anagram, a new dimension is possibly added to the view of death to be found in facetious literature.[18] However, I am in doubt that the phrase should be interpreted in this way. Rather, I am inclined to believe that the passive is indeed intended. Still, it is interesting to observe that in the midst of this conviviality the potentiality of death is ever

18. Porter, p. 46.

present, and that, by extension, death plays host to this gathering of *sages* and *fous*.

If, then, I am on the right track in construing « parvenir » as « to attain (heaven) », the upshot of the matter is: *Et in Arcadia ego!*[19] It is hoped that although all of this may at present seem somewhat *tiré par les cheveux*, the reader will indulge the hypothesis long enough to make still additional steps with me into the « mystic » areas of *Le Moyen de Parvenir*, and will finally come to entertain notions of the novel's profundity, even though he may not entirely agree with the interpretations of texts presented with the intention of demonstrating these hidden depths.

Is it not significant, for example, that right toward the beginning of the book the first speech of Alexandre revolves around death? It is a curious passage, in which a tone of unreality dominates and in which, furthermore, the word « tuer » is heavily enlisted:

> Alexandre y vint tout ralu, mais il nous fit tant de rauoire, que les dames d'Orleans en furent esmeues : vramant i'en fus tout aise, & ma ceruelle s'en espanouyt philosophiquement : de sorte qu'il m'estoit auis que l'on m'enclissoit les reparations, porce que l'on nous auoit raporté qu'il auoit esté tué, ce que nous luy dismes, & il se prit à rire & s'excuser, nous disant qu'il estoit vray, qu'il s'estoit battu auec son ennemy, mais qu'il n'auoit pas esté tué, & qu'il le prouueroit par ceux qui l'auoient veu faire. Il s'en raportoit à Aphtonius son secretaire, qui nous raconta la cause de son absence, qui estoit, qu'il auoit voyagé pour voir toutes sortes de sages, & que s'estant trouué avec les gymnosofistes, il auoit seiourné auec eux, & y auoit tant profité, qu'il en estoit reuenu sçauant, dautant que suiuant leurs maximes il auoit inuenté les haut-dechausses sans braguettes en despit des Turcs, pour fauoriser les Veniciens & Souisses (I, 18-19).

But these are far from the only references to death in *Le Moyen de Parvenir.* Note, for example, the following coarse analogy which makes of death a burlesque, a trivial event that occurs in the course of things: « La pauurette reuint auec

19. Gilbert Highet, *The Classical Tradition* (New York, 1949), p. 614.

grand frayeur, & se mit au lict, où elle ne fut que cinq jours, finis lesquels elle mourut comme vne vache qui trespasse » (I, 66). Shortly afterward comes further burlesque description of the manner in which this woman has died (« a changé d'air »): « Voila comme la pauure Laurence a changé d'air, & auoit à sa mort vne merueille notable, vne chose esmerueilleuse : C'est que son ame sortit de son corps par l'endroit proportionnel & semblable à celuy par lequel toutes les autres ames s'en vont » (I, 67). This description of death and transfiguration aside from its burlesque merits, belongs in the realm of « unreal » or « improbable » features of *Le Moyen de Parvenir,* and could be referred to in a treatment of the baroque (but emphatically *baroque satyrique*) metamorphoses found in the novel.

One of the most violent and shocking references to death in *Le Moyen de Parvenir* is an apparent allusion to the actions of the Catholic women following the Saint Bartholomew's Day massacre. According to Paul Lacroix, thanks to whom we may see the connection [20], the Catholic women uttered crude insults and disparaging remarks over the corpses of the Protestants, when they were gathered and stretched out along the bank of the Seine. The text of *Le Moyen de Parvenir,* which is delivered by Scanderbeg (a 15th century king of Albania) in the Paul Lacroix edition, but, by way of contrast to another speaker named « Moy » who is present in the dialogue at hand, by one « Vovs » in the Royer edition, follows:

> Acoutez, messieurs, accoutez vn peu, ie vous dirai vn conte pour vous apaiser; ardé, i'estois à la fuite de l'armee de Montcontour, où i'eu beaucoup de despouilles, dont voici des restes; ainsi que nous estions à ce mesnage, voila la plus grande de la Court, qui passant & voyant les morts deçà & delà, pource que c'estoient Huguenots, n'en dit rien : mais en voyant vn estendu le ventre au soleil, & considerant la grandeur de son membre viril, va dire, « Voila grand pitié de cettui-là ». Et nous de sortir de là & de nous en aller; aussi bien on nous attendoit à disner chez vn prelat (II, 243-244).

The story is, among other things, not to the credit of womanhood, by any means, and would seem to tie in with the generally

20. Paul Lacroix, p. 388.

misogynistic tone of the work, already asserted. Leaving aside possible misogynistic interpretations, the violent and shocking use of death here is, in my opinion, much like the kind of violence demonstrated by Buffum in his study of the baroque elements in Agrippa d'Aubigné's *Les Tragiques*[21], though in this passage from *Le Moyen de Parvenir,* there is, of course, humorous intent. The appropriate description would thus be extended from baroque to the *baroque satyrique.*

The pun on one of the names of the characters seen in the following exchange seems to pinpoint that haunting refrain of man's mortality which is presented in so many different ways in the novel: « (Le MORTEL.) On void bien que vous n'estes gueres sages de nous conter tout ceci. (STADIVS.) O pauure animal mortel mon amy, ne sçais tu pas bien qu'ayans vn corps il faut qu'il se vuide... » (II, 162).

There is some possibility that Le Mortel is, as Paul Lacroix mentions, a real person; for in this same passage reference is made to the « doyen du chapitre de Saint-Gatien de Tours », who, « comme le plus vieux des chanoines, semblait destiné à mourir avant les autres ».[22] I am not satisfied, however, with the suggestion that it might be Thomas More, for, as I have already indicated, I strongly suspect that along with many other works, Béroalde had Erasmus' *Praise of Folly* in mind when composing *Le Moyen de Parvenir,* and that for this reason Béroalde would more likely have fallen upon the pun on More's name already afforded by Erasmus in his dedicatory letter to Thomas More. I am even less content with Jean Mortis, « chanoine de la Sainte-Chapelle », for regional reasons and because nothing much is gained by that obscure reference. The proposal that this character might represent the printer Morel seems to me to be even less satisfactory. But inasmuch as there are other figures suggestive of the medieval farce on the scene, possibly the devil, possibly even stock allegorical figures from the miracles and the mysteries, I do not think it too unlikely that, even admitting the possibility of a real person, Le Mortel also represents, if not exclusively at least by extension, death properly speaking. « La Cène des Dieux », first represented in Caen about 1492 and found in the modern edition of *Le Recueil Trepperel,* is really less a farce and

21. Imbrie Buffum, *Agrippa d'Aubigné's Les Tragiques* (New Haven, 1951), p. 28.
22. Paul Lacroix, p. 473.

more in the vein of Renaissance satire; but what interests us is that it gives us the allegorical figure La Mors, whose lines are hardly more menacing than those of Le Mortel in *Le Moyen de Parvenir,* for these figures are in neither case really running the show. In « La Cène des Dieux » La Mors is a sort of henchman. Phoebus, for one, passes sentence on the human race, which has turned so vicious, and La Mors is to carry out the orders. Says he: « La sentence n'est pas petite, Juge, je vous en remercie. »[23]

My argument is slightly embarrassed by the fact that I do not find a counterpart, La Vie, La Vita, or some such name, as one would (and does) in a farce like « La Cène des Dieux ». It is supported, however, by the presence in *Le Moyen de Parvenir* of other characters of the farce whose identity has perhaps needlessly baffled us. Among these we might easily include Le Curé (see Farce VI, *Le Recueil Trepperel*), in *Le Moyen de Parvenir* « Notre curé »; Le Moyne (see Farce IV, *Le Recueil Trepperel*), in *Le Moyen de Parvenir* Le Moine; (la) Magdaleine (see Farce IV, *Le Recueil Trepperel*), Madelaine in *Le Moyen de Parvenir;* Margot (see Farce II, *Le Recueil Trepperel*), Margot in *Le Moyen de Parvenir;* perhaps even Gille (see Farce III, *Le Recueil Trepperel*) who may be our as yet only tenuously identified Messire Gilles of *Le Moyen de Parvenir.* I bring these to bear to indicate the likelihood that death may very well have an allegorical spokesman in Béroalde's curious gathering. However, I realise that further analysis of the utilization of farce in *Le Moyen de Parvenir,* not only for interlocutors that fall so neatly in line as the above, but, too, for such possibilities as the use of the name Gautier, of Sacerdos, which may be another way of saying le Prestre (see Farce V, *Le Recueil Trepperel*), etc. should one day be made. This is not to forget, either, the exploitation of the farce for obscene jokes and comic situations, as well as the probable use of other forms of medieval drama by the author of *Le Moyen de Parvenir.*

If we may conclude, then, that Le Mortel is an allegorical figure standing for death, it is of utmost significance that this figure should be present at this strange symposium, and such an interpretation might assist us in establishing some sort of rationale in the guestlist.

23. *Le Recueil Trepperel,* ed. E. Droz and H. Lewicka (Genève, 1961), p. 122.

For the present, let us be satisfied with this admittedly tentative solution to the identification of Le Mortel, and proceed to other observations on the treatment of death in *Le Moyen de Parvenir.* Frequently, the subject of death is treated lightly, sometimes facetiously, often with burlesque obscenity, but, I think, always with the *arrière-pensée* that it is, as Béroalde would say, « la fin finale ». An example of such treatment can be seen in the passage quoted below in which sin and death are triply involved in a licentious pun. It is from a tale told by Comines in an early chapter of *Le Moyen de Parvenir* entitled « Iovrnal »:

> A ce propos vne apres-disnee la Roine d'Egypte estoit à deuiser en sa chambre auec quelques Dames, sans autres personnes, c'est qu'il n'y auoit ny hommes, ny Prestres, ny Moines, ny Ministres, le seigneur de Danois se presenta pour entrer; comme il eut veu qu'il n'y auoit point d'hommes, il se retira. La Roine qui l'auoit apperceu, l'appela; « Ho Monsieur le grand Prieur entrez, vous y pouuez bien ». Au commandement il s'approche. Elle lui dit, « Nous estions sur le sujet des Dames. — Vraiment Madame, le sujet est vnique en perfection. — Mais qu'en dittes-vous ? — Tout bien, Madame. — Et encores, dittes-nous en à bon escient vostre opinion. — Puis qu'il vous plaist, Madame, par la mordong toutes les femmes sont putains. — O ho, dit la Roine, & moy ? — A ha, Madame, Vous estes la Roine. — Et vostre mere ? — Madame, ne parlons point des trespassez » (I, 72).

Or again, note the intricate punning on the words « mort » and « tuer » (used with their Renaissance meanings) in the speech of Pindar, « ...& la tue de la douce mort » (I, 88).

Similar passages could be quoted from almost anywhere in the novel, but what strikes the reader most about the treatment of death in *Le Moyen de Parvenir* is the fact that the death themes grow heavier toward the end of the second volume, to such an extent that one might well wonder if there is not a subconscious or even an intentional implication that the book is nihilistic, and is showing the reader the « moyen de parvenir à la mort ». If this is so, the more idealistic idea of « paradise » which I earlier advanced would have to be rejected... unless we were to extend our definition of this paradise to a « *fool's* paradise », and that notion is certainly not without support, what is more.

Whatever explanation we can find for it, however, the essential fact does remain that references to death increase towards the end of the novel, and that the whole problem of time erupts, leaving the reader in utter dismay. Those hints at the rapid passing of time, with its inherent relationship to mutability, to mortality and immortality, to man's theological position in connection to all this — his unstable lot, his penchant in the face of this to be hedonistic and heathenish — all of these matters, which are early introduced and, at that, boldly, even in the first pages of the book, certainly by the end of the very first chapter take on full-bodied statement by the end of the book.

Now, in *Le Moyen de Parvenir,* death is quite obviously tied to the theme of time; time is given the same unreal character it will have had through the dialogues between the long-dead or the lately-dead and the still-living (in any combination), or that it will have had, too, through such curious anachronisms as will have been seen at various points in the novel. In considering the presence of anachronism, one should bear in mind that while nothing can be more universal, at the same time, in *Le Moyen de Parvenir* its absurdity is of baroque stamp, the impossibility being related to the kind of disconnected vision described as « absurd » by Odette de Mourgues in her excellent book *Metaphysical, Baroque and Précieux Poetry.* The speech of Bellarmin, in a chapter entitled « Ordonnance » is one of the best and most frequently quoted examples of out-and-out anachronism in *Le Moyen de Parvenir.* In full knowledge of the anachronistic absurdity of the scene he is describing, he says: « Il estoit exact comme celui qui fit la belle tapisserie du Verger, où il y a vne Iudic qui prie & est à genoux deuant vne nostre Dame, ainsi que l'on voit aux Minimes de Tours vne Vierge Marie qui dit ses heures de nostre Dame agenouillee deuant vn crucifix, & l'Ange est de l'autre costé qui dit son Aue » (II, 254). In this passage it is Judith who is referred to, and the portrayal of her as praying to the Virgin Mary represents in some sense a telescoping of the type Odette de Mourgues represents in her discussion of the myopic or disconnected vision which ultimately leads to a depiction of a mad universe.[24]

It is, however, toward the end of *Le Moyen de Parvenir*

24. Odette de Mourgues, *Metaphysical, Baroque and Précieux Poetry* (Oxford, 1953), p. 100.

that the virtually parallel themes of death and time are rounded together with the theme of eroticism, to receive their final and most complete statement. Indeed, there are no two chapters that more clearly reveal the intentions of our author than the first and the last. For this reason, I now propose to do a rather thorough analysis of both, starting, in fact, with the opening quatrain and the first word of the novel, then the first chapter, and juxtaposing the last chapter of the novel, with its summation of the themes and its closing quatrain, already commented upon in another light. As a preliminary remark I might reiterate that the first chapter or so along with the last form a very loose frame around the more clearly defined frame seen in the form of a banquet. The looser frame shows the author's commentary on the piece of work, or, more properly, the narrator's. Another general observation which should be made is that *Le Moyen de Parvenir,* though it is frequently classified as Mennippean satire, has a much less even distribution of verse and prose than should be the case for a strict classification of the work within this genre. Hence, the presence of verse, especially in the quantity found in the last chapter is particularly noteworthy. With all of the foregoing in mind, let us now explore minutely the first and the last chapters.

CHAPTER IV

THE FIRST AND LAST CHAPTERS

What the title *Le Moyen de Parvenir* hints at, or suggests, in the way of central themes, such as time and mutability, religious satire, satire of pedantry, eroticism and so forth, the opening quatrain and the first chapter of the novel boldly announce. The opening quatrain

> Si Madame m'eust suruescu
> I'eusse commencé cet ouurage.
> Quand la Mort s'en torcha le cu
> I'eu le cœur mou comme fromage (I, 2).

leaves one in no doubt about the tone of the work he is about to read. It further suggests the peculiar time setting, by the implication that the book has never been begun, and seems to dedicate the work to « Madame », an unidentified person who seems more than likely the « Madame » who has brought the figures of the book together. The symbolism of this quatrain recurs later in the book, for example in the following passage, where the reference to the left-handedness of the Arabs, and to the Talmud as well as the Arabic-like form of the name « Cyriaque » reinforce my earlier statement that there is an Oriental quality in parts of *Le Moyen de Parvenir:*

> Tandis que l'on murmuroit le receuant, voicy arriuer le bon Demosthene. « I'y suymes, dismes nous, j'en fusmes bien aise, dautant qu'il est certain que j'apprendrons beaucoup de bonnes choses, comme desia il y parut. » En entrant il se mit à discourir, & nous enseigna que c'est qu'honneste homme, le definissant ainsi qu'il se trouue au Talmud; honneste personne est celle qui ayant fianté se torche le cul auec vn torchoir le tenant de la main

> gauche. Aristote depit de n'auoir trouué ceste belle definition se noya, & luy deroba celle de bonne menagere, qui est inseree en ses Œconomiques, comme l'a remarqué Cyriaque Strosse. Bonne menagere est celle personne qui s'estant torché le cul resserre le papier en sa pochette, le gardant pour vne autre fois, ou pour empaqueter des confitures pour donner aux mignardes (I, 20-21).

The action of the housewife is similar to that found in many of the « novelle » of the Renaissance, even to a story told in the earliest known French collection of this type, the *Cent Nouvelles Nouvelles* of Philippe de Vigneulles.[1] What should be noted in the above passage from *Le Moyen de Parvenir*, in addition to the Oriental factors already mentioned, is the sub-standard language of Demosthenes, which gives irony to the fact that he is about to define the *honneste homme* for us. That we are to have such a definition is also indicative of intentions to satirize the *précieux* hero, and the one which we receive corroborates our suspicions.

The « torche-cul » of the opening quatrain again occurs in the dialogue between Vldric and Madame which follows:

> VLDRIC. — Ie le veux bien puis qu'il vous plaist, ie ne l'eusse sceu demander plus honnestement, ny vous plus joyeusement l'accorder, ce sera quand il vous plaira, Madame; employez Moy tandis que ie suis ieune, quand ie seray vieil ie n'en pourray plus; mais ce dementi que deuiendra-il ?

1. Herbert Reiche, in his *Le Moyen de parvenir von Béroalde de Verville mit vesonderer Berücksichtigung der Quellen-und Verfasserfrage* (Coburg, 1913), p. 27, has also found grounds to refer to Philippe de Vigneulles in relation to *Le Moyen de Parvenir*. The *Cent Nouvelles Nouvelles* of Philippe de Vigneulles, « inédites » and only partially printed, are referred to, for example, in Jean Plattard's *La Renaissance des Lettres en France* (Paris, 1925), p. 17. The story I refer to here, containing reference to an « estron gelé » and more especially to « pièces d'estron » is the 24th Tale, found in Charles H. Livingston's « The Heptaméron des Nouvelles of Marguerite de Navarre: A Study of Nouvelles 28, 34, 52 and 62 », *Romanic Review*, XIV (1923), pp. 111-113. On p. 105 of this article, Professor Livingston states : « We have evidence to show that several manuscripts of his [Philippe de Vigneulles'] tales were extant in the seventeenth century. It does not seem unreasonable to believe that during the sixteenth century such manuscripts circulated even beyond Philippe's adopted city Metz and so may have been known to the circle of the Queen of Navarre. » Hence, we may reason that Béroalde will have known Philippe's work, also. For the analogy of this tale of Philippe, the 24th, see the *Heptaméron* of Marguerite de Navarre, Tale 52, the comparison having been already made by Professor Livingston in this same article.

> MADAME. — I'entends que ce soit vn dementi de musnier, vn asne le portera.
>
> VLDRIC. — Voire mais plustost de papier, ie m'en torcheray le cul (I, 157).

Furthermore, the « fromage mou » of the opening quatrain can also be found internally in a dialogue between Gesser and Pausanias, some while later in a chapter entitled « Sof passuc »:

> GESSER. — Vous proposez vne cabale de resuer en soupant; ie voudrois, tant ie suis ennuyé de la fracture de mon fourneau, que nous fussions en estat parfait de resuerie, ie serois aise & n'aurois non plus de mauuaise passion que le patissier Rigole qui songeoit, tant il estoit aise en resuant, que sa grande mere lui donnoit du fourmage mou.
>
> BACON. — Iamais fourmage mou ne gasta gorge, non plus que cul chaut ne gasta iamais linge, & ie ne ry iamais tant de fourmage mou, ou de cresme, que de celles de Manasses secretaire du Patriarche de Constantinople, ce grand esprit; il acheta vn iour vn fourmage de cresme qui ne lui cousta rien... Manasses ayant eu en main son fourmage, prit vn des cheualiers de la fleur de lys, i. des quinze vingts, & le pria de dire vn salut à son intention : pour ce faire il lui mit vn beau ietton au creux de la main. Le pauure ayant accordé ses badigoinces, griguenotoit ce Salue auec vne voix horrifique, à laquelle Manasses s'accordoit : comme il fut venu au verset qu'il se faut esqueuler de crier, & qu'il eut ouuert amplement la gorge, & desserré la goule assez grande pour y enfourner vn demi alloyau de bœuf, les babines estant desiointes bien demi pied, demeurant ouuertes en ceste belle extase de chant Royal, Manasses lui va flaquer ce fourmage mou dans le bagoulier si proprement, qu'il entra tout, & rien n'en sortit que ce que malheureusement le triste criard fit choir, estimant auoir la bouche pleine d'vne autre mixtion de plus haut goust.
>
> PAVSANIAS. — Ie pense que ce iour-là estoit fait pour rire (II, 22-23).

The opening quatrain, then, serves multiple functions, but above all it sets the tone of the book and states the major themes of death and time. Thus, the reader is impressed from the first sentence forth by the chaotic progressions of style, by the curiously exotic vocabulary, the shifting paces of tempo, the richness of theme and the intricate intentions which are obviously those of this fertile and esoteric mind: « Car est il, que ce fut au temps, au siecle en l'indiction, en l'Aere, en l'Hegire, en l'hebdomade, au lustre, en l'Olimpiade, en l'an, au terme, au mois, en la sepmaine, au iour, à l'heure, à la minute, & iustement à l'instant, que par l'auis & progrez du Daimon des spheres les esteufs descheurent de credit, & qu'au lieu d'eux furent auancees les molles balles, au preiudice de la noble antiquité, qui se jouoit si joliment » (I, 3-4). That is the way the first chapter, entitled « Question I », begins. The sentence is long, intricate, held in suspense by the opening word, followed instantaneously by the inverted present tense of « être » and that present by the preterit of « être », thus recalling the subtitle of the book, with its shifting tenses of « être ».

It is not surprising that previous commentators on *Le Moyen de Parvenir* have frequently underlined the fact that the word « car », the lead word of the novel, does not again appear in the entire text.[2] What seems to be lacking in this inevitable commentary is any explanation as to why the fact is important, not even the obvious reason that for the period it is rather unusual to begin one's story with a conjunction. The nature of that conjunction is every bit as interesting as the mere presence of the conjunction, for it is a resultant conjunction, and leads us directly to one of the central themes of the novel, that of time. In what way can we deny both its baroque quality, that of eruption, instability, and (a not uncommon character of the baroque) its excessively modern quality, both from a stylistic or a philosophic standpoint?

A random sampling shows us that this is an unconventional form of departure. Try so unusual a piece, even, as Cyrano de Bergerac's *Voyage dans la Lune:* « La lune était en son plein... »[3] We might refer, also, to Scarron's *Le Roman comique,* whose beginning, mock-heroic in tone, is consequently of

2. See Paul Lacroix, p. 1, footnote 1; but also see in particular Royer's introduction, p. lviii, where he cites from an edition of « around 1640 » containing the word *car*. It is a passage which has evidently been added to the story of the « femme bercée ».

3. Cyrano de Bergerac, *Lettres-Théâtre,* etc., éd. Charles Simond (Paris, n.d.), p. 83.

necessity written in smooth, flowing syntax: « Le soleil avait achevé plus de la moitié de sa course, et son char, ayant attrapé le penchant du monde, roulait plus vite qu'il ne voulait. »[4] We might also note the admittedly parodic but, even so, syntactically normal beginning of Furetière's *Le Roman bourgeois:* « Je chante les amours et les aventures de plusieurs bourgeois de Paris... »[5]; we might also observe the appropriately smooth style of the first line of *La Princesse de Clèves:* « La magnificence et la galanterie n'ont jamais paru en France avec tant d'éclat... »[6] Even the great teacher of style, Flaubert, begins his masterpiece, *Madame Bovary,* with a sentence which interrupts contiguous action, but is, even so, of normal syntax: « Nous étions à l'étude, quand le Proviseur entra, suivi d'un *nouveau* habillé en bourgeois... »[7] Sterne, in fact, launches *Tristam Shandy* with a perfectly normal sentence: « I wish either my father or my mother... »[8]

Indeed, seldom before modern times do we find novels which open in a manner ressembling the opening of *Le Moyen de Parvenir.* Syntactically less curious, but every bit as disturbing from the standpoint of time as a perspective, including the impossibilities we conventionally ascribe to time is the opening sentence of Henry Miller's *The Tropic of Capricorn,* which, together with *The Tropic of Cancer,* does not lack other analogies with the novel at hand. Says Miller: « Once you have given up the ghost, everything follows with dead certainty, even in the midst of chaos. »[9] Still it seems to me that James Joyce in *Finnegan's Wake* is the one we need to evoke, for he has taken that extra step beyond Béroalde, and, in his desire to defy the accepted logic of chronology implied by ordered syntax, has begun the novel not even with a conjunction, but simply in the middle of the sentence: « riverrun, past Eve and Adam's... »[10] To fill his novel with his own time dimensions, Joyce completes the sentence at the end of the novel: « A way a lonc a last a loved a long the », hence taking us one step

4. Paul Scarron, *Le Roman comique* (Paris, 1941), p. 13.
5. Antoine Furetière, *Le Roman bourgeois* (Paris, 1941), p. 13.
6. Madame de La Fayette, *La Princesse de Clèves* (Paris, 1941), p. 13.
7. Gustave Flaubert, *Madame Bovary* (Paris, 1929), p. 1.
8. Laurence Sterne, *The Life and Opinions of Tristram Shandy, Gent.* (New York, 1950), p. 3.
9. Henry Miller, *Tropic of Capricorn* (Paris, 1957), p. 9.
10. James Joyce, *Finnegan's Wake* (New York, 1939), p. 3.

further in the technique of time-eruption than Béroalde had done.[11]

I should add that I am quite aware that the psychological reality of seeming interruption of one character by another, or of the reader's entrance upon a scene already in motion was quite adequately exploited by other of Béroalde's contemporaries. Shakespeare's opening lines of *Othello* immediately come to mind: « Tush, never tell me. I take it much unkindly... »[12], says Roderigo to Iago in the opening scene. Indeed, neither was Racine ignorant of the effectiveness of this technique, for let us not forget how Orestes says, at the beginning of *Andromaque,* « Oui, puisque je retrouve un ami si fidèle... »[13] and how the dramatist again uses the technique in *Iphigénie* (« Oui, c'est Agamemnon... »[14]), as well as in his *Athalie* (« Oui, je viens dans son temple... »[15]), while Corneille, on the other hand, begins his *Pertharite:* « Oui, l'honneur qu'il me rend... »[16] No doubt we could compound these examples, but I wish to stress, beyond the dramatic and psychological effects which Béroalde has gained by beginning the novel with the conjunction « car », the importance of its being a conjunction, and, furthermore, a resultant conjunction, which, thereby, is extremely close to the concept of time, directly to follow. The gains of this unusual opening are multiple: they include the establishment of the sylistic and structual character of the work, which is chaotic and eruptive, the peculiar sense of the natural which will come and go throughout the work, and, above all, that which I consider to be the major theme, that of time.

So it is that the novel begins with this conjunction — not an uncommon word in and of itself, but outstanding as an opening, in that it is a conjunction. The word « car » is, I repeat, directly followed by first the present tense and then the preterit of the verb « être ». Subsequent to these two tense-time manifestations, the reader is confronted with a series of terms, some of them erudite, but all having to do in one

11. Joyce, p. 628.

12. William Shakespeare, *The Complete Works,* ed. G. B. Harrison (New York, 1948), p. 1059.

13. Jean Racine, *Œuvres complètes* (Paris, 1951), I, p. 264.

14. *Ibid.*, p. 693.

15. *Ibid.*, I, p. 895.

16. Jean Racine, *Andromaque* (Paris, 1941), p. 19, footnote 1.

way or another with time. The first of these terms, « temps », pinpoints the central-most theme. It is probably not a coincidence that the initial noun of the novel be precisely this noun, « temps ». Yet it and the following noun, « siècle », offer little problem in comprehension. They are general and generic; the word « siècle » remains non-specific. However, these are followed by the far more obscure time designations, « en l'indiction », « en l'Aere », « en l'Hégire », « en l'hebdomade », « au lustre », « en l'Olimpiade ». Each one of these terms is characterized by its connection with some religious event, some holy day, some feature of some religious calendar. The words « en l'indiction » tell us that a set day for the convocation of an ecclesiastical council or synod is involved. Thus, the themes of time and of religion are doubly evoked, and the concept of a gathering is almost immediately established thereafter.

Continuing on, we find the expression « en l'Aere », perhaps here meant to be non-specific like the words « temps » and « siècle », but even so surely intended to communicate some such notion as « l'Ére chrétienne ». Notice might be taken first of the capital, and then of the fact that the word « ère » ordinarily has the meaning of the point of departure of a *particular* chronology, so that various fixed phrases are frequently built on it, such as « l'Ére des Olympiades », « l'Ére d'Alexandrie », etc. Next comes the phrase « en l'Hégire », certainly the most exotic word yet, coming from the Arabic *hidjra.* It is the name given to the flight of Mohammed from Mecca to Medina, and by extension to the Mohammedan era. Now, the reference to an event from which the Moslems date their era serves to incorporate pagan religion into the general scene, to remove it, in other words, from a forcibly Christian context, to introduce in an altogether specific manner the Oriental or more precisely Arabic culture, and to ready us, in particular, for the presence of Mohammed as one of the guests at this motley convocation.

A new theme, perhaps already hinted at, is clearly visible in the word « hébdomade », a pseudo-erudite word coming from the Greek and used for week, a word which, in addition to having religious connotations, effectively contributes to the already mounting impression of mock erudition. Literary satire is hence under way at this juncture.

The words « au lustre » continue in the vein of specific and theological reference, this time to a period of five years, and more precisely to the expiatory sacrifice which took place in Rome every five years, following the census count. There is probably a touch of irony intended here, but we are thrust forth so rapidly to the next item, « en l'Olimpiade », that we need not stop to meditate too long on any one of the terms, Béroalde's gain coming as it does from abundance and overstatement here as elsewhere.

The « Olimpiade » again is a Greek term, this time referring to a period of four years, or the space of time elapsing between two celebrations of the Olympics. Religiously speaking this word could refer to the holy day for Zeus Olympios, on which day the Olympics would take place. This term, however, first designating only the holy day or festival, ultimately came to be used to designate the four year interval, & thus became part of the system of chronology. (The point of departure of the system was the victory of Coroebus in 776 B.C., which, then, was the first year of the first « Olympiade ».) Not only is a new type of chronology effected by this new term, but this is our first real encounter with the recurrent use of games for erotico-comical purposes in *Le Moyen de Parvenir.*

After these specific expressions comes another general one, « en l'an », which in its turn is followed by the more specialized « au terme », the time of parturition, or the period at the end of which a payment might be due. In Catholic liturgy this expression is used for the fixed date used as a basis for figuring the holy days which would be movable. This expression is, therefore, also open to various interpretations: it, too, suggests theological satire; it has erotic overtones; it evokes the world of business.

The listing again grows non-specific in reference now, but, in so doing, the exact instant is pinned down, through a process of elimination: « au mois », « en la sepmaine », « au iour », « à l'heure », « à la minute », « & iustement à l'instant ».

Not without interest, too, is the fact that much of this terminology (hebdomades, Olympiades, l'Ère, l'Indiction, l'Hégire) occurs in the serious, largely theological *Chroniqua* of Matthieu Béroald, father of François, according to the account given in Vol. II, Columns 402-403 of Haag's *La France protestante.*

Similar uses of time can be seen throughout James Joyce's *Finnegan's Wake,* which we think of as extremely modern, but which is more likely an outpost of the type of novel already undertaken as early as *Le Moyen de Parvenir.* I would hesitate to name *Le Moyen de Parvenir* as an actual source, but find, even so, that there are devices so similar that Béroalde's novel can stand, at least, as a spiritual forebear. The following passage from *Finnegan's Wake* will perhaps solidify the argument: « What was thaas? Fog was whaas? Too mult sleepth. Let sleepth. But really now whenabouts. Expatiate then how much times we live in. Yes? So nat by night by naught by naket, in those good old lousy days gone by, the days, shall we say? of Whom shall we say? while kinderwardens minded their twinshed, therenow they — stood, the sycomores, all four of them in their quartan argues... »[17]

I do not wish, on the other hand, to overstate the analogies between Béroalde and Joyce. The two men are as much of their time as not, and in the final analysis, the work of Joyce is apparently more serious and possibly more profound than that of Béroalde.

To return to *Le Moyen de Parvenir,* and specifically to the first sentence, what is especially salient in this list of epochs and time designations, is that the forms of religion evoked are varied, and, apparently, arbitrary. Here, already, however, that aura of orientalism which I have already mentioned is present. Rounding out the rest of the sentence are the spherico-sexual images of the hard and the soft balls — also involving the game (the sexual game, the game of life, or just a game) — and the mention of « la noble antiquité ». The juxtaposition to this last phrase afforded by the first few words of the next sentence, « Confuz soient ces inuenteurs de nouueautez » shows us that there is hostility toward change and evils brought by change. The quarrel of the ancients and the moderns is evidently alluded to, too. Mutability, though, has already been indicated by the « dedicatory » quatrain and the first sentence, where the stage has been set; we are to find within these covers the themes of death, time, mutability, religion, eroticism, pure verbal sport. We note, too, that there is to be an « indiction » — a gathering or assembly of sorts. We are sure, too, that the tone is racy and facetious, and we are aware that the style, felt in the first word « car », in the shifting tenses, in the bizarre cataloguing of time expressions, and in the structural complexity of the first sentence, is chaotic and eruptive. In addition, we have a vague inkling through the rather dense

17. Joyce, p. 555.

vocabulary that the book will be difficult, so that its obscurity or its hermetic nature is rather immediately suspected.

The burlesque atmosphere created by the opening quatrain and by the long string of chronological terms which quite obviously mean to overstate and to over-particularize are too rapidly dismissed as an imitation of Rabelais. There is much in *Le Moyen de Parvenir,* both in style and in content, that has its mainspring in the works of Rabelais. But in Béroalde's novel, one should look further, even, than in Rabelais, to a rejection by means of exaggeration and burlesque or mordant satire, of Renaissance style. What is more important is that the mannerist characteristics of the baroque period, such as overstatement, exaggeration, obssession with time, etc. are from the outset under attack. Here then is another dimension to be added to *Le Moyen de Parvenir.* It is apparent from the beginning that we do indeed have a « satyre universelle », and that the literary world is far from excluded. The same claims can be made in explanation of the excessive obscurity of the work, of its themes of death and time. The trait of obscurity in particular is satirized, and the author insists upon pointing out the obscurity to the reader, hence giving to the obscurity an added twist: it is not only a baroque feature, but a baroque feature under satire. This obscurity and this strange dislocation of time can be seen, too, in *La Pícara Justina,* a close relative of *Le Moyen de Parvenir,* and possibly one of its sources. The first book of the Spanish work opens with the same peculiar death-life, life-death and time disorientation motifs that are dominant in Béroalde's novel: « Nació Justina Díez, la Pícara, el año de las nacidas, que fué bisiesto, a los 6 de agosto, en el signo Virgo, a las seis de la Boba allá. ¿Yo soy nacida? ¡Oh que hace frío! Tapajija [vísteme], que me verán nacer desnuda. Tórnome al vientre de mi señora madre, que no quiero que mi nacimiento sea de golpe, como cerradura de loba. Más vale salir de dos golpes, como voto a Dios de carretero manchego. »[18] One cannot help but be reminded of the opening of *Tristram Shandy,* more closely related to *La Pícara,* I think, than to *Le Moyen de Parvenir,* but having something in common with both of them (perhaps Barclay's *Euphormio Satyricon* which was to be found in Sterne's library)[19]:

18. Angel Valbuena y Prat, *La novela picaresca española* (Madrid, 1946), p. 722.

19. See *A Facsimile Reproduction of a Unique Catalogue of Laurence Sterne's Library* (New York, 1930), item 1892.

> I wish either my father or my mother, or indeed both of them, as they were in duty both equally bound to it, had minded what they were about when they begot me; had they duly considered how much depended upon what they were then doing; — that not only the production of a rational Being was concerned in it, but that possibly the happy formation and temperature of his body, perhaps his genius and the very cast of his mind; — and, for aught they knew to the contrary, even the fortunes of his whole house might take their turn from the humours and dispositions which were then uppermost... [20]

It is very likely unnecessary, however, to single out these parallels, except to elaborate on what is otherwise a demonstration of the baroque currents seen in the author's wish to mystify, to imply that the book holds a secret, to advance manifold themes of time and mutability which are, in fact, tacit. That these last two themes immerge through the shifting tenses, the eruptive style, the reflections on time stated by the characters, and in many other ways, we have already seen; and we shall be seeing further instances of these characteristics.

In the meanwhile, let us turn our attention to the next few sentences: « Confuz soient ces inuenteurs de nouueautez, qui gastent la jeunesse, & contre les bonnes coustumes troublent nos jeux. N'est ce point au jeu où l'ame se dilate pour faire ses conceptions ? Si vn diable jouoit auec vous il ne se pourroit feindre, il vous feroit voir ses cornes. Mais qu'est ce que jouer ? C'est se delecter sans penser en mal. Beaucoup de maux sont auenus à cause de ce changement qui troublera l'intelligence des histoires, & gauchira toute la mappe-monde » (I, 4).

Paul Lacroix explains the word « inuenteurs » of this passage as meaning « Les ministres protestants qui proscrivaient sévèrement les jeux et les spectres ». [21] The theory is not without merit, but I am not thereby willing to abandon the more extensive concept that there is, here, a juxtaposition of antiquity and modernity. Added to these themes are those of the recording of history and the exploratory conscience of Renaissance man. The word « mappe-monde », incidentally, recurs as the title of a chapter in *Le Moyen de Parvenir.*

20. Sterne, p. 3.
21. Paul Lacroix, p. 1.

I have already said that there is, here, a link of the juxtaposition of the ancients and moderns with the theme of mutability, which to my mind is fully explored in the foregoing lines, as also in the following sentence: « Voyez combien desia en sont venus de troubles, guerres, maux, veroles & telles petites mignardises qui chatouillent malheureusement les personnes pour les faire rire » (I, 4).

Thus, Béroalde is advancing condemnation of those who have changed the rules of the game, and is listing the evils brought about by a change in the rules of the game. Far from making my theory that the work is predominantly a religious satire invalid, these lines only add to the argument. They are said, I believe, with reverse intention; their content is ironic and bitter. We may note, in passing, that the verb « aduenir » of the subtitle appears in the passage quoted.

Other facets of the subtitle and other dominant themes are evoked in the passage quoted below:

> Tant de sages qui estudient aux auantures attribuent tels effects à d'autres causes, comme au retranchement des dix jours, depuits quoy on n'a fait vendages que par rencontre de saison, aux pullulations d'heresies, depuis lesquelles les bosses n'ont peu estre plattes, aux reuoltes des grands qui font occasion que fillettes ont hanté les cloistres & les menagers les tauernes, aux haussements des tailles, durant quoy les vieilles gens ne font que rechigner, & infinitez autres soties, dont ie ne suis point controlleur, dautant qu'il ne m'appartient pas d'entreprendre sur vous (I, 4).

The learned men, here called « sages », who will shortly be back on the scene, are pictured in this passage as studying the *causes* and the *effects,* which latter word appears in the subtitle where the author claims that *Le Moyen de Parvenir* contains a demonstration of the « effects de la VERTV ». I have already discussed at length this word as it appears in the subtitle. The philosophic problems of « causes » and « effects » are again Renaissance concerns, suggesting the dogma of the great chain of being. Bacon, for example, in his *Advancement of Learning,* argues that second causes when contemplated lead away from God, who is the first cause.[22]

22. Francis Bacon, *Essays, Advancement of Learning, New Atlantis, and Other Pieces,* ed. Richard Foster Jones (New York, 1937), p. 175.

As a consequence, the opening sentences of *Le Moyen de Parvenir* soon reveal the taunting parody it is the author's intention to establish by the rapid-fire use of this terminology.

Other than this, we also have within the passage a new time designation, « le retranchement des dix jours » which Paul Lacroix says is an « allusion à la réforme du calendrier, en 1581, par le pape Grégoire XIII, qui retrancha dix jours dans l'ancien calendrier pour fixer d'une manière certaine l'équinoxe du printemps et la fête de Paques ».[23] The remark directly following this time designation — « depuis quoy on n'a fait vendages que par rencontre de saison » — seems to me to reflect another theme of *Le Moyen de Parvenir,* once more ironically. The author is being somewhat snide in saying that since spring has now been officially set by the Pope, Mother Nature follows course. The point is, in reality, that in Béroalde's mind Nature has its own inviolable laws, and there is even some cause to argue that *Le Moyen de Parvenir* may be classified, because of certain passages, as Adamitic.

Within this same passage Béroalde moves from specific time designations, and uses certain words in a construction parallel to « au retranchement », thus giving them the force and amplitude of time designations: « aux pullulations », « aux reuoltes », « aux haussements ». These words are, in reality, elliptical for something like « during the period of the multiplications of heresies », etc., but by using them in the manner that he does, the author gains another kind of time dislocation. Suggestions of heresy, alchemy, of the diabolical or supernatural begin to people the canvas in a way not unlike the content of some of the paintings of Bosch.

Finally, in this passage the *old* people are recalled, and shown to do nothing but withdraw in repugnance before the changing times.

The trailing syntax of the sentence leaves the words « infinitez autres sotises » somewhat up in the air, but, on the other hand, puts them into a relief which is desirable; for one of the principal antitheses of this chapter, as of the book, is formed by a juxtaposition of « le sot » or « le fou » and « le sage », « le philosophe », or « les enfans de la science », an expression soon to appear.

Next comes the author's testimony that all that he is about

23. Paul Lacroix, p. 1.

to say is true, and we note that over and over the author or one of the interlocutors swears to the truth of his story, even when it is a completely preposterous one: « Et bien en cet excellent periode il auint ce que vous sçauez, & ie vous iure sans iurer, que tout est vray. Si vous me pressez ie vous defonceray trois ou quatre ruades toutes brodees de cremoisy, & iureray comme vn homme, ou bien ie priray mon voisin de iurer pour moy, ainsi que feit le sire Guillaume, qui pressé du Iuge de iurer luy dit ainsi : " Monsieur ie ne sçay point iurer, parce que ie n'ay pas estudié ny esté à la guerre, & ne suis docteur, ny gendarme, ny gentilhomme; mais i'ay vn frere qui iurera pour moy " » (I, 4-5). It appears that in this passage Béroalde is mocking the narrators of the Renaissance who would swear to the authenticity of their tale, even when it was clearly obvious that it was a current joke, or a legend, which could be found from one author to the other. This desire to give to the story an air of reality is related to the problems of *vraisemblance,* which were to be so carefully worked out during the coming Classical period; the device can be found in Philippe de Vigneulles, Marguerite de Navarre, Bouchet, etc. Part of the trick was the use of real names, to heighten the air of truth and thus engage the listener's or reader's belief, or at least his suspension of disbelief. What makes the passage of *Le Moyen de Parvenir* not only satirical but even farcical is that in swearing to the truth of his story, he echoes a passage from Rabelais, as Paul Lacroix indicates. Lacroix refers the reader to *Pantagruel,* Book III, chapter 35, and says: « Panurge prie un jeune page de jurer pour lui. »[24] The pun on the word « iurer » and the threat of violence serve to heighten the farcical tone of the passage. In addition, the circular logic of « ...il auint ce que vous sçauez » is highly effective in setting the comedy, for, if the reader knows, why tell him? (Again the curious verb « advenir » of the subtitle appears, by the way.)

Without further delay, the author thrusts us back into a given time which has truly not been clarified, and tells us what occured:

> Il fut donc en ceste saison sonné, trompé, trompeté, corné (comme vous voudrez, prenez au goust de vostre ratte) & crié, huché, dit & proclamé auec la trompe philosophique,

24. Paul Lacroix, p. 2, footnote 2.

que toutes ames qui auoient serment à la Sophic se trouuassent au lieu susdit, ainsi qu'il auoit esté ordonné & promis auec serment solemnel, comme il est ordinaire és affaires serieuses de la benoiste coustume des Sages; pour asseurance dequoy les enfans de la science auoient mis la main au symbole de la conscience. Parquoy nous fusmes tous resolus de nous trouuer chez le bon homme nostre pere spirituel, parce qu'il auoit esté ordonné & iugé en dernier ressort de serrure, d'horloge, de cranequin, de rouet, de routissoir, d'arbaleste, & que les deffaillans seroient mis à la nois, à la noisette, au noyau, & à l'amende. A cet esclat de mandement ie ne faillismes à nous trouuer, aussi auions nous promis de nous bien chercher pour cet effect; & puis ie l'auions iuré, & sçachez que c'est vn grand peché de faillir parmi nous, pource que nous suyuons uniquement la regle de perfection en promesse. Et bien que ce soit vne ordinaire, glissee de pere en fils pour gens de bien, coulée de mere en filles pour femmes d'honneur, d'oncle à neueu pour gens d'Eglise; ordinaire (disie) comme ces docteurs qui enfilent leurs discours; que promettre & tenir est tout ce qu'vne personne de bien peut faire, & qu'il n'appartient qu'à ceux qui sont issus de damoysellerie & de gentilhommetté, si en a ton menti vn petit, & ie vous diray aussi honnestement que fit Coquereau à monsieur le President son maistre. Il estoit sommelier & nous boyuions frais & bon, ie disois que le vin estoit bas, monsieur disoit qu'il estoit à la barre, madame dit, « Et bien sommelier qu'en est il ? — Ha ha, dit il, monsieur n'a menty de gueres. » Promettre est facile, mais effectuer difficile, de tenir il est aisé, tenir ce que l'on promet est faire comme le seigneur de nostre parroisse, qui ne vous refuse rien, & baille encor moins (I, 5-6).

The foregoing passage vividly amplifies the concept Béroalde has early invoked by the word « indiction ». It is my feeling that commentators and critics of *Le Moyen de Parvenir* have not insisted enough upon the obligatory nature of this meeting. The mandatory character of the reunion enlists both religious and political satire, and the intermingling of these two regimes is altogether characteristic of the period. The degree to which the problems of the Catholic Church (especially the Ligue) and the Reformers were involved in the choice of the French king and the degree to which the Spanish Inquisition and Philippe II had their hand in disturbances not only in France but also in England are well know, and form the basis of the *Satyre Ménippée*, not a little of which doubtless provided the author of *Le Moyen de Parvenir* with material.

One certainly senses, however, that pressure is brought to bear upon this group, evidently by some religious institution. We note, for instance, that the catalogue of verbs calling the group together has the ring of the militant — leaving aside the erotic implications of the list. The gathering does not take place as a matter of free will, or so it appears. On the contrary, the characters of the book, including the narrator, are brought together by a « mandement », are directed to « muster out », as it were, to be present at the « lieu susdit », which, it is quickly revealed, is the headquarters or home of the mysterious « bon homme nostre père spirituel ». All of the members of the group are said to have in common their dedication to Sophie, either a real or an allegorical person, perhaps both, but more than likely only the latter. What is of interest is the fact that any defaulting members of the group are in danger of torture, the nature of which constitutes one of the most complex and obscure puns in the entire novel *(se puisse tuer)*. In this catalogue of verbs we have a sequence of punishments or threats. As a matter of fact, the defaulting members « seroient mis à la nois, à la noisette, au noyau, & à l'amende ». Now, if one passes over the obvious lascivious color of these terms, and if one leaves aside the pun on the word « amande », which involves the concept of monetary punishment, one comes to realize that this catalogue, taken together with its neighboring sequence, « en dernier ressort de serrure, d'horloge, de cranequin, de rouet, de routissoir, d'arbaleste », constitutes a listing of outdated and contemporary forms of weapons, including firearms and forms of primers or projectiles for various types of hand weapons and firearms. Thus, a new theme, already suggested, no doubt, by the quotation from the *Æneid* found on the title page, and by the early time designations is introduced. This new theme is the theme of war, and especially the satire of the « art of war », which is merely another form of *préciosité*. Under the circumstances we might well conclude that Béroalde is alluding to the decadent nobility and more particularly the Civil Wars. Then the implication would be that a gathering, dedicated to Sophie, to wisdom or philosophy, if you will, is similar to a religious gathering of the times: either one is suspect of heresy; but more salient is the fact that either one is brought about by internal pressures. Any dissenter is in mortal danger, for « c'est vn grand peché de faillir parmi nous ». The word « peché » together with the expressions « la benoiste coustume » and « serment solemnel » become key to the passage.

Though in some ways one might be reminded of the Abbé de Thélème, such an analogy is not too valid, by virtue of the implicit danger, torture and duress of the gathering. The people here, like those in the Abbé de Thélème are, true enough, said to have liberty... but the fact is questionable; and even granted this fact, it is questionable that they use the liberty at their disposal within the dictates of good taste, as we are told is the case with the people in the Abbé de Thélème. The polyglot abilities of these people are not really analogous, either, for trenchant satire is at stake in *Le Moyen de Parvenir,* and not in this particular passage of Rabelais. While the people of the Abbé de Thélème may bespeak an almost Epicurean life, the people in *Le Moyen de Parvenir* are victims of unbridled excess in all forms, and I think we would do well to seek comparison instead with a satirist of the stamp of Viret, whose *Satyres chrestiẽnes de la cuisine papale* depict a gathering which is both religious and unbridled in its behaviour. Indeed throughout this work of Viret the over-all vocabulary and the general tone (more vitriolic than but similar to that of Béroalde) announce more than one feature of *Le Moyen de Parvenir.* Through Viret, in fact, we spot Béroalde's symposium as being, probably, papal, and many of the problems of *Le Moyen de Parvenir* begin to be less troublesome. A passage from Viret will illustrate the truth of these statements, and in order to maintain the analogy with an abbey I have selected the opening lines of Satyre IIII. Viret's glosses should be noticed for additional similarities, as, for example, the very first gloss in this passage, in which the ironic statement that the convent is the place of perfection can be readily related to the sole rule of the guests in *Le Moyen de Parvenir,* the « règle de perfection en promesse ».

Il faut commencer par les retraits, comme par le lieu de perfection.	LECTEUR escoute vn autre vice. Ces Conuents du monde retraits, Sont de ce manoir les retraits, Et cuuier a buer les linges De ces singesses & ces singes Abominablement puans.
Conuẽts.	Regarde de puis trois cens ans Quelles vieilles sempiterneuses, En leurs cloaques veneneuses, Font buée a ces Venerables. Regarde (choses miserables !) De messieurs les Pharisiens Qui ne sont tous Parisiens, La forte & ferme hypocrisie : D'Achab l'auare frenesie A vsurper la propre vigne De Naboth, qui luy est voisine.
Lesciue Papale. Orgueil & luxure buãdieres principales.	Regarde ce chapeau doré Qui veut de tous estre adoré, L'orgueil d'Aman, & la luxure, Soix en Euesché ou en Cure, Vuident, & de façon lasciue Espanchent en bas la lesciue.
Yurõgnerie & gourmãdise baillent les eaux.	L'yurongnerie de ces prestres, Et gourmandise de ces traistres, Auecques leurs vomissemens, Fournissent a tous lauemens.
Rage & Tyrannie tordent & batẽt.	Rages & fureurs trescruelles, Auec tyrannie, sont celles Qui les fardeaux tordent & batent.
Ruse & finesse estendẽt & destendẽt.	Ruse & finesse s'entrebatent A qui mieux tendra les drapeaux, Qui sereunt d'amuser les veaux.[25]

As I have said, attack on *bienséance* is unquestionably present in *Le Moyen de Parvenir,* even if we disregard the term as applying to the papal see or « siège » in which the Pope may or may not be firmly fixed. We have also seen that satire of affectation may even be implicit in the title of the book. For

25. Pierre Viret, *Satyres chrestiẽnes de la cuisine papale* (imprimé par Conrad Badius, 1560), pp. 47-48.

this reason, the language of the narrator is of utmost interest. « A cet esclat de mandement », says he, « ie ne faillisme à nous trouuer, aussi auions nous promis de nous bien chercher pour cet effect; & puis ie l'auions iuré... ». The narrator, then, is not endowed with the « art de bien dire » which is supposedly a prerequisite for such a group as is gathered together here. I do not entirely agree with Paul Lacroix, however, when he says that Béroalde here reflects a « Critique de cette façon de parler... ».[26] Instead, I suspect that it is Béroalde's intention to show the narrator as disengaged. His speech then is a way of revealing him as different from the rest of the group, as a person who has possibly happened along, and insists upon attending the banquet only because he has promised to do so. Somehow or another, his whole heart is not in it, at any rate. His identity is not entirely clear; he is of mysterious origin; the quality of his French reveals that he is not well-educated. There are reasons to suspect that he is a *pícaro,* a rogue, a wanderer, and that this explains in part his sub-standard speech. In fact, he holds « learning » in a certain amount of scorn, it would appear. At least, in regaining the thread of his sentence in the passage just quoted, he likens himself mockingly to « ces docteurs qui enfilent leurs discours ». Indeed, this curious narrator again berates precious speech in the very next chapter. He says, « Alons viste, la souppe se mange, ie pindarise, ie cuidois dire on mange la soupe » (I, 8).[26 a]

That the « soupe » in question is a sort of theological stew offered up by dissenting theologians, especially papists, is ever so likely. The following lines of Viret's *Satyre chrestiēne de la cuisine papale* support this theory:

Le premier seruice diuin
Cloches & matines commencent.
Et Primes en toussant s'auancent
De preparer la souppe grasse.[27]

Of significance to us is that the « soup » Viret describes takes on various forms, including that of « salmigondins »:

26. Paul Lacroix, p. 3.

26 a. The announcement of the soup course is a convention in the satires of « learned groups » brought together for a supper. See Régnier's « Souper ridicule », lines 247-8. But in *Le Moyen de Parvenir* the word « soupe » is probably charged, as in Viret.

27. Viret, pp. 59-60.

AGIOS, HIMAS sõt andouilles,
Saucsisses, ceruelats, boudins,
Hastereaux & salmigondins.
Fressures, hachis, saupiquets,
Sont Exorcismes, bourriquets,
Adiurations, sortileges
A ceux qui suyuent leurs colleges.[28]

The eagerness of the narrator to get to the soup tells us that he is a famished *pícaro,* a representative of the Spanish « épicos de hambre », but there is reason to view in him, too, the type of novice described by Viret: « Si faut-il que ie me marrisse/ Qu'vn ieune Reuerend nouice/ Veut toute la souppe humer. »[29]

Be this as it may — and it is hard other than by this clue from Viret to see in the narrator a clerical identity — the view of this person as a type of rogue will help to explain away his cynical *grossièreté*[30], which, in Chapter V, entitled « Proposition », permits him to utter the following obscene and bitter indictment of the party of story tellers, who are predominantly « scholars » gathered before « La bonne Intention »: « Nous estions là deuant elle pour faire preuue de nos esprits, cela fut cause que je m'y trouvé, & m'assis aussi bien qu'vn autre, dautant que j'ay vn cul, joint que sans cul nul ne pourroit auoir seance entre gens d'honneur » (I, 22).

The satire of precious manners and court etiquette also seems to be on the horizon in an early passage (Chapter III) where Béroalde describes the way in which the people greet one another, unctuously, while bowing deeply:

> Mes gens sont là qui m'attendent; sont messieurs dea, ils sont à moy, est il pas vray, ne sommes nous pas les vns aux autres, dittes vous pas bon jour monsieur ? il est donc vostre sieur... ainsi nous disons bon jour, ou adieu Madame, ma comere, & on nous dit mon amy, mon hoste; & de mesmes nous sommes aux autres, & nous à eux, & pource ils sont à moy, ils sont donc mes gens, qui

28. Viret, p. 61.
29. *Ibid.*, p. 32.
30. His cynicism and the fact that he is apparently of low origins fit the description of the Thessalian Myrtibus the cynic who makes attacks on all philosophers in Athenaeus' *The Deipnosophists.* See in particular Athenaeus, *The Deipnosophists,* ed. E. Capps *et al.*, trans. Charles Burton Gulick (London, 1927), vol. I, pp. xiii-xiv.

> auec moy & moy auec eux trouuasmes tous, & toutes, chez nostre pere se Puissetuer... Chacun y entrant auisa à son debuoir, par ce moyen nous exerçasmes vn notable conflict de reuerences... & pratiquant mille vetilles d'humilitez, auec vne friponne escopeterie de langage curtisannisié fismes plusieurs belles entrees & rencontres à la façon que l'on porte les barbes... (I, 9).

A similar satire of (court) manners among members of the small nobility — specifically the court nobility — can be found in Molière's « La Comtesse d'Escarbagnas » when the countess and Julie go through all sorts of contortions as to which of them will seat herself first. The countess is first speaking to her *suivante* Andrée, and then to Julie:

> LA COMTESSE. — Otez-vous de là, insolente; je vous renverrai chez vos parents. Apportez-moi un verre d'eau. — Madame. *(Faisant des cérémonies pour s'asseoir.)*
> JULIE. — Madame.
> LA COMTESSE. — Ah ! Madame.
> JULIE. — Ah ! Madame.
> LA COMTESSE. — Mon Dieu ! Madame.
> JULIE. — Mon Dieu ! Madame.
> LA COMTESSE. — Oh ! Madame.
> JULIE. — Oh ! Madame.
> LA COMTESSE. — Eh ! Madame.
> JULIE. — Eh ! Madame.
> LA COMTESSE. — Hé ! allons donc, Madame.
> JULIE. — Hé ! allonc donc, Madame.
> LA COMTESSE. — Je suis chez moi, Madame, nous sommes demeurées d'accord de cela. Me prenez-vous pour une provinciale, Madame ?
> JULIE. — Dieu m'en garde, Madame ! [31]

31. J.-B.-P. Molière, *Œuvres complètes*, éd. Maurice Rat (Paris, 1956), II, pp. 727-728. This analogy between « La Comtesse d'Escarbagnas » and *Le Moyen de Parvenir* is not the only one. Long since, Reiche noted Molière's evident borrowing from *Le Moyen de Parvenir* for the scene in which the tutor of the Countess' son has him recite the following lines from Jean Despautère: « *Omne viro soli quod convenit esto virile. / Omne viri...* » (Ibid., pp. 735-736). The tutor, by the way, promises the Countess that in educating the son he will try to inculpate into the boy « les semences de la vertu ». (!!) (*Ibid.*, p. 736). Of course, the idea that a child should be reciting this line before polite company is very comical, since the citation amounts to a statement that « all that which has to do with man only is of the masculine gender. » Béroalde's use of the line is, however,

The narrator in *Le Moyen de Parvenir,* by virtue of his apparent status as a *pícaro,* or at least as an onlooker, would have something of that same natural outlook we associate with the members of the servant class in Molière's plays. He would automatically view the greetings and the ceremony of the assembling dinner-party as further evidence of affectation. But because ours is baroque satire, an extended (and, as it so happens in this particular instance, a deeper) form of criticism lies beneath Béroalde's portrayal of this false protocol. We gain these deeper insights into Béroalde's depiction of this insincere behavior first through the presence of the key word *reuerences,* and, after this, through Viret's *Satyres chestiênes de la cuisine papale.*

It is clear that the word *reuerences* has a religious connotation here. The « conflict de reuerences » passes beyond a simple depiction of awkwardness produced by unctuous encounters into the realm of a clash of ideas, thus alluding to religious conflicts or ideological dissension. Supporting an interpretation of this passage as a satire of the kind of insincere pomp and circumstance found in the *papal* court is Viret's satire of what he calls « courtoisie sorbonesque ».[32] In his « Satyre V » (« Banquet papal ») he underlines the hypocritical etiquette of the priests and other servants of the Pope, the theologians, or, as he significantly labels them, the « abstracteurs de la quintessence »: [33]

more scatalogical, and more satirical; for he is satirizing the learned doctors' ability to make such neat distinctions in gender. In fact, we should relate this item in *Le Moyen de Parvenir* to the whole subject of baroque mutability and metamorphoses — sexual or otherwise. The allusion to this precept of Despautère is found in *Le Moyen de Parvenir* in a chapter entitled « Minute »: « Mais pourquoy le con d'vne femme est il masle ? Omne viro soli quod conuenit esto virile; les Docteurs de Paris l'enseignent ainsi aux escolles, ie vous asseure ô vous qui entendez cecy qu'il est vray, & que comme ce bon pere le dit il n'y va point de sa faute » (I, 141). In *Le Moyen de Parvenir,* then, satire of the grammarian and, in fact, of the clergy (the Doctors of the Sorbonne, at any rate) is accomplished by use of this passage. I do not claim that similar satire is not present in Molière's use of the line, but I *do* feel that in Molière's play the use is more limited, a difference we might expect between baroque satire and classical satire. Limitations are, of course, set on Molière, simply through the difference in genre. The fact that the above passage from *Le Moyen de Parvenir* issues from the mouth of Le Bon Homme will make the satire present even more trenchant. For identification of Molière's probable borrowing from Béroalde see Reiche, p. 25.

32. Viret, p. 57.

33. *Ibid.,* p. 11. The expression « quinte essence » used by Rabelais as an epithet for M. Alcofribas (« Abstracteur de Quinte Essence »), supposed author of

Non Monsieur, vous irez deuant.
Mais vous, Monsieur le plus scauant:
Voire mais si c'estoit a prendre,
Maudit qui se feroit attendre
Et puis Messieurs ces deslauez
Nous preschent que sommes lauez
Par sale & salé lauement.[34]

We can find further evidence that the word « reuerence » in *Le Moyen de Parvenir* is intended to satirize false etiquette among the theologians in the explanation as to why Madame has selected Socrates as toastmaster of the banquet: « ...Madame luy donna la charge d'expédier la bienseance dont il s'acquitta galemment, dautant qu'il estoit expert aux proportions du manage reuerencieux de la Court & auoit fort bien estudié les circonstances des similitudes, ceremonies, fadaises, & miracles qui se pratiquent entre ceux qui s'aident des specialitez d'honneur que l'on se fait, entrant ou sortant, s'asseant ou se leuant, se rencontrant ou passant » (I, 18). Socrates, in his role as sophist, can belabor either side of the theological debate, in other words. As sophist and toastmaster, he is a kind of moderator, although his high knowledge of the papal « court » would imply he is perhaps a cardinal. Other signs that he is a papist are present, but we are concerned principally with the function of the words « reuerence » and « reuerencieux » in the early chapters of *Le Moyen de Parvenir.*

Another proof of this double meaning for « reuerence » is seen in the deeply allegorical tale of Marciole. Without trying to analyze the symbolism of the story, notice that the virgin's presentation of the basket of cherries along with her « reuerence » has the ring of one entering a church, for, it is said, Marciole « ...vint en la salle faire la reuerence à Monsieur qui disnoit & luy presenta ce fruict de par son pere » (I, 27). This Monsieur is Monsieur de la Roche, who, I believe, can be identified as a papist. I base this on several factors in the story, but especially on the statement « ...dautant qu'il estoit le protype de l'Antechrist... » (I, 27-28). « Antechrist » is frequently used

La Vie Très Horrifique du Grand Gargantua and of *Pantagruel, Roy des Dipsodes,* does not seem to me to have quite the same implication it does in Viret and in Béroalde. See François Rabelais, *Œuvres,* ed. Louis *Moland* (Paris, 1950), I, p. 1 and p. 155.

34. Viret, p. 57.

as a synonym for the Pope in *Le Moyen de Parvenir*, as it is in Viret.[35]

Let us not forget, either, how the duty of the reader toward *Le Moyen de Parvenir* is clearly spelt out: « ...vous deuez porter honneur à cet ouurage, que si vous n'estes assez forts pour luy en porter assez, trainez-le, ou luy enuoyez, ou le roulez, ou luy faites tenir en reuerence » (I, 42). This admonishment is advantageously recalled here in support of the argument that the word « reuerence » has in it a probable pun which lifts the allusion from the realm of a simple satire of affectation and into the realm of a satire of religious affectations and hypocrisies, which are, I should think, more serious faults in mankind. At any rate, by seeing the duality and even multiplicity of the term, we catch another glimpse into that excessive complexity of *Le Moyen de Parvenir* which gives to the work its richness and its universal applications.

Le Moyen de Parvenir (like the *Satyre Ménippée*) also presents a type of processional, an order of appearance (Chapter VI, « Proposition », I, 17-22). That such a processional exists in the book is significant, and when Béroalde ascribes to the story of Marciole the title « Cérémonie », these « reuerences » and this processional, including the set order and progression in the papal court, and even in the celebration of the mass are all reflected. A re-examination of Socrates' qualifications for master of ceremonies will serve to strengthen this assertion.

The processional proper is linked rather loosely to the question of whether man is responsible solely to God, or to some other human being who in turn is responsible to some other human being, and so on, till responsibility finally falls on the Pope, who, in this complex hierarchical chain is responsible to God. For external evidence that the papists are designated in Béroalde's procession, we may again turn to Viret, who in his gloss places the word « Processions » and in the text writes:

> Le confanon est mis au vent,
> Pour defêse aux assauts des mouches,
> Lors brayêt de toutes leurs bouches,
> Presentans a tous leurs viandes.

35. Viret, p. 4.

Les volatilles plus friandes
Sont par les Cardinaux portees.
Toutes delices apportees
En dernier mets par Courtisanes.
Garçons sur mulets & sur asnes,
Ganymedes, pociallateurs...[36]

These and many others are ready to come from near and far, « Tans sont-ils gentils faucõniers ».[37]

The above passage and others in Viret also duplicate the fanfare of the first chapter of *Le Moyen de Parvenir:* « Il fut donc... sonné, trompé, trompeté, corné... & crié auec la trompe philosophique... » The difference comes in Béroalde's essentially baroque variations on the same theme.

Now if we take fanfare, bowing and scraping (here, probably scrapping, as implied by the word « conflict de reuerences »), the oily greetings, the subtitle « Cérémonie », along with dubious heroics and artificiality of language, we may ascribe to the totality the term « ostentation », a term often used in baroque nomenclature. Ostentation is said by Rousset to be an essential ingredient of baroque art, and specifically in the character of the hero in baroque theater.[38] However, its presence in *Le Moyen de Parvenir* is not simply baroque in and of itself but, couched as it is in a satirical *genre*, is quite likely a satire not only of the characteristic but also of the taste for it in literature. A great many passages in *Le Moyen de Parvenir* can, as I have said, have the added interpretation of literary satire. For that matter, we might even wonder if the dichotomy we note between interlocutor and tale told is not due strictly to a cynical view of the « learned » doctors and what their *real* concerns are, according to the author (or narrator), but entails a mordant statement on the current taste for stercoraceous literature. To regard the eroticism of *Le Moyen de Parvenir* in this light is not entirely unreasonable, and were we to give serious consideration to this theory, the unjustified stigma of « pornography » from which Béroalde's name and his great work suffer would be removed.

Returning to the last sentence quoted from the first chapter

36. Viret, p. 28.
37. *Ibid.*
38. Jean Rousset, *La Littérature de l'âge baroque en France* (Paris, 1954), pp. 214-217.

of *Le Moyen de Parvenir,* I should like to point out that there is good reason not to make the narrator seriously when he states the high dedication of this group of people to « Sophie ». While this is what we are supposed to believe, the claim is beguiling. Within the confines of *Le Moyen de Parvenir,* no one of these celebrated « scholars » will in truth fall into the category of « ames qui auoient serment à la Sophie », including the narrator; those who should fit the definition do not behave accordingly. In addition to the intentional and evident religious satire, an adjacent but tacit literary satire is present in the very form of the book. This is all the more true if we consider that the excuse trumped up by authors to get a group of people together for purposes of providing a frame to hold together a series of otherwise disconnected tales which the persons purportedly tell to one another is frequently feeble, lame, or preposterous. Thus, if the *raconteurs* in *Le Moyen de Parvenir* do not by the tales they tell seem to fit with the frame (which Béroalde states to be a gathering in the name of Sophie, standing for *Sagesse, Philosophie, Sainte Sophie* or some other abstraction altogether), then that is exactly the point! Contradictions between purpose and result are basic to the *modus operandi* of *Le Moyen de Parvenir* and recall in part the discrepancies between the station of some of Chaucer's pilgrims and the tales they tell. However, the inconsistency in *Le Moyen de Parvenir* is so much greater than that found in the *Canterbury Tales* that if one is forced to make a distinction, one feels compelled to say that the lengths to which Béroalde goes tax the imagination. To such an extent is this the case that the very point of departure of *Le Moyen de Parvenir* is rather more cynical than satirical, its tone and color approaching the stercorous — but for a reason — and a profound scepticism, at least with respect to the perfectibility of man.

Leaving aside the question of Béroalde's *Weltanschauung* for the moment, and to continue with considerations on form and content, we might summarize the technical problems posed by the relationship of frame to tale by saying that since, over and above the tales, the frame itself is evidently satirical, while the collective work presents a vast mixture of genres drawn on for one or another satirical purpose, major prisms are established. It need only be added that such prisms, be they minor stylistic ones or major structural and/or thematic ones, abound in *Le Moyen de Parvenir*, and their presence is one of the many good reasons for characterizing the novel as baroque. The fact that we are dealing with a many-faceted satire even leaves open the possibility that the very procedures of baroque literature, such as antitheses, prisms, etc., may be under attack. If this is the case, then we should properly set upon the definition of baroque as it applies to *Le Moyen de Parvenir* the restriction of satirical baroque, or *baroque satirique.*

Further to this, as we go along in our examination of the guest-list and the tale told by the guest, we discover there is greater plan, greater correlation between the two than first appears to be the case. By minute inspection of the interlocutors, their very presence to begin with, and after that, what they seem to represent and even what they say, it becomes apparent that virtually all the themes I have indicated in the foregoing will show up in one way or another. This fact will be all the more clear once we have established the dominant trends of the final chapter. As it is an extremely telling chapter (ironically entitled « Argument »), I shall first reproduce it in entirety, and then proceed to a commentary on it.

> He bien, à propos de vous, Messieurs, vous direz que ie suis fou; ie voudrois le pouuoir deuenir; pource que si tost que ie le serois, ie serois exempt du feu si on me disoit heretique; deliuré de prison, si ie deuois; non suiect au Consistoire ou à la Mercuriale, ou à la reprimende.
> — Et pourquoi les fous ont ils de si belles libertez & priuileges?
> — Pource que l'Empereur Iustinian qui gouuerne encor le monde fou, est deuenu fou durant sa vie, par ainsi les fous sont empereurs & è conuerso.
> — Et ie ne m'esbahi pas si mon pere mourut par faute de gouuernement, crede michi. Quand ie reuins de voyage, ie ne trouuay point d'eau dans le sceau, encore moins en la seille; il mourut comme à Dole à la dance Macaber, il y a la Mort qui parle à vn beau ieune homme, & lui dit,
>
> A, galan, galan
> Que tu es fringan,
> S'il te faut-il meurre.
>
> Et il respond :
>
> Et, mort arrogan,
> Pren tout mon argean,
> Et me laisse querre.

— Or bien, si vous me calomniez, c'est tout vn, il n'y a point de ma faute; le vallet de l'Aumosne, à qui les autres faisoient la guerre, le dit bien à messieurs du Bureau : « Vrament, messieurs, il n'y a que les pauures que l'on canonise. »
— Or bien touche là, Vignau, ta femme est femme de bien, ie le croy, si l'ay-je besongnee aussi bien que toy.
— O le niays ! elle est si laide, que ie ne voudrois auoir affaire à la femme non plus qu'au mari.

Passons outre, ie sens desia que ce liure nous eschappe; & me semble que ie voy desia vn frippon de proposant qui s'est joint auec vn aspirant à la Prestrise mediante coquedindo, & ils disent que ie suis nigromanchian, que ie fais parler des morts; ie suis bien plus habile que cela, les morts ont parlé, ils le sçauent bien; mais ie fais parler les bestes, & beaucoup parleront, si Dieu plaist : mais auisez, s'il vous plaist, à tout ce qui se fait, ou que l'on fait en ce monde : tout cela a vne fin certaine, & ie vous en feray vne demonstration notable : allez chez vn peintre, & voyez lui broyer les couleurs. Sçauez-vous bien pourquoy on prend tant de peine à les broyer diligemment ? Ie vous vay dire vn grand secret, auisez y; prenez la molette & la leuez, & vous verrez de beaux arbrisseaux & branchages qui se font haut & bas. Et voila la cause pourquoy, la fin pour laquelle, les aueugles se cognoissent en couleurs : & pource, si tu crains la goute, abbas-là, fou là. Ma fille, o, belle seruante, si mon vallet te prie vn peu de resiouissance, prens vn baston & lui en donne, tandis que ie m'amuseray à ces gens de reputation, qui sont pleins d'honneur, comme vne truïe de poiure. Or ça, mes bons amis, viuons en liberté, nostre conuiue s'acheue, ils sont sur le dessert : ie suis vn peu sorti pour vous le dire; d'autres pourront recueillir le reste que i'ay oublié pour mon plaisir & vostre commodité, dautant que les yeux vous feroient mal, qui seroit fort au desauantage de vostre veuë. Bien donques, dittes moy, auez-vous enuie de paruenir ? lisez ce volume de son vray biais; il est fait comme ces peinctures, qui monstrent d'vn, & puis d'autre. On m'a dit qu'il y a eu quelques malotrus qui ont dit, « Voici des traits d'Ateiste. » En dea ie n'en sçay rien, ie m'en raporte à eux : si i'ay rencontré à dire leur naïueté, ç'a esté sans le sçauoir, ie joue au colimmaillard, ie prens ce que ie trouue. Mais eux qui sont sages, & pleins d'intelligence, ils sont tout par election & cognoissance, il est tousiours auis au chat breneux que la queuë luy put. Ne vous desplaise, si i'ay dit quelque chose qui regarde ou oye de costé, & sente mal à vostre goust, ce n'est pas ma faute, c'est vne perspectiue d'oreilles qui est gauchie : & puis, les parfaits sont aux Cieux. Si ie m'esbats à me mocquer de vous, esbatez-vous à dire bien de moy, afin que ce ne soit pas vous dont ie parle : & puis qui sçait en bon escient ce que ie veux dire, s'il n'a veu & leu le tout, & n'a requis le vray sens de mon affaire ? Et par la double fressure de mon petit chien, i'ay quasi iuré comme vn Connestable, & pris Dieu par tout : mais ie me suis retenu par vostre exemple. Et vous direz doncques que ie suis vn moqueur, vn contempteur : il est vray, si vous le prenez selon vostre folle fantaisie, qui ne vaut pas vne foutee de chat; aussi ie controolle vos sottises, & condamne vos impudences. Or chacun iuge selon le poids de sa charité, & de là les bonnes religieuses qui apprendront ceci par cœur, diront : « Il est bon homme, il taxe les vices d'vne belle façon » : & pour l'amour de cela, ie me mettray à faire vn beau liure, où ie vous diray la verité tout au rebours des autres, & d'vne façon si belle que ie le publieray apres ma mort, afin que l'on voye que i'y diray de bonnes choses, que ie n'entendray non plus que vous autres : & si deuiendra tant authentique que le monde de son temps le priseront tous, & le diront vnique : tellement qu'ils tiendront tous les autres auteurs, ainsi que vous, comme vrais fous qu'ils sont, se trauaillans pour neant, & pour penser acquerir vne reputation, qui se porte à Paris sur des crochets, comme fagots benits. Malheureux sont ceux qui se donnent de la peine pour auoir bruit d'estre, ou pipeurs, ou flateurs, ou mercenaires, ou dicteurs des folies d'autruy. Et afin que ie puisse vn iour commencer ce volume, ie mettray ici vn tronc, tel qu'il est en nostre ville, aupres le portail de la grande Eglise :

> Vous qui auez mine d'estre homs,
> Et qui semblez estre hommasses :
> Apportez quatre gros ès troncs,
> Afin que l'œuure se parface.

Et ie vous promets que vous y gaignerez : & dauantage, y apprendrez tout ce qu'il y a de bon en ce monde;

> ce que ie vous prouueray en toutes & maintes sortes (II, 257-261).

One can immediately appreciate that in this last chapter Béroalde has brilliantly avoided the temptation to impose a conventional ending for his frame on the sophisticated and ingenious time dislocations which he had set down on the title page, in the opening quatrain, and in the first chapter, and which he had consistently and successfully sustained throughout the whole book.

The very title of the final chapter — « Argument » — again displays the rampant irrationalism we have already spoken of at length. This is self-evident when one recalls that any early chapter of *Le Moyen de Parvenir* — Chapter XIII — is entitled « Conclusion », and that another early chapter — Chapter XI (like « Conclusion », ironically entitled « Pause dernière ») — begins with the imperative « Or commençons de conclure ». These and all the other ironic upheavals of time sequence as well as the defiance of the rational seem to attain full expression by Béroalde's giving to his last chapter the title « Argument ». In some ways this title is quite justified, since in the last chapter we do find the chief propositions of *Le Moyen de Parvenir*. Nevertheless, its position at the end of the book is capricious, startling and unorthodox.

It is not just the title of the last chapter, however, that contributes to a re-enstatement of the time ironies in *Le Moyen de Parvenir*. It seems to me that the greatest time absurdity of the entire work comes at the very end, where the author promises that one day he will write the « unique », the « authentic » book — or breviary — which he has over and again in the course of *Le Moyen de Parvenir* claimed it to be. In addition to some day writing this book, he will publish it after his death, says he. When we pit the opening quatrain and the promises of the final chapter against the simple fact of the book's existence, we know we are being brainwashed or at least presented with the kind of disclaimer affidavit we examined earlier from *Le Palais des Curieux*. Like that passage this final chapter seems designed as a publicity stunt, to stimulate those who tend to read the last chapter of a book into reading the whole of *Le Moyen de Parvenir*. This, of course, is conjecture; it is not essential to an understanding of the chapter. Leaving the conjecture aside, let us recall that in the opening quatrain of *Le Moyen de Parvenir* we are told that the work we are about to read was not begun because « Madame » did not survive. Now, in this strange coda, beginning with the words « Passons outre » (cf. I, 8), and continuing through the promise of the last sentence of the book — « Et ie vous promets que vous y gaignerez : & dauantage, y apprendrez tout ce qu'il y a de bon en ce monde; ce que ie vous prouueray en toutes & maintes sortes. » — we are being told that the book which we have just read has not yet been written, but one day will be. At no point in the « novel » is our imagination more heavily taxed than here. But, even so, at no point is our whimsy more delightfully enlisted, nor is Béroalde's fancy pushed to a greater extreme.

To summarize the time motifs of « Argument » we may say the final chapter's title and content reveal that the conclusion of the book is really at the beginning while the beginning is at the end — if, indeed, we are even permitted to say that we *have* a book. This is largely what gives to *Le Moyen de Parvenir* the effect of break-down in form and structure which are at once associated with baroque literature's refusal to compose and with « innovations » of the Joycian type, to be found in twentieth century literature. Analogies with this latter have, of course, already been drawn. The confession of refusal to compose found in the text of *Le Moyen de Parvenir* will be dealt with in the treatment of the book's style. Time eruptions have been pointed out in abundance. No more need be said, then, of the presence of these features in the last chapter of the novel. Their appearance is simply in the order of things. Having therefore recognized the place of the final chapter in the temporal plan of *Le Moyen de Parvenir* we are free to turn to the structure and ideology of the chapter proper, which, in turn, will lead us back to other themes and tendencies of the book.

The final chapter is divided into two sections, the one still carrying out the dialogues, the second recovering the frame, in so hasty a manner that it risks telescoping the work. This second part may conveniently be called a coda. Those who consult the Paul Lacroix edition will note that this « coda » is (incorrectly, I believe) divided among the speakers L'Autre, Le BonHomme and Quelqu'un. That is why Paul Lacroix is able to identify « Quelqu'un » with Béroalde.[39] Although this

39. Paul Lacroix, p. 486.

identification is risky, and even suspect, it does not do irreparable mischief to this particular section, since I feel that it is the « author » — not the narrator and maybe not even Béroalde himself, except facetiously — who is addressing the reader.

In both sections of this chapter the themes of time dislocation (with accompanying manifestations of nonsense or irrationalism) and death are thoroughly explored, from a variety of viewpoints. The dominant themes are recapitulated; the humor and satire are not only retained; they are heightened, and to some degree translated. To the extent that this is true, the whole last chapter is a foil. It reveals the satire as one on the folly of mankind, held in the grasp of mad and inefficient government by church and state and then caught in his own traps of self-inflation. In the first part of this chapter, the use of Justinian as a symbol of madman, soldier, legislator, author, ruler and even as a liaison between Church and State, by virtue of his part in the erection of the church of Saint Sophia, is more than happenstance. He represents a rounding up in one name of most of the facets of society under attack in *Le Moyen de Parvenir.* Furthermore, by the special achievements of his life, he unquestionably stands for one particular contemporary of Béroalde. For this reason, we have in the final chapter, alongside the major themes of time, mutability and mortality (with accompanying time eruptions and anachronisms) the two chief antitheses of *Le Moyen de Parvenir:* wisdom versus folly and the ancient versus the modern. These antitheses, it need scarcely be added, are conspicuously related to the major themes of time and mutability.

We can further subdivide this final chapter so that in the first part, which continues the dialogues, we have a discussion of folly, especially of the « mad » Justinian, who symbolizes bad government, characterized by folly and producing folly. Further, we have the death of a father (perhaps linked to the « pere spirituel » ?) as a result of bad government, and ultimately we have the effort of a lover to buy off death. In both the case of bad government and in the scene from the Dôle Dance of Death, the examples and the results are individual and specific. Nevertheless, they seem to tell us of certain certainties: folly and bad government, folly which even makes conceivable the effort of a mortal to buy off the inescapable reaper, death, whose handmaid is time. The « coda » of the chapter, on the other hand, reviews the time absurdities we have just examined, and broadens the death theme to a real Dance of Death, in which all the characters — interlocutors and otherwise — are implicated. In this tableau, the author includes himself, and even the reader, for that matter, since the reader's reactions toward a completed book the author will write and publish some day after he is dead are predicted and prescribed.

The certain certainties proposed on an individual basis in the first part of the last chapter are generalized in the coda. We see that through the folly of self-glorification, some clergyman — the author, or Béroalde, if you will — may claim to write the only authoritative book, a sort of Aristotelian *summa,* a compendium of human knowledge. The book of this scholastic *arriviste* would be one by which we should live, and it would guide us to the kingdom of heaven. Still another type of folly or self-glorification would cause this book to be misunderstood by his readers and critics. At least each one would have his own private theory concerning it. In the quatrain at the end of the chapter we also see that the mad but all too human desire to bribe death may easily be exploited by the clergy. People are persuaded to bring their money assumedly for masses, bulls of indulgence, etc., so that they may buy their way « in » — the exact place being intentionally left vague. Such vicious practices, it seems implicit, can only result from the folly of bad government, ecclesiastical or otherwise... and, too, from the death of the father, which, I think, is symbolically linked to the resultant ills of bad government. The coda, it appears, seeks to point out universal folly and universal guilt: the victim is barely less culpable than the parasites who feed upon him. However, depth examination of the allusions and vocabulary in this chapter show still another and more trenchant kind of satire at work. That is why I believe that a minute analysis of the chapter, both of the dialogue continuum, and of its coda, will be worth our while. It will be profitable not simply for the understanding we can come to of the chapter itself, but for the light it can shed on the totality of the novel, whose whole orientation has, with the exception of M. Saulnier's sympathetic appreciation, been historically misrepresented, if not even mistaken.

The satirical intention of the last chapter is not so obscure as some of the other parts of *Le Moyen de Parvenir.* The author is apparently telling us that no commentary (on the Bible), no missal, no guide to « perfection » exists, and that its composition could only come about in another setting. That the human race will ever achieve such an environment is, however, doubtful. In addition, even if it were possible to attempt to write a book of this nature, the effort would wind up in a *débacle;* for the book would be misunderstood and misused. The reasons for this potentiality of misunderstanding are manifold, but they can be condensed into the corruption of two inter-related human institutions — government and religion — and the corruption itself into one basic human folly or vice — egomania.

The combined institutions of government and religion are pictured in this chapter as coming under the temporal power of the madman Justinian. This emperor stands as a symbol, since, in accordance with the endlessness of our « satire perpetuelle », he still governs « le monde fou ». The mutuality of the madness is a factor which merits our attention just as much as its perpetuity. If Justinian refers to a contemporary sovereign it is hard to say which one. In some ways he seems to suggest Philip II of Spain, but I think that taking Justinian at face value, and treating him as pure symbol will be the safest approach, until absolute identification of this person can be made.

Restricting ourselves to Justinian as Justinian will reveal a great deal for us even so. For example, if « Madame » of the opening quatrain is to be identified with « Sophie » — as I think she is — then « Sophie », or wisdom, i. e., the source of the author's inspiration, is dead. Even more significantly, if « Sophie » is to be connected with the Church — and I think she is — then the fact of dissension and schism, of heresy and vice among the clergy and the intelligentsia renders the creation of a reliable guide to self-perfection impossible. The name Sophie in connection with the Church is very subtly introduced here under the name of the emperor Justinian, who as emperor of Constantinople was responsible for the construction of the Santa Sophia at Constantinople. Thus, Justinian's madness as it is depicted in the first section of the final chapter is allied with the madness of all those who reign. The fall of Constantinople, the Eastern schism, and all forms of political and religious dissension are clustered around his name. He is a universal symbol here, but he may also stand for a contemporary leader, possibly one who was opposed to the Pope, or sought power over the Pope, who might then be the father who has died as a result of bad government. On the other hand, he may be the Pope himself, and the father a simple abstraction either of an earthly parent or of the heavenly Father.

But there are other things in Justinian's biography which make him a significant symbol in *Le Moyen de Parvenir.* His connection with religion extends beyond his part in the construction of the Santa Sophia, for he is also remembered for having called together the Council of Chalcedon to deal with the monosophysite heresy, which would represent in later times governmental efforts to quell the Eastern Schism, and in still later times, a fight against the onset of Protestantism.

As a lawgiver, too, Justinian would be doubly involved in church and state, and his *Justineaneus Codes,* or his *Digesta* (cf. the chapter title « Diette ») would be monuments to this function. The emphasis here could be the folly of the Pope's intervention into matters of state or a government leader's intervention into church affairs. In either case the folly of any effort to bring order to chaos by artificial fixing of times for fasting, of moral law, or determination to hold the straying lambs in the fold through forced council and the issue of ineffective policies resulting from such a meeting is associated with the figure of Justinian. Again, Philip II's interference with the papal see, his (or for that matter any other sixteenth century monarch's) long list of councils, synods, pacts, etc., concerned with the people's religious rights and practices would make him as good a candidate as any for a contemporary Justinian.

It seems to me important to recall the exact relationship of state to church, both as a natural fusion from the early Middle Ages and as a subject for discussion during Béroalde's period. Lucas most vividly points out that for all intents and purposes there was no real division during the sixteenth century, nor did any faction conceive of it as such:

> The relationship of church and state is an important subject in the history of liberty. According to medieval conceptions, the two institutions were parallel, each supreme in its own sphere. But as the church was of divine foundation and possessed authority over man's moral nature, it was superior to the state in secular matters which involved man's eternal welfare. Upon this conception rest the practices of the medieval Inquisition,

> and also the explanation of the fact that the state was willing to punish heretics without a trial in its secular court after they had been condemned by the courts Christian. But Luther had very different ideas; he held that the Christian prince should direct the work of reformation and control the church. Thus Luther helped to create the territorial church subjected to the will of secular Christian princes, the state church of the Reformation. Calvin, however, did not move so far away from the medieval conception, for he held that the church and state were ordained of God and that the former was independent within its own sphere. His followers were loath to recognize the right of the state to dictate matters of religion. Both Luther and Calvin believed that princes, instructed by the clergy, should uproot heresy and labor for the purity of the faith. For this reason it is impossible to hold to the idea, still very popular in some quarters, that the great reformers inaugurated a régime of religious toleration. The belief that men were not to be molested because of their religious convictions was not a sixteenth-century conception, but arose later when states found it utterly impossible to make all men think alike in religion. Catholic princes were also intolerant; if they were more severe in repressing heresy it was due not to the character of Catholicism as much as to the jealousy which the outraged majesty of old conservative ruling houses felt toward heretical ideas.[40]

As I have said, it is difficult to distinguish whether the Justinian of the final chapter of *Le Moyen de Parvenir* represents a papal monarch or an imperial (governmental) figure. The above quotation from Lucas will help to explain this perhaps. In one way, it might be best to regard Justinian merely as a ruler. Even so, his title « emperor » will justify our correlating him with « La belle Impéria », and therefore with the church. Impéria in *Le Moyen de Parvenir* (I, 23-26) is unlikely to be the courtisan discussed by the Balzacian editors Bouteron and Longnon.[41] She is no doubt the point of departure for the

40. Henry S. Lucas, *The Renaissance and the Reformation* (New York, 1934), pp. 695-696.

41. Honoré de Balzac, *Œuvres complètes*, éd. Marcel Bouteron and Henri Longnon (Paris, 1932), XXXVII, pp. 290-297.

Impéria of *Les Contes drolatiques,* for Balzac in writing of the illustrious literary past of Touraine admits his debt to Verville. Touraine, says Balzac in his Prologue, « ...ha fourni sa grand'part des hommes de renom à la France avecque feu Courier de piquante mémoire; Vervile, autheur du *Moyen de Parvenir;* et aultres bien cogneuz... ».[42]

However, in *Le Moyen de Parvenir* Impéria is, like Marciole whose story follows hers, deeply allegorical. On the fictional level, Impéria is roughly identified with Bonaventure Des Periers' noble lady in his Nouvelle LXXVIII.[43] « La belle Impéria » of Verville is indeed a courtisan, but the word has the double meaning of a *meretrix bonesta* and a lady-in-waiting at Court. Her connection with the court is established when Béroalde associates with her a certain flower, the « couronne imperiale » (the « lis royale », as it is also called, according to Paul Lacroix).[44] But here as elsewhere in *Le Moyen de Parvenir* the word « court » has every sign of referring to the papal court. In brief, the story of « La belle Impéria » juxtaposes the practices of the Dames Françoises and the Dames Italiennes (the French and Italian churches) in the administration of the mass. The mass is disguised by the word « vesse », so that insight into the meaning of the story is only gained through such things as the name of the lady, or the following passage from Viret:

> Quand Messire Jehan porte chappe
> La vesse a faite, & Messe dite.
> Ie ne veux vser de redite,
> Messe, vesse, si tu as sens,
> C'est tout vn, ils ont mesme sens.
> I'ay tant trauaillé que i'en sue.
> En deux mots acheuons l'issue.[45]

In the gloss to this passage Viret writes: « Mots vileins a choses vileines ». This seems to give us the key to Béroalde's story of « La belle Impéria ». In the amours of Impéria, for example in « La belle abbaye de Turpenay » or in the sketch

42. Balzac, XXXVI, pp. 3-4.

43. Bonaventure Des Periers, *Contes ou Nouvelles Récréations et joyeux devis suivis du Cymbalum Mundi* (Paris, 1872), p. 203. From the footnote on this page we might postulate a vocabulary borrowing by Béroalde.

44. Paul Lacroix, p. 15, footnote 5.

45. Viret, pp. 74-75.

entitled « L'Archevêque », Balzac approaches theological satire[46], but even so, he has a tendency to sacrifice the satirico-allegorical features of Verville's Impéria for the straight story-line.

As a rule, and at that very much in accordance with baroque techniques, one finds a complement to any one characteristic or phenomenon of *Le Moyen de Parvenir* in some other passage of the novel. Thus, the following passage seems to bear on the reference to church and state evoked by the mention of Justinian: « ...& pource que, entendez que ie voulois parler bref, l'Espitre, c'est le Roy d'Espagne, & l'Euangile, c'est le Roy de France, d'autant que deuant le Pape disant Messe ils sont Diacre & Sou-diacre, & ie dy que ie ne me soucie pas de leurs debats, d'autant que demeurant à Basle, i'estois Chanoine de Sainct Paul » (I, 147-148).

The allegory of Impéria, on the other hand, receives this variation: « ...vous trouuerez en ce liure, si vous le lisez, que la Royne signifie damoiselle; & vesse vaut autant à dire que fille d'honneur : aussi pour l'honneur qu'on porte à l'Église, on appelle leurs contubernales vesses; depuis ce temps là les dames qui ont eu de la reputation & ont esté grandes par le monde, & releuees en honneur, ont voulu estre putains... » (I, 286).

Whether he is to be associated with a prince of the church or not, the mad Justinian clearly feeds on the madness of those who support him, « è conuerso ». The presence of court fools and emperors among the interlocutors at the symposium in *Le Moyen de Parvenir* will corroborate the apparent sententia, « ...les fous sont empereurs... ». One of the most interesting features of this diatribe on favor shown to fools in general and to the mad monarch Justinian in particular is the death of the interlocutor's father. It is a question once again of cause and effect. Here the cause of bad government is madness or folly, and its effect is death to those who are victimized financially and spiritually.

A similar satire on civil and ecclesiastical government and its relation to the people is seen in the body of the text as follows:

> Et de là i'infere que si le Roy defendoit de mettre des febues aux gasteaux des Rois, & qu'il prit ces febues là, & les semat, il en tireroit vn grand soulagement du peuple.

46. Balzac, XXXVII, p. 225 ff. and pp. 291-294.

> Or sans nous amuser à ces gueux de Rois, si tu veux estre libre n'aye iamais de femme, pource que si tu es marié tu seras obligé, tu payeras la taille & la tauxe aussi, & faudra que tu le fasses par contract : ainsi sont tenus les gens mariez; ce à quoi les libres Ecclesiastiques ne sont obligez, n'ayant affaire au particulier ny à la raye publique que pour leur plaisir & recreation, & ce les apres disnees, & au temps d'esbat, non pour tenir femmes auolees toute nuit; parce qu'a leur resueil ils sont obligez de dire leurs heures à ieun, & ils auroient beu de l'ordinaire comme les Ministres, & on les accuseroit d'estre heretiques : tellement qu'ils auroient beu la façon de leur iournee ayant beu de l'ordinaire.
>
> LVCRECE. — Ie mourus par ce poison : toutefois c'est tout vn (I, 199-200).

The story of this interlocutor's homecoming rehearses the themes of departure and return which abound in *Le Moyen de Parvenir,* despite the fact that we have basically the static scene of a banquet. These voyages animate the novel, and give it the shifting geography which it has in common with the picaresque novel and which reveals the baroque stamp of either. In this final passage one is mindful, too, of the parable of the prodigal son, an archetypal *pícaro.*[47] Indeed, reference to the prodigal son occurs in our text (II, 218).

Conversely, the voyage may be pictured in *Le Moyen de Parvenir* in the framework of nonsense, as in the following passage, where the implication may be that the « sage » of our novel is not really very well travelled: « — Puis que tu es cordonnier, si tu veux ie t'apprendray vn beau secret, que m'enseigna l'Empereur des Turcs, quand ie le fus voir durant mon grand voyage à Chastelleraut, où ie vis l'origine de toutes les nations, estats, sexes & gens du monde » (II, 233).

The statement of the interlocutor in the final chapter that he did not find any water in the pail or bucket appears to be a fragment of some verse or song. It has an erotic implication which, under the circumstance of the death of the father is

47. This view of the prodigal son as an archetypal *pícaro* is reinforced by Gide's portrayal of trials borne during absence, among which was bitter servitude. The prodigal son says to his mother, « ...j'ai dû servir... De mauvais maîtres qui malmenaient mon corps, exaspéraient mon orgueil, et me donnaient à peine de quoi manger ». André Gide, *Le Retour de l'enfant prodigue* (Paris, 1948), p. 194.

grotesque in its humor and yet profoundly symbolic, seeming to suggest Orpheus, or any other maimed father symbol. Sexual impotence and death are humorously and tragically inter-related and the humorous connections are not overlooked by Béroalde, as I have previously pointed out.

There is also reason to see in these lines about the pail and the bucket a hidden reference to the communion rites, the water representing humanity. This sacrement is frequently in Béroalde's mind — which is understandable, in view of the current arguments about every aspect of it, especially the question of transubstantiation so thoroughly satirized by Viret. In *Le Moyen de Parvenir* one of the best examples of apparent satire of the watering of the sacremental wine is found toward the end of the story of Democritus and how he found truth in the well (I, 15-16). In any event, there appears to be some theological reference, and the words « seau » and « seille » may represent puns on the words « sceau » and « selle » — e.g., the « sceau de confession » or « selle » meaning « siège » or « chaise », the latter to be taken either in a vulgar sense (cf. I, 211; I, 248) or as a rendering of « bienséant », referring to court manners or to the papal see. An equally complex pun of similar construction occurs in another passage of *Le Moyen de Parvenir*, where the pun includes the meanings « to seal », « to conceal », perhaps even « to seat ». Speaking of « le Liure », the interlocutor says, « ...d'autant qu'il aduiendra ainsi qu'il est aduenu plusieurs fois, & que les grands, au detriment des plus foibles, le trouuant, & craignant qu'il soit veu du petit & bon monde, le seelleront comme Chanceliers à simple queuë, ou à double, ou telle que le temps admettra » (I, 47-48).

Of all the persons who figure in the Dances of Death, it is characteristic of Béroalde to quote the lover in this Dance Macaber which we are told is at Dôle. The overt mention of the Dance of Death is of utmost importance to us, no matter which of the persons speaks; no matter, even, if this is apparently the only knowledge we possess of any Dance of Death at Dôle. The same can be said for the Danse Macabrée at Fubourg mentioned in an earlier dialogue (II, 82).[48] Allusion to the Dance will eventually assist us in explaining the presence of certain interlocutors. In the meanwhile, we may note that

48. E.-H. Langlois, *Essai historique, philosophique et pittoresque sur les Danses des Morts* (Rouen, 1852), I, pp. 218-219. On pp. 218-219 Langlois assures us that the Fubourg of *Le Moyen de Parvenir* is indeed Fribourg in Switzerland.

through specific reference to one individual dancer the whole tradition of the Dances of Death is called upon. All persons who participate in the dance, that is, all levels of humanity, unfold through this single figure, and if one is familiar with this tradition, one is hesitant to think its presence here amounts to anything but another form of satire. Langlois has pointed out that the Dance of Death attains greater satiric value as it advances historically to the point where the artists even dare to ridicule the pope when he attempts to bribe death for a little bit of time, just like any other human being.[49]

Without belaboring the fact of the reference to a Dance of Death in the final chapter of *Le Moyen de Parvenir,* we should observe, even so, how the lover's plea to the stern summons pulls together innumerable issues which are the novel's concern. The summons of death is similar to the summons of the guest to the banquet. The effort to buy off the crier invites satire. It also announces the terminal quatrain in which bribery is again at stake. Then, too, social stratification all the way from the Pope and the Emperor on down to the court galant and the peasant is evoked by this single point of reference.

In short, the death of the father and that of the young lover are individual accounts of the human condition, generalized in the Dances of Death and also in the Dialogues of the Dead to which the author will next allude. In the dialogue continuum, as in the « coda » the themes of time and death (time's greatest reality) and the satire of theology and philosophy are sustained in the by now familiar climate of unreality and irrationalism. This climate was examined earlier in connection with other passages, and Mr. Porter's statements on the function of death in *fatras* and *fatrasie* should be consulted again for the additional understanding they can give us of the role of death in this final chapter. But now, let us examine the role of death in the theological satire of the « coda ».

The break in the final chapter effected by the imperative « Mais passons outre » constitutes an abrupt shift to another plane. We have moved from the specifics of Justinian, the father, the young man of the Dance of Death to generalizations. Yet the themes of folly and death are cautiously retained. The idiom « passer outre » has the basic meaning of « to go on to another subject ». But here, as in other parts of *Le*

49. Langlois, II, pp. 104-105.

Moyen de Parvenir (e.g., I, 8) I think one is allowed a metaphysical reading. Thus, we have the idea of passing from this world to one beyond, into the other-world, the afterworld. The facetious « ...ie sens desia que ce liure nous eschappe... » is carefully placed so that it bears upon the rather Pythagorean concept of passing beyond or escaping the wheel of birth, while it also has bearing upon the grim reality of this world. When the « author » expresses the feeling that the book is getting out of hand, we may say that he is confessing its lack of composition, or its baroque nature. But there is more to the statement than a simple effort to characterize style. The « author » is facetiously, sardonically expressing his fear that this sacred missal (whose mysic secrets were to be held under lock and key, and revealed only to the elect) is about to fall into unsympathetic hands. As a result, the secret will out: the « pot-aux-roses » will begin to bloom (i.e., the apotheosis), and theological discourse, to say nothing of Scripture itself, may begin to appear in French, rather than in some unintelligible dead language.

But even more grotesque than the potential revelation of these secrets is that the clashes of doctrine between protestant (un frippon de proposant) and Catholic, here Jesuit (*coquedindo,* or *Codinde,* i.e., Jesuit), will impair the proper understanding of the book.

At this point the theme of folly is reintroduced and extended. Justinian's folly and that of the young lover who tries to buy off death are complemented by the retort the « author » has ready for those who may accuse him of being a necromancer, simply because he has caused the dead to speak.

Intense irony is present in the statement that the « dead have already spoken ». When we stop to consider that the majority of the speakers are theologians or learned persons, we see that death-in-life and life-in-death juxtapositions are being established. The recurrent allusions to sloth and sleep are thereby clarified.

The word « nigromanchian » contains burning satire of a theological order. It doubly involves the condition of these « dead » theologians (« chiens ») and — insofar as the « author » himself is evidently a theologian — the idea that one can « raise the dead », buy the dead out of purgatory, buy one's way out of sins that would otherwise put one in hell, even buy one's own masses for the dead before one's death, etc. Satire of these pecuniary practices of the clergy is so rampant in the period that one needs no documentation. And not only is the « author » prepared to answer the accusation of being a necromancer. He is prepared to say that these are no ordinary dialogues of the dead: « ...ie suis bien plus habile que cela, les morts ont parlé, ils le sçauent bien; mais ie fais parler les bestes, & beaucoup parleront, si Dieu plaist... » The *double-entendre* involved here is not of Béroalde's own invention, but it assists in the identification of certain interlocutors and assuredly hands over the key to the true satirical intentions of *Le Moyen de Parvenir's* author.

Taken literally, he has indeed made « beasts » speak. This will, for example, explain the presence of the interlocutor Pacolet, the *cheval de bois* which served as a mount for the hero of the popular novel *Valentin et Orson.* The horse is referred to in Rabelais, too[50], but I submit that in *Le Moyen de Parvenir* Pacolet represents in burlesque what Des Periers has in mind in inserting into Dialogue III of his *Cymbalum Mundi* « Phlegon Le Cheval », who has been variously construed as the *bas clergé,* the people, etc. Des Periers' groom, Statius (another interlocutor in *Le Moyen de Parvenir*) has also undergone a number of interpretations. In the light of *Le Moyen de Parvenir,* it seems quite appropriate to construe Phlegon as *le bas clergé,* and Statius as the papacy which rides him. This is all the more likely since the « bestes » who speak in *Le Moyen de Parvenir* are the clergy, the learned doctors, the professional fools. Assuming we can reason from Des Periers to Béroalde, the part of the dialogue in *Cymbulum Mundi* in which Phlegon le Cheval and Statius appear illuminates greatly the claims of the author of *Le Moyen de Parvenir*

50. Rabelais, I, p. 250. Varying accounts make of Pacolet the mount itself and the dwarf who rode a wooden horse. Taken in this second meaning, our argument would be somewhat invalidated, and Béroalde would be alluding to a contemporary who might either be small in size or characterized by speed of action, speech, etc. Paul Lacroix (p. 378) attributes the piece of dialogue in question to a Patolet, but in his *Notices Historiques,* p. 478, he writes: « On ne trouve pas un personnage de ce nom; c'est peut-être *Pacolet,* enchanteur qui avait fabriqué un cheval de bois volant à travers les airs et conduit à l'aide d'une cheville : ce cheval joue un grand rôle dans les vieux romans de chevalerie et surtout dans celui de *Valentin et Orson.* Il y avait aussi au seizième siècle un Jean *Patouillet,* protonotaire apostolique, habitant Dijon où il mourut en 1585, *homme de grand jugement et de grande lecture, savant dans les langues et dans l'histoire,* dit Rémi Belleau; *grand philosophe et vraiment démocratique,* dit le sieur de Flavigny. Béroalde avait-il en vue ce contemporain ? »

that he has caused « bestes » (animals or fools) to speak. Phlegon says: « Il a esté ung temps que les bestes parloyent; mais si le parler ne nous eust point esté osté, non plus qu'à vous, vous ne nous trouveriez pas si bestes que vous faictes. »[51] We can compare here the following passage from a chapter of *Le Moyen de Parvenir* entitled « Enseignement »: « ...voila le moyen de faire la barbe aux heretiques, que d'accorder les textes : dis que tu en as, Huguenot : tu n'es qu'vne beste, comme dit l'interprete d'Aristote qui traduit disant : Aristoteles aux liures des bestes, parlant de l'homme & de la femme, dit, &c » (I, 96).

Furthermore, Ardelio in *Cymbalum Mundi* sees the monetary advantages of such « animals », and he says he will go tell this to Cerdonius: « Or jamais je n'eusse creu qu'ung cheval eust parlé, se je ne l'eusse veu et ouy. Voila ung cheval qui vault cent millions d'escuz. Cent millions d'escuz ! On ne le sçauroit trop estimer. Je m'en voys compter le cas à maistre Cerdonius, lequel ne l'oblira pas en ses annalles. »[52]

Cerdonius has been explained as coming from the Greek for « lucre », and would therefore be a person who seeks gain from unworthy endeavors. Some believe that he may be identified with either Bouchet or Bourdigné.[53] Be this as it may, the stupidity, the avariciousness, the effort to buy off, to pay off, to get money for that which is undeserving of pay is unquestionably one of the *bêtises* alluded to under several guises in the last chapter of our novel. Béroalde's juxtaposition of wisdom or reputed wisdom and of folly or stupidity is again completed through this pun, probably taken from Des Periers, but improved upon by Béroalde's incorporation of stupidity's infinity. Béroalde accomplishes this through the addition of the phrase « ...& beaucoup parleront... ». This added flourish and the extra time dimension are the sort of thing that would distinguish *Le Moyen de Parvenir* as baroque, if it were opposed to the humanistic Renaissance work of Des Periers.

In view of the foregoing, the dialogue between Apulee and Cardan, involving metamorphosis and reincarnation is telling:

51. Des Periers, pp. 335-336. The footnote informs us that Rabelais uses a similar device in *Pantagruel*, Book II, ch. XV, when Pantagruel says, « Au temps que les bestes parloient (il n'y a pas trois jours)... ».

52. *Ibid.*, p. 339.

53. *Ibid.*, pp. 339-340.

APVLEE. — I'ay esté asne comme chascun sçait, mais mon compere Cardan a bien esté vne autre beste.

CARDAN. — Ouy, dea, i'ay esté de trois sortes de bestes, & ie ne fu iamais asne; mais ie me souuiens du temps que i'estois beste ainsi que vous; tesmoin Theuet, & quelques semblables pour estre bestes de bon esprit, & ayant mis en memoire la promesse faite a Pythagoras, i'ay plus fait que lui; d'autant que i'ay bien retenu ce que i'auois en rencontre : & de fait i'ay engraué en mon esprit ce que i'ay veu és institutions & ceremonies des bestes, & sur tout en leur cabale qui est notable, en laquelle il y a vn article du plus de consequence, & sur tout en ce qui est de leur creance; d'autant que comme i'ay sceu d'elles qu'elles croyent que les hommes sont plus bestes qu'elles ne sont, bien que quant à elles, elles soyent les martyrs de nature. Il est vray qu'il y a de meschantes bestes, comme il y a de meschans hommes; si i'osois ie passerois outre, parce qu'elles ont vne religion, mais ie n'en veux pas parler, d'autant que la declarant elle se trouueroit semblable à celle de plusieurs sots (II, 210-211).

Thus, the words « nigromanchian » and « bestes » have further satirical meanings in *Le Moyen de Parvenir* which do not take their inspiration from Bonaventure Des Periers. When the « author » says he is afraid that the intruding clergymen will call him a « nigromanchian » is he not really saying that he will be called a papist? The following passage from an early part of the novel will help to clarify the use of the word « bestes » in connection with the clergy: « ...gardez-vous de ces entrelardeurs de Theologie alegorique, de ces effondreux d'argumens, & de tous ceux qui aiguisent les remonstrances sur la meule d'hypocrisie; fuyez telles bestes, & ne leur communiquez point ce rare thresor, ains le commettez à gens de bien... » (I, 51).

Viret in his *Satyres chrestiẽnes de la cuisine papale* frequently uses the word « bestes » to refer to the clergy. Then are not the fear of being called a necromancer and the request for the money in the terminal quatrain inter-related? Are not both the fear and the request for money reflections of the young lover's effort to buy off Death? Viret, for example, had written a work entitled *La Nécromancie Papale* and in his *Satyres chrestiẽnes de la cuisine papale* he attacks the church's practices of taking exorbitant sums from the people for bulls of indulgence, for masses for the dead, etc.

Folly, it appears from this « coda », is synonymous with the celebration of the ego; and several forms of egomania can be spotted in the concluding statements of the book. We have first of all the egomania of the hermetic writer — probably a theologian — who intentionally writes in a steganographic manner, so that no matter how closely we read, we are bound to be confronted with a *trompe-l'œil*: « ...lisez ce volume de son vray biais; il est fait comme ces peinctures, qui monstrent d'vn, & puis d'autre » (II, 259). The device of the *trompe-l'œil* is baroque, of course, but under the circumstances it seems safe to say that here the device is used as much to satirize baroque style as it is to mock hypocrites « qui monstrent d'vn, & puis d'autre ». Every statement made and every device used by the author is meant to mislead the reader; that is one of the kinds of egomania under attack. The « author » of this missal which he has enough conceit to consider unique and predicated on universal truth (cf. I, p. 46) has intentionally made it impossible for the most cautious of readers to read the book « de son vrai biais ». The reader can't understand: he's not supposed to! And even if he were to see and read the entire book, or like Oronce, study it for fifty years (I, 214) — though at one point he's been told that it isn't essential to study it in any order — he will not know what the « author » means.

Nevertheless, another form of egomania — on the part of the reader this time — will make innumerable interpretations of the book possible. According to his own « folle fantaisie » he will see mockery, atheism, satire of vice, etc. Thus dissension among the learned is inevitable. Man will not ever understand man's work for want of true desire to understand. In some ways this concept seems to echo the cry of man's inhumanity to man to be found in another place in the text: « Voila, il n'y a que telles gens qui ayent les bonnes graces des grands; si c'eust esté quelque homme qui eut eu de la doctrine, on l'eut enuoyé rostir le balay; il ne faut qu'estre effronté pour obtenir faueurs : & à dire vray, c'est pitié absoluë, que pour estre grand & gaigner, il faut ruiner la vertu & le prochain. O quelle misere ! que les hommes sont diables aux hommes ! quiconque ne croira point qu'il y ait de diables, qui aille au Palais & à la Court » (I, 152).

Another type of folly found in the concluding lines of *Le Moyen de Parvenir* echoes the foolish notion the young lover has that he may pay death a certain sum to stay death's reaping.

This is symbolic of universal folly, springing from vain, egotistical concepts that one may in any way control through his will or worldly wealth the hand of Providence, particularly for some such idle purpose as lovemaking. It in its turn gives rise to another kind of folly which feeds upon it. The curse of the « author » rests predominantly on any and all (theologians) who might pass judgement on the folly of others, or allow others to think that through their reimbursed intervention serious errors can be set right. Says the « author »: « Malheureux sont ceux qui se donnent de la peine pour auoir bruit d'estre, ou pipeurs, ou flateurs, ou mercenaires, ou dicteurs des folies d'autruy » (II, 261).

In quoting the quatrain, the « author » reinforces his criticism of the church's exploitation of humanity, in the name of « perfecting » what by now seems to be « imperfectible » man.

Thus, folly in *Le Moyen de Parvenir* seems to be equivalent to celebration of the ego, to vanity in all forms, from the false acquisition of reputation to one man's exploitation of another man's vice or error. In short, we may say that perhaps the greatest folly unnamed but implicit in this final chapter, as in *Le Moyen de Parvenir* as a whole, is man's use of time. In other words, the sense of the chapter seems to be that all these mad efforts to gain reputation — on false grounds — to baffle rather than to counsel, to pretend to understand what is not meant to be understood, to quarrel and dispute over doctrine, to try to stay with worldly goods the will of Providence, to capitalize on another's fear of death and the hereafter — all these mad efforts are nothing but a waste of precious time. Indeed, through time dislocations and through the denial of the existence of his composition the author refutes time. He « kills time » and throws the book back on itself. He projects it into the future, so that we of the twentieth century, in reading this book (printed this year) are made painfully aware of the vice and corruption of these pursuits and even more painfully aware of their timelessness. The most certain of all certain certainties — next to taxes which are certainly alluded to in this chapter too — in death. No matter what one does, says the « author » — giving baroque emphases through these stylistic variations on the same thought — all has « une fin certaine » (cf. « la fin finale », I, 54). Of this he promises to give a « demonstration notable », a scientific or mathematical proof. The promise echoes the claims of the subtitle; it ridicules scientific claims to prove the obvious; but on the other hand, the promise is unnecessary. We are convinced that this is the case, and that all efforts to escape death are a form of folly and vanity which waste time, but are nonetheless ever present. Once more, then, time proves to be the principal theme of *Le Moyen de Parvenir.* An essential untruth concerning the guests has been told (« on s'assagit, on deuint, on paruint »), since we learn from the terminal quatrain that the « work » must still be « perfected », and from the last chapter that « les parfaits sont aux Cieux ». On the other hand, an essential truth concerning the guests has been told: « ...on passa le temps... » Hence, within this context, the stratification of activities at this banquet should be taken less seriously, if in the end we may even say that any of it exists or ever did exist or ever will exist — banquet, guests, stories told, or book in which the deeds of the gathering are recorded.

CHAPTER V

THE CHAPTER TITLES

Just as the title page, the first word, the first and last chapters of *Le Moyen de Parvenir* reveal upon close examination satirical intentions against political, theological or philosophical institutions and methods, as well as the inter-related themes of time, mutability and death, so do the titles of the individual chapters. The choice of chapter titles, like the allocation of names to the interlocutors can be interpreted as a horizontal satire which is borne out by the vertical (the text, properly speaking). Such an approach is convenient and telling, for otherwise there would seem to be no connection between the speaker as we know him through history, and the story he tells in *Le Moyen de Parvenir*. The same incongruity seems on the surface to exist between the chapter titles and the contents of the chapters.

Before discussing the titles, let us list them off as they stand in the Royer edition, and add to them the Roman numerals and variants from the Lacroix edition:

I. Question I.
II. Poinct.
III. Parafrase.
IV. Axiome.
V. Songe.
VI. Proposition.
VII. Couplet.
VIII. Cérémonie.
IX. Coqalasne.
X. Circoncision.
XI. Pause dernière.
XII. Vidimus.
XIII. Conclusion.
XIV. Correlaire.
XV. Dessein.
XVI. Homélie.
XVII. Journal.
XVIII. Mappe-monde.
XIX. Métaphrase.
XX. Paragraphe.
XXI. Occasion.
XXII. Plumitif.
XXIII. Problème.
XXIV. Enseignement.
XXV. Resultat.
XXVI. Liure de raison.

XXVII. Parabole.
XXVIII. Fen.
XXIX. Chapitre général.
XXX. Rencontre.
XXXI. Cause.
XXXII. Minute.
XXXIII. Remonstrance.
XXXIV. Généalogie.
XXXV. Notice.
XXXVI. Parlement.
XXXVII. Verset.
XXXVIII. Arrest.
XXXIX. Passage.
XL. Glose.
XLI. Sermon VI.
XLII. Diette.
XLIII. Annotation.
XLIV. Bénédiction.
XLV. Texte.
XLVI. Synode.
XLVII. Tome.
XLVIII. Allégation.
XLIX. Advis.
L. Commentaire.
LI. Distinction.
LII. Partie.
LIII. Section.
LIV. Epistre.
LV. Canon.
LVI. Théorème.
LVII. Sommaire.
LVIII. Stance.
LIX. Absolution.
LX. Article.
LXI. Risée.
LXII. Coyonnerie (I, 339-341).
LXIII. Exposition.
LXIV. Emblesme.
LXV. Sof passuc.
LXVI. Dictionnaire.
LXVII. Elégie.
LXVIII. Respect.
LXIX. Couuent.
LXX. Apostiles.
LXXI. Leçon.
LXXII. Superstition.
LXXIII. Thesme.
LXXIV. Tèse.
LXXV. Chapitre.
LXXVI. Consistoire.
LXXVII. Commitimus.
LXXVIII. Reuers.
LXXIX. Chartre.
LXXX. Concile.
LXXXI. Instance.
LXXXII. Production.
LXXXIII. Exploit.
LXXXIV. Suitte.
LXXXV. Défaut.
LXXXVI. Rémission.
LXXXVII. Discours.
LXXXVIII. Folie.
LXXXIX. Contract.
XC. Parantaise.
XCI. Doctrine.
XCII. Bail.
XCIII. Transcrit.
XCIV. Copie.
XCV. Confession.
XCVI. Original.
XCVII. Sentence.
XCVIII. Démonstration.
CXIX. Histoire.
C. Attestation.
CI. Sommation.
CII. Kalendrier.
CIII. Palinodie.
CIV. Satyre.
CV. Mémoire.
CVI. Fantaisie.
CVII. Tiltre.
CVIII. Reprise.
CVIX. Archiue.
CX. Ordonnance.
CXI. Argument (II, 361-363).

While Chapter I in the Lacroix edition has no title, in the Royer edition it is entitled « Question I ». The only other important variation is that Chapter XXVIII in the Lacroix edition[1] is entitled « Jamais », while the same chapter is entitled « Arrest » in the Royer edition. These variations are not of great consequence, especially when one notes that either « Arrest » or « Jamais » can be linked to the time theme so noticeable in several different aspects of the novel.

Leaving aside Lacroix's modernization of spellings — which, of course, is present throughout his edition — we might also note in passing that in the Lacroix edition the term « Sof passuc » is written as one word, while « Commitimus » has a double *t*. These mechanical matters recorded, we may proceed to an analysis of the evident purposes of the chapter titles.

In *Le Moyen de Parvenir,* the chapters themselves are of varying lengths, with no formula as to the amount of speakers for any one dialogue, as to the over-all structure of the dialogue itself, as to a balance or connection with other dialogues which have preceded or which follow, etc. Thus from a functional point of view, the titles of the chapters seem to provide little more than a break. One might liken them to a musical pause, perhaps. As can be seen, these titles constitute ornament, but ornament which is assuredly related organically to the motifs of *Le Moyen de Parvenir,* and such organic relation of the ornament is quite in keeping with baroque style. No one part of a successful baroque creation — in the plastic arts, in music, or in literature — is ever really unrelated to the substructure or to the totality of the work. It is often up to us, however, to find the connections. Wölfflin is making much the same claim, I believe, when he writes: « The a-tectonic style does not fall into lawlessness, but the order on which it is based is so much freer that we may well speak of a general contrast of law and freedom. »[2] Hatzfeld approaches this same statement in writing that baroque literature is characterized by « The principle of an unlimited gradation in a motivistic and nontectonic structure ».[3]

Not only are the chapter titles of *Le Moyen de Parvenir*

1. Lacroix, p. 116.

2. Heinrich Wölfflin, *Principles of Art History* (New York, 1932), trans. M. D. Hottinger, p. 134.

3. Helmut Hatzfeld, « A Clarification of the Baroque Problem in the Romance Literatures », *Comparative Literature,* I (1949), p. 114.

related to the principal motifs, but, in addition, they can occasionally be described as ligatures, and by this function as well as by virtue of their being purposeful ornamentation (that which not only adds to but probably cannot be dispensed with), the titles are manifestations of baroque style. That they are farcical, burlesque, ironic, gives to them the even more specialized designation of manifestations of satirical baroque.

An excellent example of the merging together of chapters, artificially split by a title, which in turn becomes a type of ligature can be found near the end of *Le Moyen de Parvenir.* At the end of a chapter called « Reprise », one of the interlocutors (according to Lacroix, L'Autre)[4] says: « Estant à disner & faisant bonne chere il falloit selon la coustume rapporter quelque chose d'edification; & nous de dire notre fortune » (II, 244). Directly following this interlocutor's very brief story, a new chapter, bearing the title « Archive », begins with a sentence which plainly echoes the one just quoted: « Passant ainsi de propos en autres sur les discours d'edification, Monsieur le chantre tira de sa manche vn canon fort excelent, & disoit que c'estoit l'Abesse de Rousserai qui le lui auoit enuoyé... » (II, 245).

We can observe a quite similar process at other points in *Le Moyen de Parvenir,* as, for example, in the reverberations of the last few sentences of the chapter entitled « Diette » (I, 202) occuring in the first sentence of the chapter directly following — « Annotation » (I, 203). For all intents and purposes, the insertion here of the title « Annotation » does little more than provide a break or pause. At the same time, because the first paragraph of this chapter provides us with a facetious definition, the title « Annotation » is not entirely irrelevant to the chapter content in and of itself. Yet another example of the same procedure can be seen in the uninterrupted flow of the end of the chapter called « Canon » (I, 279) into the beginning of the following chapter, « Théorème » (I, 280). This technique of linking one chapter to the other gives the same kind of continuance from chapter to chapter that the reversal of beginning and ending, or the presence of anachronism or time dislocations give to the novel as a totality.

The above, however, are not the only examples of ligature found in *Le Moyen de Parvenir.* Another quite similar procedure can be noted at an earlier point in the novel, when a chapter

4. Paul Lacroix, p. 388.

entitled « Plvmitif » ends with the words « ...de mon Chapitre ». The next chapter, entitled « Probleme » begins with the words: « A ce mot de Chapitre... »

Several other examples of ligature or liaison appear in *Le Moyen de Parvenir,* and among these, as I have just pointed out, is the curious circular motion of the book, arrived at by the author's saying in the opening quatrain that had Madame lived he'd have written the book, while stating toward the end of the book that some day he intends to set about writing the book. The technique is so tied to the problems of the irrational and of time dimension set forth by the ideology of *Le Moyen de Parvenir* that here, as everywhere, the form and essence are quite inseparable, which is merely another way of saying that the ornament — the chapter title, the name of the interlocutor, etc. — is functional in good baroque art.

The principal concern at present is to show how the same circular effect, the same timelessness, is created through some of the chapter titles. That is why we must underline the fact that the *dénouement* or at least the conclusion of *Le Moyen de Parvenir* appears to occur very near the beginning of the work. « Commençons de conclure » (I, 42) are the words that open the chapter called « Pause derniere ». Shortly thereafter, interrupted only by a chapter whose title is « Vidimvs » (I, 45), we have a chapter entitled « Conclvsion » (I, 53). Yet the title of the last chapter of the book is « Argvment »! The ironies of this procedure are abundant, and the artistry involved indicates that our author is by no means jotting things down in a haphazard fashion. On the contrary, his is a strategy behind which reigns a rational plan and an intelligence of the first magnitude.

Further to the juxtapositions effected by the particular placement of the titles « Conclvsion » and « Argvment », the importance of certain words found on the title page of *Le Moyen de Parvenir* is pointed up by the echoes of them in the titles of the individual chapters, as I shall soon demonstrate more fully. Meanwhile, it should be taken into account that this, too, is a form of ligature, as are the cross hatchings we are able to make from the chapter titles to the text proper.

By like token, in the first chapter of *Le Moyen de Parvenir* we find the word « mappe-monde » which I conjecture to be an allusion to the papal « mappe-monde » portrayed by Viret. A type of ligature is manifested by the repetition of this word as the title of one of the chapters (I, 76). Many examples of this could be cited, but I would prefer to treat the recurrence of the book's vocabulary in the chapter titles (and vice versa) as something more significant than mere ligature, and shall do so accordingly.

All in all, then, the chapter titles perform a range of tasks from functional ornament to ligature, from emphasizing to reiterating theme and satirical intention. Like the names of the interlocutors they are to be read as the horizontal satire of the book, the meat of the satire coming on a vertical line through the actual text. As we read back and forth or up and down, we see the range of interpretations possible, and the countless means Béroalde has employed to drive home his satire of political, philosophical and theological dissension. The variety of his methods, the convolutions often resulting in ambiguity or obscurity, antitheses, the point and counterpoint, the ironies, the infinite variations on a single theme all work in the direction of a style we characterize as baroque.

Although the titles usually have an erotic *double-entendre* (e.g., « Sermon VI » in which the Roman numeral is to be construed as a word), and perform some stylistic function such as ligature, it is their relation to the other, the deeper concerns of *Le Moyen de Parvenir,* such as the themes of time and mutability, the religious satire, the satire of pedantry, the baroque manifestations and techniques of the novel, which are of primary interest to us in this study. The connection between satire of pedantry and these farcical titles has not been overlooked by Saulnier, who writes:

> En conclusion, le choix des titres de chapitres n'est pas fait au hasard; il révèle un double dessein. Un dessein d'humour superficiel, par l'inadaptation du titre à la matière, la parodie formelle des traités savants en un livre de sujet facétieux et l'introduction de quelques titres burlesques dans une suite de termes doctes; plus profondément, une critique chère à Béroalde de l'abus du Culte de la Forme que la routine scolastique imposait à tous domaines, et contre qui depuis Rabelais tous les Renaissants avaient exercé leur verve.[5]

5. V.-L. Saulnier, « Étude sur Béroalde de Verville », *Revue d'Humanisme et Renaissance,* V (1944), p. 298.

I am quite in agreement that this choice of titles is not random. The same hiatus occurs between title and content of chapter as between interlocutor and alleged utterance. Indeed, the chapter title and the interlocutor are in direct relation one to another. The vain titles echo the formulae by which these vain « sages » operate. Their works would and indeed do bear similar titles, to such an extent that it may even be possible to work out a correlation between the titles and the interlocutors. Under such a scheme we might allocate « Glose » or « Dictionnaire » to Calepin; we might see in the title « Folie » a reflection of Erasmus' work; to Marot we might grant the title « Paraphrase »; to Viret we could give the title « Mappemonde », as a satirical reflection of shifting geography and particularly of the special kind of map needed to find one's way around in the Pope's world. Similarly, the title « Songe » may be linked to Artémidore for his *Traité des Songes,* or might suggest the interlocutor Poliphile who is the hero of Colonna's *Poliphili hypnerotomachia* (Combat de l'Amour et du Sommeil). Béroalde himself had in 1600 presented an edition of an old translation done by Jacques Gohory under the title of *Tableau des riches inventions, couvert du voile des feintes amoureuses qui sont représentées dans le Songe de Poliphile,* as Paul Lacroix reminds us.[6] By like token, the title « Epistre » might be ascribed to Tixier (who appears in *Le Moyen de Parvenir* under the name Textor); that of « Commentaire » to Caesar. « Histoire », on the other hand, might reflect the beginning of a title by Rabelais, or the works of any one of the historians numbered among the guests. To Messie we might afix the title « Leçon » and to Menandre (if we read this name given by Lacroix rather than Méandre as the name appears in the Royer text) or to Ausone the title « Sentence ». In like fashion the titles « Satyre », « Mémoire », « Stance », « Kalendrier », or even « Commentaire » might any or all apply to Passerat. As there are only one hundred and eleven chapters, and there are well over three hundred interlocutors, I am not proposing any absolute connection of a given title with a given speaker. The notion that any of these theological and philosophical impostors would readily give to his discourse — no matter what its subject — one of these pompous titles is nevertheless quite within reason; if the titles are, as Saulnier says « scolastiques », the inter-

6. Paul Lacroix, p. 483.

locutors are quite noticeably sophists, in the pejorative sense of the word.

More interesting and revealing than this particular similarity between chapter title and interlocutor is the extent to which Béroalde manages to express ironies and states themes through these chapter titles. With them he says « little » what in other places he will say « big ». Simple ironies and antitheses are accomplished through the choice of such titles as « Transcrit », or « Copie », opposed to « Original ». Recalling the internal claims that *Le Moyen de Parvenir* is the center of all books, « l'unique breuiaire », etc., we begin to spot the intentional inconsistencies between one chapter title and another. The purported disorder of the book's composition is in this way ironically confirmed — ironically because quite planned. Analagous antitheses can be seen in the titles « Elégie » and « Risée », « Epistre » and « Apostiles », or « Verset » and « Sof passuc » — which according to Royer are « Mots hébreux » meaning « Fin de verset » (II, 352). We cannot fail to observe, too, the deeper irony and the Joycian absurdity of entitling the final chapter « Argument », with the title « Conclusion » appearing early in *Le Moyen de Parvenir*. That the word « Satyre » appears as the title of one of the final chapters is in itself a revealing fact, and here irony is achieved by the tardiness of the word's appearance.

Furthermore, these titles announce the main currents of the novel, and the minute analysis we have made of the title-page makes possible the spotting of similar terminology in the chapter titles. Given a certain arrangement of some of these titles, for example, we can very nearly reproduce the spirit of the subtitles, and even of the title. So that my reader can clearly visualize this correlation, I would propose something of the following as a title page for *Le Moyen de Parvenir* in which italicired items indicate vocabulary taken from the chapter titles.

TEXTE et/ou *CANON* (de) *DISTINCTION*

Généalogie, Histoire, Original (et) *Liure de Raison*
(contenant la)

Demonstration (de la) *Cause* (de la) *Folie* (et du) *Défaut* (comme) *Résultat* (d'une) *Rencontre* (d'un) *Exploit,* (d'un) *Arrest,* (d'une) *Sommation,* (d'une) *Ordonnance,* (etc.).

Dictionnaire (de) *Songe* (avec) *Glose* (et) *Annotation.*

(A ce) *Parlement* (on n'est) *Pas/sage.*

(A l') *Instance,*

Vidimus; Commitimus.

— *Sermon VI.*

(Imprimé cette) *Minute*

The reader will readily note that where duplication of vocabulary does not occur, we have something which is at least synonymous, or, still more telling, a strict antonym. Incidentally, such substitutions as « Cause » for « Effect » can be textually justified, I believe. The following speech of Gorreus to Fernel supports this argument quite adequately: « — Pource que selon vostre doctrine au liure 'De abditis rerum causis', où vous deuiez mettre 'effectis', d'autant que vous ne parlez aucunement des causes, mais des effects, il faut considerer ceste belle vente de foye qui palpille imperceptiblement... » (I, 107). As can be seen, my simulated title page made up of chapter titles is not, like Béroalde's, burlesque. Rather, it is a transliteration from the comic to the serious.

All of the dominant satirical strains of *Le Moyen de Parvenir* show up in these chapter titles, which, like the book's title and so many other of its aspects, are ambiguous. We can subdivide these terms according to themes, etc., but must keep in mind that over and above their erotic implications, which Lacroix has in part explained in his « Sommaire Analytique des Chapitres du Moyen de Parvenir »[7], they slip easily from one category to another.

Recalling that *Le Moyen de Parvenir* is built around a symposium which the people are compelled to attend, we may ask ourselves what signs of this we find in the chapter titles. The immediate answer is that signs of forced assembly are abundant. The compulsory nature of the meeting is seen in the use of legal terms, such as « Ordonnance », « Arrest », « Sommation », even « Tiltre ». Here we may include a world of special interest, « Exploit », which, like « Ordonnance », has military connotations as well as legal. More specifically, the word « Exploit » can be extended to mean *exploit d'huissier.* Now, when we consider the role of the *huissier* in *Le Moyen de Parvenir,* as keeper of the gates, as the one who will not

7. Paul Lacroix, pp. 403-427.

permit escape, assumedly from the fold of the Catholic church — though the setting is other-worldly and so the symbolism of the gates is more extensive — the presence of the chapter title « Exploit » takes on great significance. When we further consider that another chapter title, « Sommation », has as its very definition an *exploit d'huissier,* resulting in a *mise en demeure,* an arrest, a halt made by a sentinel, we begin to feel that the titles are not a simple parody of « scholastic » terminology, as Saulnier says, but sharply bespeak the exact nature of the inner satire of *Le Moyen de Parvenir,* a satire which extends far beyond a mere satire of pedantry into all phases of religious and philosophical expression, to all professions and levels of society.

Thus, through orders from some official body — legal, papal, etc. — the group assembles. They have a « Rencontre », a « Diette », a « Parlement », all of which may be construed on both legal and religious levels. But it is no doubt religious satire and parody which are primarily intended. The word « Parlement » is probably an allusion to the « Parlement des États Généraux à Blois » of 1588; the word « Diette », of course, suggests in addition to its medical connotations (cf. the title « Ordonnance ») the papal fixing of the rules of fasting which are frequently parodied in *Le Moyen de Parvenir;* and so it is not merely the meeting that is alluded to, but also the « Résultat » of this meeting.

Additional titles indicate gatherings that are clearly of a religious nature. Among these is « Concile », of special interest because we can assume that it refers to the Council of Trent, reasoning from internal allusion to this particular assembly. Such allusion is found in the following statement of Tostatus, for example: « Vrament ie vous escoutois, mais puis que i'y suis remis sachez s'il vous plaist, qu'apres ou aussi tost ou enuiron le temps, ce fut quand ce fut que le Concile de Trente fut publié, ie ne dis pas celui de Monsieur le Granger, qui est intitulé le Concile de XXX » (I, 110). In addition, Ciceron, of all people, expresses the infallibility of the Council, of which he claims to be a member: « ...ce que ie ne voudrois commetre en lieu tant sainct & membre specifique du Concile qui ne peut errer... » (I, 98). Furthermore, the Council of Trent is at one point in *Le Moyen de Parvenir* facetiously referred to as the « Concile de Trois Dizaines » (II, 70) and in another passage mention is made of the « Concile de Quarante » (I, 253).

Viret, in his *Satyres chrestiēnes de la cuisine papale,* takes issue with banishment by the Council[8], and reference to the Council is also found in *La Satyre Ménippée,* where, however, the main concentration is on the League. The League is frequently referred to in *Le Moyen de Parvenir,* too, often as a point of fixing time. The interlocutors, in telling a story, will preface it by saying « Durant la Ligue... » (e.g., II, 86).

Any of these gatherings, and especially the League, constitute a point of reference for the interlocutors of *Le Moyen de Parvenir,* and so are incorporated into the time theme as a manner of dating a story or anecdote. Numerous examples of this can be found, as, for instance: « ...durant que la Ligue estoit en vigueur... » (II, 17) and « ...durant les Estats... » (II, 51). The latter, Paul Lacroix says, may refer either to the Etats de Blois of 1589 or to the Etats de la Ligue of 1593.[9] Reference to the assembly at Poissy can also be found in *Le Moyen de Parvenir:* « Ce fut le Coloque de Poissy, ce venerable Concile racourci, qui fut d'auis d'instruire les ieunes Religieuses de telle sorte » (II, 245); and the gathering of the Etats-Généraux at Blois is not overlooked: « Ho ho, gardez-vous de prononcer ainsi que fit Charlotte à Blois durant les Estats que nous estions auec ce moine de Bourmoyen... » (I, 208). This same group is mentioned by the interlocutor Chose, who says, « Cela me fait souuenir qu'estant à Blois auec mes amis à faire bonne chere durant les Estats... » for which remark Chose is cautioned by the words « — Garde Concile » (II, 133).

Now, in addition to the distinctly religious significance of the title « Concile », we have as one chapter title the word « Synode »; what is more, we have a « Chapitre », suggesting a gathering of *chanoines,* and recalling the liaisons we just recently saw with the expression « ...de mon Chapitre... » (I, 91-92). The word is labored in the text: « A ce mot de Chapitre chacun presta l'oreille, surquoy SIMPLICIVS dit tout haut, 'Hola Messieurs auant que passer sçachons que c'est que Chapitre, oiseau, poisson ou beste' » (II, 92). To this Zabarel answers: « ...Chapitre est vn corps, non corps, vn certain composé dissoluble en ses elemens... » (II, 92), and so forth. Most telling of all, perhaps, is the chapter title « Consistoire », which may refer to a convocation of cardinals called by the Pope, an

8. Pierre Viret, *Satyres chrestiēnes de la cuisine papale* (Paris, 1540), p. 25.
9. Paul Lacroix, p. 253.

assembly of rabbis, or of protestant pastors. Hence, the concept of a gathering of the ancients and the moderns, interpreters of the Old and the New Testaments, of the different, indeed conflicting religious sects and faiths unfolds through the use of the word « Consistoire ». In order to epitomize these chapter titles reflecting types of meetings for political and religious discussion (debate), deposition, advancement of some cause, and arrival at some decision, we may justifiably focus on the following text from *Le Moyen de Parvenir,* which through a burlesque harangue delivered by Budée satirizes these « reunions », one of which is, of course, the symposium in the novel:

> ...de moy ie ne veux point de disputes, i'en parle au vray. Il y auoit vn certain Monsieur de la Tour, Ministre en ce Poictou, lequel par hazard, comme le Diable est subtil à seduire les enfans de Dieu, ayant aduisé vne belle femme qui ne luy appartenoit pas, & qui auoit pere & mere, il la conuoita suiuant l'intention du canon 17. du 11174. Concile, qui demonstre que la fille d'autruy n'est point defendue... mais ie hay ces paraphrases, il faut donner dedans : il commit adultere; ce qu'estant cognu du Consistoire, il fut corrigé & aduerty fraternellement, dont il ne tint conte, par ce qu'il continua, tellement que le scandalle fut grand, & fut passé par les Consistoires, puis par le Sinode, & en fin deposé comme vn pot en tez... (I, 104).

Having seen through the chapter titles that the symposium is a « papal banquet » à la Viret, which we may also label a « Concile », a « Synode », a « Consistoire », etc., we might wonder how the chapter titles indicate where this meeting takes place, what the people do, how they are subdivided, what the outcome of their meeting, is, etc. Not only might we wonder how the chapter titles answer these questions, but also how the chapter titles announce that satire is involved, and, for that matter even reveal to some extent what the main targets of the satire are.

The place of the meeting is suggested, I think, by such a chapter title as « Couvent ». It, like the title « Chartre », suggests both the place of meeting and the outcome of the meeting. « Couvent », a convent or monastery, seems to disguise the word « covenant », and therefore to lead to an important aspect of *Le Moyen de Parvenir* — the political and religious conflicts of the Spaniards with the English, the Scotch and the French. Allusion to the Covenant or Pact of 1588 between the Presbyterian Scotch and Philip II of Spain may very well be Béroalde's intention here. I would question, however, extension of the term to include the theological meaning of divine promise revealed through scripture. A less specific but quite similar device could be found in the word « Chartre », which doubly involves the words *chartreux, chartreuse* (monk, as well as charterhouse) and *charte,* the rules of a monastery, or even a political pact such as the *Magna Carta.*

Whether we are told through the subtitles the exact place of meeting or not, I think the type of place is suggested, just as is the nature of the meeting. We are reassured that a meeting did take place, incidentally, for « Commitimus » says one title: « We join, or gather. »

But « Commitimus » also implies « we give battle », and so it refers simultaneously to the « manly art of war » and to the concept of religious dissension with subsequent changes of religion. For the first interpretation one can compare the title « Exploit » and its possible opposite « Reuers ». Other allusions to the *homme de bien,* the gentleman who is not only an accomplished soldier characterized by his « vertu » but also by his elegant manners and traits, may be present in the titles « Cérémonie », « Distinction », « Poinct » (i.e., *poinct d'honneur*), « Respect », « Tiltre » (i.e., *tiltre de noblesse*), « Emblesme », etc. Let us not forget in this connection that, satirical though the claim may be, self-improvement, perfection, *bienséance* are all stated goals of the group gathered together in *Le Moyen de Parvenir.* The artifical manners of the Court (probably the papal court) are reinvoked by these titles, as are a decaying nobility or clergy. Thus concepts of liberty and a republic are present by negatives in such titles as « Sommation », « Exploit », « Arrest » and by evident satire of precious procedures. Indeed, the Latin titles « Commitimus » and « Vidimus » suggest pedantry and affectation, as well as the polyglot claims of the guests of the symposium, and even the use of Latin for official or theological purposes, while the title « Fen » — assumed by both Lacroix and Royer to be a dialectical rendition of the oath *foin* — would offset the pedantry with a kind of linguistic naturalism which corresponds to the tales told by the pedants. For both types of contrast the term

« vertical » may be applied, I think, as opposed to the « horizontal » lines — the text proper. The presence of the word « Fen » as a chapter title also seems to correspond to the plea for the French language over and against Hebrew, Greek, Latin, Chaldean, and what will you. In addition, it establishes the same juxtaposition of the ancient and modern, the Old and New Testaments, etc. which abound in *Le Moyen de Parvenir*. Over and above contrasts of pedantic and natural language or of the ancient and modern, allusion to grain in one of the subtitles is appropriate, since one of the points of satire in *Le Moyen de Parvenir* is the use of grain for the fattening of the « rats », the « diables », the « ventrus » — i.e., the clergy. They, by some manœuvring, manage to escape the very fasting laws which they establish.

The law-giving powers and purposes of this assembly of people with vastly disparate points of view, as well as their questionable efforts to reach a truce, are also implicit in the chapter titles. A moment ago, we explored these facets in the two words *Couvent* and *Chartre*. The gathering has, for example, a « Plumitif », if we are to judge from the titles. This is, of course, a type of stenographic notebook, and recalls the claim of the author that *Le Moyen de Parvenir* itself is a collection of hermetic — therefore, sacred — records. The deliberations and decisions of our assembly would then be collected in a « Plumitif ». (But when, incidentally, we take into consideration that *plumitif* has the extended meaning of « mediocre writer », the literary satire found in *Le Moyen de Parvenir* is also announced by the word.) Now all issues of the gathering would go into this « Plumitif », by virtue of its being a record, including, for example, « Question I », or the « Poinct », or the « Argument », or the « Discours ». One can compare here the various *discours* and *harangues* in Rabelais, but a still more advantageous comparison would be with the *Satyre Ménippée*.

In such a « Plumitif » one might even find systematized the opinions expressed by certain professional groups. For instance, the « Plumitif » might reflect that the mathematician, colored by his own professional orientation, has presented his « Poinct », or maybe his « Axiome », whereas another mathematician may have stated a « Proposition », since this is, from the geometer's point of view, somewhat antithetical to an « Axiome ». Furthermore, the mathematician's statement of his « Problème » might be in the form of an « Argument ». In fact, he might seek through « Démonstration » (or even « Production ») to illustrate a « Parantaise », a « Sommation », a « Partie », a « Section », perhaps the « Parabole » (parabola) as one of the conic sections (the others being the circle, the hyperbola and the ellipse). He might advance his « Théorème », or maybe just a small theorem, a « Correlaire ». Like all mathematicians, he would insist on the uniqueness of his definitions, thus claiming to advance the « Original », containing the primitive terms which permit him to claim a « Distinction ». He might support his statements with the « Copie » of an angle, with a « Dessein » or with a geometric notation, or « Annotation ». The « Plumitif » would then, logically, have a record, too, of the mathematician's « Résultat », or his « Conclusion ».

Now, if nothing other than the mathematicians' viewpoints were to be recorded in our « Plumitif » we would have a « Liure de raison ». The same would be true if we took all the terms we could away from the field of mathematics, applied them to philosophy (e.g. « Argument », « Conclusion », etc.), meanwhile adding to them other terms found in the chapter titles which properly belong to the philosopher's field. The same could be done in the field of literature. A man of letters might, at that, produce little more, in a lifetime than a mere « Plumitif »; on the other hand (the « Reuers »), he may have composed a « Tome » in which we could find the « Elegie », the « Verset », the « Sof Passuc », the « Palinodie », even a « Satyre ».

From the point of view of the scientist, the mathematician, the historian, the rhetorician, the physician, the magistrate, the author, etc., the « Plumitif » of their « Parlement » would be a « Liure de Raison », and would contain the following: « Question I », « Poinct » (cf. « Allegation », « Attestation »), « Parafrase », « Axiome », « Proposition », « Couplet », « Conclusion », « Correlaire », « Mappe-Monde », « Paragraphe », « Problème », « Résultat », « Cause », « Notice », « Verset », « Glose », « Annotation », « Texte », « Tome », « Commentaire », « Distinction » (cf. « Poinct »), « Partie », « Section », « Épistre », « Théorème », « Sommaire », « Stance », « Sof Passuc », « Exposition », « Dictionnaire », « Élégie », « Apostiles », « Thesme », « Tèse », « Chapitre », « Instance », « Discours », « Démonstration », « Histoire » (cf. « Journal », « Mémoire », « Archiue », « Généalogie », « Kalendrier »), « Sommation », « Palinodie », « Satyre », « Tiltre », « Reprise », « Ordonnance » (cf. « Arrest » vs. « Passage »), « Argument ».

Through the evaluation of such minutiae the learned doctors might even be able to enter into a « Contract », a pact or covenant. This contract might more specifically be a « Bail » (a lease of property at a fixed price for a fixed period of time). But there is little likelihood that agreement could be reached; for there is, after all, the problem of human vacillation (e.g. « Attestation » or « Allégation » vs. « Palinodie »).

It would seem that for this reason — human weaknesses — the learned theologians and moralists are enlisted. They only could administer the sacrements, for example, the « Ceremonie » of « Circoncision ». To them « Confession » is made; through them one seeks « Absolution » and « Rémission ». One may receive from them a « Remonstrance » or a « Benediction ». They provide for us the « Mappe-monde » — they are our apostolic guides, as is suggested in the word « Apostiles » (in reality, a type of *post scriptum*). From them we also receive « Doctrine ». After study of the biblical « Texte », possibly an « Épistre » of St. Paul, they might provide their own « Glose » or « Commentaire ». Among these theologians is one, the pope, who interprets for us the « Article(s) », establishes what is « Canon ». And these men provide us with a « Leçon » or an « Enseignement », sometimes couched in an « Emblesme », a « Sentence », or in an « Advis », often in a « Parabole », a « Sermon », a « Homélie », even in the tale of an « Exploit ». These are all by way of a « Démonstration », and should lead to an « Allégation ».

The « Parlement » of the theologians should, then, result, not in the recording of a « Sommaire » — a mere brief or an *abrégé* — not in a « Transcrit » or a « Copie » or a « Plumitif ». On the contrary, through this group of men we should be presented with the valid kind of text which *Le Moyen de Parvenir* is, or claims to be. It is therefore logical that internally we find Béroalde assuring the reader that these are not the fragments, the epitomes, etc., contained in false texts; careful examination of *Le Moyen de Parvenir* and comparison of it to false « copies » will prove that *Le Moyen de Parvenir,* and only *Le Moyen de Parvenir* is genuine:

> Apres l'exhibition de ces apozemes ie pense que ceste preuue est de merite; auisez doncques bien, & diligemment espluchez, & voyez auec curieuse conference tous les autre pretendus liures, cayers, volumes, tomes, œuures, liurets, opuscules, libelles, fragmens, epitomes, registres, inuen-

> taires, copies, brouillars, originaux, exemplaires, manuscrits, imprimez, esgratignez, bref les pancartes des bibliotheques... sont icy en lumiere profetisez ou restituez (I, 49-50).

In the above passage the words « tomes », « copies », « originaux » and even « brouillars » which can be compared to « Plumitif » are notable. But in the passage directly following, Béroalde, in rehearsing to us what we will find in this « CENTRE DE TOVS LES LIVRES » (I, 51), practically reiterates the terminology of the chapter titles:

> De perdus sont retrouuez & recouurez, & s'il y a bien dauantage, si quelqu'vn a desrobé vn œuure il sera icy decouuert, comme il se presume en verité, par vne bonne reuisitation de textes, parafrases, commentaires, metaphrases, homelies, annotations, recensions, notes, aduersaires lectures, leçons, & autres telles negoces & inuentions de gloses & interlignes pedentines, & les calculez, vous les trouuerez icy, sans qu'il soit plus besoin de tant de liures, romans, poesies, prosnes, & bauarderies, qui occupent les esprits mal à propos, & lesquels apres que l'on les sçait, ne laissent pas l'industrie d'auoir vn paillard escu... (I, 50).

Indeed, says Béroalde, the worthlessness of much material has caused « ...beaucoup de gens de bien... comme i'en ay veu de doctes & sages aduancez pres les Papes, Roys, Empereurs, & Republiques, gens sans fard... » (I, 50) to be moved to compassion, and to see the need for an authoritative text such as *Le Moyen de Parvenir,* in which they will find no « ...pedantisme, comme ès autres... » (I, 51). This book will contain the secret of secrets, truth unqualified, provided the reader drives off « ...ces escorcheurs de latin, ces escarteleux de sentences, ces maquereaux de passages poëtiques qu'ils produisent & prostituent à tous venans... » (I, 51) and watches out for « ...ces entrelardeurs de Theologie alegorique... ces effondreux d'argumens, & ...tous ceux qui aiguisent les remonstrances sur la meule d'hypocrisie... » (I, 51).[10]

10. It is possible that the word « meule » here involves a pun on *mule* (i.e., *mule du pape* and *mule,* the animal), especially since the reader is told to flee « ...telles bestes, & ne leur communiquez point ce rare thresor... », the word « bestes » coming directly after the expression « la meule d'hypocrisie... » The theory is substantiated by the final sentence of this same chapter, which comes shortly after the admonishment that reader not communicate to these « bestes »

To digress a moment, in the passages just noted, Béroalde is stabbing with all possible irony at the insistence of the papists (and other theologians) upon censorship and direction of textual interpretation. He alludes to the clergy's ability to « disturb the pots of roses », or to hide the truth, partially through refusal to translate with resultant obscuring of the « Apotheosis », twice disguised in *Le Moyen de Parvenir* by a pun made on « apothéose » through the term « pot-aux-roses »: « — Si vous en parlez d'auantage vous gasterez tout, vous rendrez honnie toute la doctrine des Colleges, & n'y aura plus de plaisir de s'estudier apres les fadaises de la science des Poetes anciens; si vous declarez ainsi le secret des esprits, vous troublerez l'Apotheose, ie voulois dire, vous decouurirez le pot aux roses. Pensez vous que ce soit bien fait ? » (I, 230). The second time the pun occurs it is in a key passage, in which the violent Ligueur and arch-devil Frostibus has come to harrass Luther and is chided by Sturmius, « ce vieil resueur »: « — Tais-toy, lui dit ce vieil resueur STVRMIVS, tu n'es pas sage, tu descouures le pot aux roses, tu declares les secrets du mestier » (II, 129). The formula, like many of the formulae of *Le Moyen de Parvenir,* appears to be borrowed from Viret's *Satyres chrestiẽnes de la cuisine papale.* Viret contends that the « pots aux roses » have been uncovered despite the efforts to keep them hidden in languages unknown to the people (Hebrew, Greek or Latin), and that the sweet odor of the roses has been spread about the earth. From Viret's gloss we see that he blames the « Docteurs & beneficiez du Pape » who were « stipendiez pour cacher la verité », and for this deed Viret accuses them in the text of being « Brigueurs briquetiers » who, dashing up and down the paths of the papal garden:

> Pour rassembler brigues & briques
> Et par leurs nouvelles fabriques
> Serroyent & recachoyent les roses,
> Voire pour les tenir encloses
> Taschoyent a vieux pots radouber.[11]

I have already discussed this matter of secrecy, of the hermetic, to some extent, and have alluded in passing to the question

the secrets of *Le Moyen de Parvenir:* « Ceux qui parlent d'abuser de ce qui peut servir ne l'entendent pas, ie les renuoye au Principal du college de Geneue, i'en atteste la pantoufle du Pape que ie dis vray » (I, 52).

11. Viret, p. 9.

of the closed doors, the « huissier », the keeper of the keys, etc., all of which is obviously related to the matter of the secret text and most of which is hinted at in one way or another by the chapter titles suggesting closed cabinets and compulsory meetings. The above has served to underline the need to keep this *plumitif*, which is « LE CENTRE DE TOVS LES LIVRES », sacred, by keeping its contents secret. It is even rather surprising, under the circumstances, that we do not find numbered among the chapter titles the word « Apothéose », but in the ones existing the air of mystery is, even so, achieved.

Other internal uses of the chapter titles can easily be found in the text of the novel, but these examples serve to show the use to which the titles are put. Furthermore, the apparent disorder of the chapter titles should not surprise us, for, making ample use of the terminology of the chapter titles, Béroalde himself says that the « texte » and gloss or « commentaire » have been thrown together pell-mell, each adding its own special zest to the (papal) ragout or « souppe », which symbolizes the main course of this symposium, served along with (sacramental) bread and wine:

> Dames qui auez les oreilles chatoüilleuses, de peur de rire lisez cecy tout bas ou de nuict, durant laquelle la honte dort, & ne vous formalisez, scandalisez, ny estomirez de chose quelconque que trouuerez en ces textes & memoires meslees de toute sapience, moyens, elemens, & enseignemens à bien viure, les meslanges que vous trouuerez sont suruenus à cause de l'antiquité de ce volume, & des annotations, apostilles, & interpretations qui y estoient mises, & le Gentilhomme qui le transcriuit pour vostre auancement en toute sagesse a tout escrit d'vne suite, meslant sans distinction glose & texte; ainsi que quand vous estes à table, vous qui ne jusnez pas, vous mangez des viandes prises deça & dela, selon l'occurrence (I, 35).

As a matter of fact, Béroalde writes, there is question as to the value of text in relation to gloss and *vice versa:*

> ...le personnage qui vous produit en tout honneur ces saincts memoires de perfection, a pensé que le texte ne valloit pas mieux que le commentaire, parquoy il les a fait aller ensemble. Donques soit que vous le lisiez ou non, ou que vous commenciez icy ou là, n'importe, ce liure est par tout plein de fidelles instructions & sens

> parfait, tellement que c'est tout vn par où vous le lisiez. Il est vn globe d'infinie doctrine, il y a autant à apprendre en vn lieu qu'en l'autre, en ceste sorte-cy qu'en celle-là, il n'y a ligne, endroit, verset ou passage (afin de parler niaisement aussi bien que les doctes) qui ne soit tout farcy de science mystigorique & concluante (I, 36-37).

Béroalde's claim in the above passage that each of the parts is equal to the whole is completely farcical. The implication would be that a theologian's glosses or commentaries would be equal to (perhaps as sacred as) the Bible. On the other hand, a Bible, or at least a principal, primitive text is what the company aims for, but will not achieve. As Melvin says, the adoption of *Le Moyen de Parvenir* as « gospel » and the replacement in it of all the things borrowed from it would obviate the need for any other book:

> Il a raison, d'autant que tous ces memoires, dictons, discours, sentences & paroles, sont prises au dictionnaire à dormir en toutes langues, de l'institution à lire sans poincts, sans lettres, sans caracteres, sans accens, sans figures, sans notes : aussi bien les notes font faillir, ainsi que le prouuoit frere Ambroise, qui disoit qu'il eust bien chanté, mais la notte empeschoit. Aussi sans chifres, & telles choses, a esté fait ce liure par le fils du dernier homme : Item de l'Épitome des Bibliothèques de S. Germain & autres, du Grand Luminaire des sots, tous liures extraits de cestui ci, auquel si chacun auoit remis ce qu'il y a pris, il n'y auroit qu'vn liure au monde (II, 170-171).

However, these particular theologians and learned doctors — like those in real life, or so we are to think — could never arrive at an agreement over any issue, though an effort in that direction would be ideal: « ...vrayement vous estes docte, vous estes en danger d'estre vn iour Pape, vous aurez le benefice, vostre doctrine vous l'adiuge, il ne faudroit à la verité que vous seul pour faire tomber toute la Theologie en demonstration... que nous serions heureux si on resoluoit ainsi tous arguments, nous serions incontinent d'accord, toutes heresies seroient englouties » (I, 116). Other functions of the theologians are reflected in the chapter titles. For example, despite mutability occasioned by religious or other forms of affirmation and denial (e.g., « Défaut » vs. « Remission »;

« Attestation » vs. « Palinodie », etc.), despite mutability occasioned simply through time (e.g., « Minute »), the theologians will establish their « Kalendrier ». Equivalent to this in the text is the fixing of the time at which a tale took place by saying for example, « Mon Chapitre deuoit au iour de la solemnité Sainct Louys... » (I, 96); or, « ...ainsi que le vieil Penitencier de Paris, qui vn iour de saincte Geneuiesue donna à desieuner aux Chantres de la saincte Chapelle... » (II, 230), or « Ie m'en souuiens, nous estions à Geneuve, & folastrans en nostre logis à caresme prenant en cachette... » (II, 153), or « Certe, ce dit-il, ie n'y ay pas esté depuis Quasimodo... » (I, 252), and so forth.

The theologians will, in fact, we might surmise from the titles, make a ludicrous effort to control man's « Reprise », his « Reuers », etc., and an even more ludicrous effort to impose on the chaos of time and resultant mutability not only the artifical order of a « Kalendrier », but even to work out a « Diette » — and in the text no end of ridicule of fasting rules can be found. In addition, the theologian (and other *savants*, for that matter) will impose on the natural sequence of human events the false systematisation of an « Archiue », an « Histoire », a « Généalogie ». The following burlesque genealogy from the text will indicate this assessment of the historian who reasons moral responsibility in terms of forebears: « Et bien que ce soit vne ordinaire, glissee de pere en fils pour gens de bien, coulée de mere en filles pour femmes d'honneur, d'oncle à neueu pour gens d'Église; ordinaire (disie) ...que promettre & tenir est tout ce qu'vne personne de bien peut faire, & qu'il n'appartient qu'à ceux qui sont issus de damoysellerie & de gentilhommetté, si en a ton menti vn petit... » (I, 5-6). An even more vivid example of argumentation by historical fact is reflected in the following passage:

> ...& pource que nous sommes gens qualifiez, nostre assemblee a esté reparee de menus suffrages de la magnifique melodie de l'antiquaille & nouueauté, congregeant ainsi le plus celebre, scientifique, & venerable Senat qui fut iamais, & iamais sera; & de faict la gloire de l'antique remembrance des gestes & parure de l'enfance, & autres âges du temps, n'a fait que fueille à nostre congregation, y apportant vne gelee de sagesse, qui a fait trionphamment agir (I, 11).

Furthermore, in an effort to confront the problems emanating from the passage of time and resultant mutability theologians and other « sages » might consult the records for a « Songe », a « Pause derniere », a « Dessein », a « Journal », even for a « Métaphrase », an « Occasion », a « Résultat », a « Minute », an « Arrest » (cf. « Stance »), a « Passage », a « Production », a « Suitte », for some kind of precedent. But whether or not these « gentlemen » consult such documents or enter them themselves in the « Plumitif », whether or not we can work out a cross-reference between title and text here, the very existence of this particular set of titles is closely related to the theme of time, as can easily be seen.

The theme of death, related to that of time and mutability, as we have already seen, also emerges in the chapter titles of *Le Moyen de Parvenir,* especially through such words as « Songe » (sleep being related to death throughout the novel, and hinted at on the title page through the claim that this is a « dictionnaire à dormir »), as « Pause derniere », « Stance », « Arrest », and « Passage ». We are, therefore, not too surprised when we have entered into the book and discover that we are in a kind of Lucianic afterworld, and that many of the interlocutors are frequently caught dozing, partially because, members of the clergy though many of them are, they are well-fed and drowsy, if not indeed lazy.

Neither are we very surprised to find an extensively burlesque, sometimes satirical, even cynical tone in the book, for, in addition to the chapter title « Satyre », we have been given clues that the book is not serious (though of serious intent) through the illogical order in which the titles are arranged, as well as through such titles as « Coqaslane », « Risée », or « Coyonnerie » (« Quoi ! on ne rit ? »).[12] I think, too, that this last title revals too well the author's expectation that we will not really be laughing by the time we have hit the « Chapitre general », — the passages that provide the satire's out-branching from any specific station in life to the general human condition, which is that mankind (n'est) Pas/sage; that due to his « Folie », which he construes to be wisdom, he is ludicrous; and that no matter what stand he takes, what profession he chooses, he cannot come to any « Solution », he cannot make a « Demonstration » with which others will

12. Paul Lacroix, p. 418.

agree. Consequently, a real understanding of his universe and God will not be arrived at before he has passed beyond (cf. « Passons outre... » II, 258), or before he has « booked passage » so to speak. Life is made up of dream, or folly, of dissension, of change, and much of this is due to a form of egomania which allows one man to provide a « Sentence », another an « Ordonnance », still another a « Canon », or another a « Doctrine », all of them in conflict, no doubt, but by all of which, incongruously enough, all of mankind is to live.

I submit, then, that a considerable amount can be learned about the world view presented in *Le Moyen de Parvenir* simply by examining the chapter titles very closely and by organizing them around certain passages and precepts. What is certain from this discussion of the titles, at least, is that they perform a very vital function, by stating in a small way some larger motif, by providing ligatures and cross references, point and counterpoint, in short, a « Sommaire », or an *abrégé* of *Le Moyen de Parvenir,* which will guide us in our use of this unique breviary, this missal which taxes human vice and presents a *satyre perpetuelle,* this great book, this « CENTRE DE TOVS LES LIVRES » (I, 51).

CHAPTER VI

THE STYLE

As the title, the title page, the first and last chapters, and the chapter titles spell out the philosophical motifs of the novel and betray the baroque stamp of *Le Moyen de Parvenir,* so does the style. When we notice the restlessness of the style in the irrepressible punning, in the sentences chopped up by something akin to stichomythia, by frequent tense shifts, by catalogues, and other forms of exaggeration and emphasis, as we are led further and further afield by obscurantism, and pitched back and forth by many other stylistic devices which can be found in abundance in a baroque writer, we are surprised that Mr. Ball should tell us that efforts toward clarity are especially noticeable in *Le Moyen de Parvenir.*[1]

The style is, on the contrary, eruptive, and by that it is tied to the time upheavals of the novel. The style is baroque. It is, in fact, *baroque satyrique* (grotesque, erotic), and, departing from that it is, specifically, *baroque satirique* or satirical baroque. And while the chief aim of this study is not stylistic analysis, it is important nevertheless to show how the style bears out the themes and tendencies of the novel, and thus how the style may reflect the world view of Béroalde. The fact that the novel is baroque in style is therefore relevant and demonstrable.

To approach the question of style, we shall proceed in somewhat the same manner as Imbrie Buffum in his *Studies in the Baroque from Montaigne to Rotrou.* First, we shall see if Béroalde makes any leading statement about his own style. We shall not pause on the assumed moral purpose of *Le Moyen de Parvenir,* since we have already sufficiently examined the

1. George H. Ball, « A Study of Syntax in the *Moyen de Parvenir* » (Unpublished Ph. D. dissertation, University of California, 1938-9), p. 228.

themes of time and mutability, and the connection of these with Béroalde's probable outlook and purpose — namely, to satirize the clergy, especially the papacy, and, more generally, to show the sage to be the fool in this « satyre universelle ». Our chief concern will be to locate the presence of emphasis and exaggeration, to discover whether we have any elements of horror or incarnation — or related evidence of the macabre and realistic — to see whether the novel uses procedures that fall under the categories of theatricality and illusion, whether we can discern marked uses of contrast and surprise, whether we have movement and metamorphosis, and, finally, how *Le Moyen de Parvenir* manifests organic unity and counsels the acceptance of life. This done, our analysis of the world view of Béroalde as reflected in *Le Moyen de Parvenir* will be complete.

We are assuredly not lacking for comments by the author of *Le Moyen de Parvenir* on his own style, for, if we had no other sentence than « Passons outre, ie sens desia que ce liure m'eschappe... » (II, 258), we would even so have the overt confession of the baroque artist's refusal to compose. Béroalde himself intimates by this statement that the book is flighty, restless, and, in short, not self-contained. But we do, in fact, have further clues, even though we should leave aside the author's claim that the book is the center of all books, and, as such, can be taken as much for a literary model as for a moral and spiritual guide. Indeed, in the last chapter our artist manifests his unorganized creativity when he claims to « broyer les couleurs » so that before we are done we have, at his own admission, a book that from every point of view is like an optical illusion: « Bien donques, dittes moy, auez-vous enuie de parvenir ? lisez ce volume de son vray biais; il est fait comme ces peinctures, qui monstrent d'vn, & puis d'autre » (II, 259). And, as if he wished to demonstrate clearly that he is not engaged in presenting an orderly exposé, Béroalde tells us at the very end of the book, which we have analysed in another light, that the guests are « sur le dessert » and that he'll leave it up to others to *finish* the work: « ...d'autres pourront recueiller le reste que i'ay oublié pour mon plaisir & vostre commodité... » (II, 259). Thus, one finds examples in *Le Moyen de Parvenir* not just of Béroalde's comments on his own work, but comments which betray the baroque procedures of the novel. Refusal to compose is their major characteristic.

Emphasis and exaggeration are present in abundance in *Le Moyen de Parvenir.* For example, the claim that « CE LIVRE EST LE CENTRE DE TOVS LES LIVRES » by its bold-face type and by the hyperbole of the words « centre » and « TOVS » provides us with both these qualities.

Emphasis is gained in other ways, too. One of the most frequently used in *Le Moyen de Parvenir* is alliteration, sometimes coupled with repetition of a given word as in the following quotation, in which tense shifts also occur: « ...& ils disent que ie suis nigromanchian, que ie fais parler les morts; ie suis bien plus habile que cela, les morts ont parlé, ils le sçauent bien; mais ie fais parler les bestes, & beaucoup parleront, si Dieu plaist... » (II, 258).

Here is an example of combined alliteration and pun: « ...il est donc vostre sieur, & partant maistre du chantier où l'on sie. Ainsi nous disons... » (I, 9).

The following instance of violent conversational sound effects combines with an incomplete correlative construction illustrating the eruption of the sentence structure: « ...& au nostre [vnivers] qu'y a-t-il ? quoy, qué, qué ? vne quinte essence plus profitable, plus penetrante, plus glorieuse, plus intelligible, & plus viuificante; les sages & les paruenans l'ont recogneuë, & l'ont apprise à plusieurs » (I, 164).

However, the passage which follows will better demonstrate the degree to which alliteration and assonance are used by the author as a means of driving home a point, here seemingly the doctrine of the *bon buveur,* but doubtless also involving the eucharistic sacrifice and sacrement:

> — Mais encor, nostre maistres vous qui sçauvez que le pain est plus ancien que le vin, d'où vient qu'estant le pain en la bouche, il est long temps à se demener ça & là, auant que trouuer le chemin de la vallee, & le vin tout incontinent le trouue ?
>
> — Ce mystere n'est pas de vostre religion : C'est pour ce qu'il y a plus d'esprit en vne pinte de vin, qu'il n'y a en vn boisseau de bled. Voire, direz vous, l'eau en fait bien autant. O lourdaut, mon doux & bel amy, c'est vne folle que l'eau, elle se laisse tomber du haut en bas, elle court les rues, & fait deuenir fols ceux qui l'aiment, & là dessus mon mignon resoluez vn peu a quoy il y a plus de reputation, à se faire declarer yurongne, ou fou. Guette au paneau, & dy que tu en as. Ie vous aduertis, doctes

> beuueurs, que vous ayez des flaccons, ils sont bons vaisseaux fermans à vis, vous serez en seureté. Qui a, pensez vous, esté cause de la guerre de Troye, du siege de Babylon, de la ruine de Thebes, de la venuë de l'Antechrist, & de tant d'autre malheurs dont les vrayes & fausses histoires nous amusent ? Bouteilles cassees, & vin respandu; à dire vray, vin respandu ne vaut pas plein le cul d'eau nette pour vous débarboüiller dans vne escuelle percee. Et pource que l'on n'osoit pas en paroles vulgaires prophaner ce digne & excellent sujet, on le taisoit, & faisoit on accroire aux bonnes gens, qui ne sçauent pas les mysteres mysterieux du vin, comme nous autres philosophes, que lanternes estoient vessies, & attribuoit on ces malheurs à d'autres jolies causes pour vous emmailloter l'esprit (I, 15-16).

The echo found in the phrase « mysteres mysterieux » is noteworthy as a favorite rhetorical device of Béroalde, used for emphasis and characteristic of most baroque writers. Another example occurs early in *Le Moyen de Parvenir*, and is therefore in an ironic position, according to the analysis we have already done of the book's beginning and end — « lequel est la fin finale... » (I, 54).

Rhyming, too, plays its part in the exaggerations and emphases coming from sound, as for example, « ...tesmoin vn pauure moine... » (I, 18), which is only a near rhyme. A better example of rhyme can be found in the following: « Ce beau parfait, ceste belle estofe à faire la pauureté, ce corps tant accomply fut veu en tant de plans si delicieux, que difficilement y eust il jamais yeux plus satisfaits que ceux des assistans » (I, 29). Still another example from the same story of La Belle Marciole is « Les cerises remises au pannier, la belle reuint vers les fenestres reprendre sa chemise... » (I, 30).

One more example of sound repetition is: « Allez donc au grat correcteurs ingrats, & vous grattez... » (I, 59).

Similar sound effects are derived from puns, which are present in almost every sentence, and are too numerous to quote. These puns frequently have multiple intentions, such as the following which plays off Lent, chrism and cream: « Sçauez-vous pas que le C, est la teste de Caresme, & A est le col ? Ostez ledit A, le col sera coupé, & ainsi il demeurera Cresme; le corps ioint à la teste sans cou, est tout vif, & ce à la Catholique, d'autant que le Ieudi absolu on fait le cresme »

(II, 251). Similarly, the professions are satirized through punning on the word *sel:*

> Ie vous diray pourtant, vous demandant excuse, qu'il y aura icy assez de place pour tous les fous, pourueu que l'on les y mette l'vn apres l'autre. En Allemagne les Allemans y mettront leurs fous, en France les François, en Angleterre les Anglois, en Espagne les Espagnols, en Souisse les Italiens, en Turquie le reste; & puis que l'on fasse si grande chere qu'on voudra, soit en droit, soit en musique, soit en canon, soit en Theologie, soit en gendarmerie ou marchandise, ou medecine, ou toute telle autre sorte que vous imaginerez sans y mesler les grenetiers, pource qu'ils sont le sel du monde; ils salent les autres fous, de par le Roy (II, 199).

A final example of punning which is to be found on every page of the novel, will be the superb word play on the Geneva psalter:

> — Tu és vn sot toy-mesme, ie te recommanderay au maistre des sots.
> — Et qui est-il ?
> — O grosse beste, c'est le sotier de Geneue.
> — Quel sotier ?
> — Tu fais semblant de ne le sçauoir point, pource qu'ils escriuent Psautier ? mais ie disons sotier, non sans cause; dautant que tous les sots qui sont repris de Iustice en ce païs-là passe sous son enseigne (II, 171).

Both repetition and recurrent vocabulary also give emphasis and exaggerate the comic tone in *Le Moyen de Parvenir.* Here is a nicely ordered sermon in three parts, opening with a series of tense shifts, and showing throughout the use of repetition:

> ...ie vous diray des choses que vous ny moy n'entendrons, ni entendons, ni n'auons entendu, ou ie me tairay comme fit le Curé de Busançois, qui dit : « Ie vous prescherois auiourd'hui, mais nous n'auons pas le loisir : toutefois ie vous diray vn bout de sermon que nous diuiserons en trois parties. La premiere, ie l'entens & vous ne l'entendez pas. La seconde, vous l'entendez & ie ne l'entens pas. La troisiesme, ni vous ni moy ne l'entendons. La premiere

que i'entens & vous n'entendez pas, c'est que vous faciez rebastir le presbytère. La seconde que vous entendez & que ie n'entens pas, c'est que vous entendez que ie chasse ma chambriere, & ie ne l'entens pas. La troisiesme que vous ni moy n'entendons, est l'Éuangile d'auiourd'hui. Adieu » (I, 171).

Recurrent vocabulary is as common to *Le Moyen de Parvenir* as are recurrent themes, and contributes to the general atmosphere of exaggeration. Two such words are *éplucher* and *cymbale.* The word *éplucher* is variously used to describe the doctor's activities — « Ie dy que ceux qui s'amusent à nos folies, sont comme les Medecins qui regardent et espluchent les ejections des autres, qui sont aussi fous que nous... » (I, 21) — to relate what Bodin will do with the maxims he is getting from Lycurgus — « i'esplucherons en passant que de ceux qui paruiennent » (I, 168) — and to tell the reader what he must do — « ...diligemment espluchez... » (I, 150). He had, by the way, in a previous passage been told that he must « succer les rainceaux » (I, 11), which is reminiscent of Rabelais' « sugcer la mouelle ».[2] The two directives to the reader are not unrelated, of course. As a matter of fact, the same vocabulary as Rabelais' is found in *Le Moyen de Parvenir* (« succer la moelle de doctrine ») (I, 194).

The word *cymbale* recurs both as a word and as a sound, and is ultimately linked with the words *lampe* and *lanterne,* all of them probably alluding to the papacy. Early in *Le Moyen de Parvenir* the word *cymbale* appears to have no other than the erotic meaning (« les cymbales de concupiscence » — I, 40), as is explained by the next two phrases (« les cailles d'Amour, les boulettes de Venus » — I, 40). Yet, in the first chapter we are told that « ...les enfans de la science avoient mis la main au symbole de la conscience » (I, 5), so that we see the possible allusion to the Apostle's Creed or the Tridentine Profession of Faith, and this interpretation is made possible by the following passage: « ...tellement que ces Messieurs ayant pris conseil, & estant assemblez ils ont fait vn (ie ne sçaurois dire ce mot des Apostres, aydez moy à le trouuer, c'est vn ? Ie l'ay trouué; qu'au diantre soit le harnois, tant il m'a cousté à fourbir) c'est vn symbole : ainsi chacun apportant son symbole

2. François Rabelais, *Œuvres,* éd. Louis Moland (Paris, 1950), I, p. 5.

ils furent ioins ensemble comme la mie à la crouste... » (I, 161-162). Again, the word *cymbale* seems to suggest something akin to Des Periers' *Cymbalum Mundi* or Rabelais' « Ile Sonnante ». As I have said, in this respect the word *lanterne,* having the meaning « papist » seems to be related, at least in their mutually evocative power. This notion is illustrated by the following passage: « Est-ce là ceste belle lanterne qui nous doit esclairer, sera-ce elle qui nous apprendra l'intelligence & solution de ce qui est proposé de l'excellence des escritures ? » (I, 110). The ecclesiastical *lanterne,* like the word *cymbale (symbole)* reappears frequently in *Le Moyen de Parvenir,* notably in a dialogue too long to be quoted (I, 103-105), but even more direct in its allusions and satire than is the above.

Thus, recurrent vocabulary gives emphasis to certain words, and by reiteration and new settings, additional innuendos. The comic effects and the satire itself become, in fact, exaggerated.

One of the most frequent and effective of devices used to give emphasis and exaggeration in *Le Moyen de Parvenir* is hyperbole. It may be found under many guises, as, for example, with the adjective « all », noted in the claim that « CE LIVRE EST LE CENTRE DE TOUS LES LIVRES » (I, 51), or the pronoun form: « ...tout y estoit auec grace fort bien retaconné... » (I, 10).

Hyperbole may be found, too, in the abundant use of negatives, as « ...& prenoit grand plaisir de nous auoir pour son contentment, sans quoy les dames n'en feroient rien, tant soient elles ferues du desir de science » (I, 12). The rather cynical negative statement of the narrator also furnishes us with an example of both rhyme and hyperbole: « ...& m'assis aussi bien qu'vn autre, dautant que j'ay vn cul, joint que sans cul nul ne pourroit auoir seance entre gens d'honneur » (I, 22).

Other examples of hyperbole may be found in the expansive use of high numerical figures, as: « O toy donc cetuy-là à qui ie parlois tantost, releué d'orgueil, bouquin qui as esté mille fois gourmandé par ta chambriere, ainsi qu'il se fait volontiers en nos cloitres » (I, 57), or « ...mille fois plus de bruit qu'ils n'eussent peu faire... » (II, 197), or again, « Cent mille petits Diablotins de deçà & delà les monts qui vous extrauaguent, vous puissent casser des noix, que la gorge vous coupe le coup, il n'i a ni rime ne raison en vostre fait » (I, 174), and « Il y a plus de trois mille minutes que ie suis apres pour vous attraper à ce poinct sans vous interrompre... » (II, 38), and finally, « I'ay beu plus de mille deux cents quatorze bouteillees de l'vn & de l'autre vin... » (II, 248).

But one of the passages which most clearly shows hyperbole and consequently exaggeration by negatives, by superlatives, by all-inclusive tense shifts, and the like is the following:

> Or entendez, belles petites mignonnes ames, qui venez icy succer les rainceaux du rameau d'or pour sauourer la science, que nous sommes, nous qui parlons, de ce temps; nous y sommes, en tenons & y viuons, si ne sommes trompez, & la pluspart de ceux du temps passé ont vescu en leur siecle, comme nous au nostre, & vous au vostre, & pource que nous sommes gens qualifiez, nostre assemblee a esté reparee de menus suffrages de la magnifique melodie de l'antiquaille & nouueauté, congregeant ainsi le plus celebre, scientifique, & venerable Senat qui fut iamais, & iamais sera; & de faict la gloire de l'antique remembrance des gestes & parure de l'enfance, & autres âges du temps, n'a fait que fueille à nostre congregation, y apportant vne gelee de sagesse, qui resplendissant par tout, nous a fait trionphamment agir (I, 11).

This same passage continues with hyperbolic praise of Madame (Sophie), the perfect pearl (see also I, 47) of Eastern origins suggestive of the Incarnation: « Madame qui est l'vnique entre les sages, la perle des entendues, & le parangon de perfection... nous festoyoit... » (I, 11-12).

The true nature of the gathering is likewise described in terms of hyperbole which carries a theological burden, so that we are not surprised to discover that our banquet is, for all intents and purposes, an ecumenical council:

> Que ne sçauois-ie ces belles responses, & ces doctrines, ie suis fort desplaisant, & meurs de regret, que ie n'attendis à escrire pour estre le secretaire de ce sympose, qui m'eut plus apporté de reputation, que n'en auront tous les escriuains ensemble. Or c'est tout vn, i'ay la copie des discours tant verbaux que couchez par escrit, comme disoit nostre Aduocat : « Ie me tiens à mes demandes, faites par requestes verbales, desquelles la copie est en mon sac »; & voila comment ie me tiens aussi à ces futures sentences qui sont ia escrites. En outre, ie preuoy pourtant que ce banquet sera le grand, vnique & vniuersel sur tous autres, & monarque des symposes œcumeniques (I, 216).

Similar exaggeration, also containing theological satire, comes through the use of long words, of which the longest in the book (longer by eight letters than any word in Rabelais, says Reiche) [3] will serve as an illustration. It is *Pseudosevangeliquolipapistoranabaptistiogiesuitanorbiterondepuritain* (II, 201).

Furthermore, the catalogues, frequently found in Renaissance and baroque literature, of which we have already seen several, serve as an example of the exaggeration to be found in *Le Moyen de Parvenir*. I will requote only the following as a reminder:

> Et que faisoient tant de bonnes gens de loisir ? voire, mais que fit-on là ? On parla, on mangea, on beut, on fit st, on se teut, on fit du bruit, on protesta, on rencontra, on rit, on baailla, on entendit, on disputa, on cracha, on moucha, on s'estonna, on s'esbahit, on admira, on gaussa, on raporta, on entendit, on broüilla, on s'esclaircit, on debattit, on s'accorda, on trinca l'vn à l'autre, on fit carroux, on remarqua, on tremoussa, on s'accouda, on cria tout bas, on se teut tout haut, on se mocqua, on murmura, on s'auisa, on se reprit, on se contenta, on passa le temps, on douta, on redouta, on s'assagit, on deuint, on paruint (I, 43).

Thus, emphasis and exaggeration are gained through sound effects, echos, repetition, tense shift, hyperbole, long words, catalogues, all of which are ingredients of baroque style. The first of Buffum's categories appears at this somewhat cursory glance to apply well to *Le Moyen de Parvenir*.

However, for the following two categories of Buffum — horror and incarnation — we shall substitute related categories — the grotesque or macabre, and efforts toward realism.

The whole of *Le Moyen de Parvenir* is grotesque, *satyrique*, Lucianic, or other-worldly, by its own admission: « ...ie fais parler des morts... » (II, 258). As we have seen, the author even suspects that he may be called a « nigromanchian » (II, 258) and indeed the following references to the Dance of Death do not seem at all out of place in *Le Moyen de Parvenir:* « — Voila de belles raisons, i'aymerois autant celles de Iannotin, qui dit qu'il faut estre sergent pour aller en Paradis, d'autant que les sergens vont deuant. — Da, da, il est bon, s'il n'y auoit que les gens de iustice qui allassent en paradis ! Et c'est le

3. Herber Reiche, *Le Moyen de parvenir von Béroalde de Verville mit besonderer Berüksichtigung der Quellen-und Verfasserfrage* (Coburg, 1913), p. 52.

contraire, & ie l'ay veu, en la dance Macabree de Fubourg, où les Presidens, Conseillers, Auocats, Procureurs, & clercs, sont par les sergents conduits en enfer, & t'en guette » (II, 82-83), and again: « ...il mourut comme à Dole à la dance Macaber, il y a la Mort qui parle à un beau ieune homme... » (II, 257).

Yet, over and against this otherworldliness we find several devices used to give to the work a tone of realism, especially in relation to speech habits, as, for example, an interlocutor's holding his listener at bay: « ALAIN. Qu'est-ce a dire ? VIVES. Vous le sçaurez tantost. Ce moine, pour le dire plus gayement, cherchoit... » (I, 73).

Another device for rendering natural dialogue is an exclamation such as the following uttered in frustration by Chilo: « Que d'interruptions ! » (I, 169).

Even more striking is the portrayal of laughter showing the enjoyment the company has over the discourse of Sapho on the seven wonders of the world: « — Aa a, ha he ! Toute la compagnie s'esmeut à rire, & nous nous trouuasmes joyeux & alegres, comme vne belle troupe de jeunes ou nouueaux Cardinaux » (I, 206).

A related speech tic is frequently used by the interlocutors in reproducing dialogue for their tales, as, for example, « 'O ho, dit la Roine, & moy ? — A ha, Madame, vous este la Roine' » (I, 72). Similarly, a bit further on in the book one finds, « 'Ha ha becasse babouine, qu'auous tant fait là haut ?' » (I, 81).

The interlocutors themselves use similar exclamations, such as, « — Ha ha, he, appelez vous cela intacta ? » (I, 87). And here is an example which combines with it an aphoristic formula, a feature not uncommon in *Le Moyen de Parvenir* or in other baroque literature: « — Ho, Monsieur, i'y suis, ne vous courcez pas, il ne se faut fascher qu'à bon escient » (I, 94). Examples of the interjection, as of aphorisms — or at least proverbs — could be multiplied endlessly, and this latter phenomenon shall presently be dealt with.

One of the most striking devices used to give to the speech a natural quality is the abundant use of colorful oaths and interjections. A partial list of these would be as follows: « Diantre... » (I, 70; II, 32), « Par le sainct sabre de castud... » (I, 86), « Par mon asne... » (I, 92), « O de par plus de cinq cens mille cornes de coquu... » (I, 120), « ...foin de par diantre foin ! » (I, 172), « Saincte Marande... » (I, 192), « Pay ! » (I, 194, 257), « Dianche... » (I, 207, 252), « ...par ma digne conscience... » (I, 209),

« Par ma finte... » (I, 212), « Cap de biou... » (I, 223), « ...par la gorge... » (I, 234), « ...bran... » (I, 236), « Par saint Picot... » (I, 282), « Corps de moi dienne... » (II, 14), « Par la Merci-Dieu... » (II, 35), « Pardé... » (II, 72), « Pargoy... » (II, 75, 84, 145), « Par mon serment, sans jurer... » (II, 77), « Pardienne... » (II, 84), « Chedienne... » (II, 97), « Par ma nanda... » (II, 98), « Ardé... » (II, 114), « ...de par le diable... » (II, 127, 137, 224, 232), « Par la certe bieu... » (II, 140), « ...par la double, triple manche de serpe... » (II, 149), « ...tous les mille diables... » (II, 201), « En nanda... » (II, 202), « O diantre soit le traistre ! » (II, 215), « Ma fine... » (II, 229), « Per meam... » (II, 244). These exclamatory expressions and oaths are used copiously both by the interlocutors when speaking to one another, and when reproducing dialogue for their tales.

Another device which gives the semblance of reality to the dialogues is the frequent interruption of one interlocutor by another, sometimes to urge him to continue, sometimes to reprimand one or another interlocutor, to criticize digression, to make an interjection, etc. Examples of this are: « Foutin, laissez dire ce Docteur... » (I, 114); « Vrament bon homme c'est bien vous qui y estes allé de biais; que n'acheuez vous ce que vous auez commencé ? » (I, 144); « Or là, laissez moy acheuer, mon analogie sera parfaicte... » (I, 163); the often-said « Taisez-vous » (e.g., I, 182, 310); « LE MAISTRE : Vous auez tort, il ne faut pas les mesler, il n'y a point de comparaison. — Paix là, paix là, paix ! » (II, 128); « BIGON : Paix de par tous les diables, taisez vous, ou ie vous couperai le cou, comme ie fis vn iour à vn Roy qui chioit. Acheuez le discours de ce Conseiller, & meshui ne vous interromperai, ou i'abomine, ie contamine, ie precipite, ie diable, ie trente mille... A ha, ie ne le dirai pas; faictes vostre deuoir » (II, 142); « Pay, ne passez pas outre, ne dites pas tout » (II, 162); « On void bien que vous n'estes gueres sages de nous conter tout ceci » (II, 162); « Tu ne fais ce conte qu'à demi » (II, 201).

Here is an example which combines with it aphoristic pronouncements on the part of the intruders: « ALAIN : Vous me faictes de l'interruption; le ciel vous en punaisira & regardez bien que signifie cela. Laissez moi acheuer. — Fou enragé qui ne l'escoute. — Et plus fou est il qui s'y amuse » (II, 12).

In *Le Moyen de Parvenir* we frequently find the interlocutors swearing to the truth of their tale, a device often found in this type of literature, for example in Philippe de Vigneulles and Marguerite de Navarre, and one which lends a false reality to the story. In the following passage, for example, the interlocutor evaluates the accuracy of his account in saying: « Mon Chapitre deuoit au iour de la solemnité Sainct Louys à Rome (si ce n'est ainsi c'est tout vn, puis que le reste est vray...) » (I, 96). Another interlocutor assures his listeners, « Omne viro soli quod conuenit esto virile; les Docteurs de Paris l'enseignent aux escolles, ie vous asseure ô vous qui entendez cecy qu'il est vray, & que comme ce bon pere le dit il n'y va point de sa faute » (I, 141). Yet another interlocutor insists that a story must have integrity, saying, « — Ie m'enquis de ceste histoire de ministre, passant par là, dautant que ie ne veux rien dire, ni presenter, ni oüir s'il n'est vray » (I, 175). The interlocutors frequently support their utterances with the adverbial expressions « voire », « vrayement », « de fait », etc., but here is a highly redundant utterance in which the speaker seems intent upon communicating the authenticity of his claim, « — Voire, ce Moine l'estoit vrayement & de fait... » (I, 235). Indeed, the interlocutor Alain is even constrained in his commentary by the need to tell the truth, « Ie ne sçaurois que faire, c'est la verité qui me contraint... » (II, 13). And how are we to doubt Renee who says, « O vere, en ma conscience ie vous iure qu'elle est vne pauure petite putain... » (II, 33).

Sometimes the devices used to give to the dialogues a natural setting are combined. Thus, in the following instance we have one interlocutor interrupting another in order to fortify the correctness of the former's discourse: « — Pardonnez moi, ce que ie dis n'est que pour rendre plus authentique vostre prolation, & de faict, ie croy que ce n'est pas lui dont ie veux parler, c'est d'vn autre qui est de Geneue, & est de mesme estat : là on ne dit pas sergent, on dit officier » (II, 214). In the following passage, however, an oath, a claim to truth (« sans iurer ») and the interlocutor's irritation at being rushed are combined to give an air of naturalistic dialogue: « Corbeau, tu me presserois trop, & puis ô de par le diantre, sans iurer, ne sçais-tu pas bien qu'il y a trois choses qui ne veulent souffrir estre pressees ? » (II, 167).

A stock comic device, but one which also gives realism to the dialogue in *Le Moyen de Parvenir* is the *lapsis linguae.* One can find examples of this in Philippe de Vigneulles' Nouvelle 91 and Nouvelle 64, as in Marguerite de Navarre's

Nouvelle 62[4], but verbal slips are even more frequently used by Béroalde. Here is an example of one in which Latin is involved:

> — Ce Latin est pareil a celui du Vicaire de Chamberi, qui lisoit l'Euangile des cinq pains; & au lieu de dire, « Vt quisque accipiat modicum », il dit : « Accipiat modium. »
>
> — Il disoit vray, il en eust fallu beaucoup de muids : ne disoit-il pas aussi : « Quid statis occisi », pour ociosi ? Ce fut lui qui nous annonçant des festes, comme tantost se voulant paillarder à bien dire, & mit-il pas sur sa tombe, « Requiescauit in pace, s'il a pleu à Dieu ? ».
>
> — Que voulez-vous, il y alloit à la bonne iniquité. Encores y a-il des gens qui ont de la conscience (II, 232, 233).

However, here is an example of a verbal slip containing a play on the words *congelé* and *congé.* The reader will also note the punning on the words *garces* and *graces* in the same passage: « Monsieur le Cardinal, les Bohemiens s'en recommandent à vos bonnes garces (i'ay la langue fourchante andistrosante), ie dis graces pour l'amour d'eux, auec vostre congelé, i'ay cuidé dire, congé, comme Bubescius, Alemant, qui disant adieu à la Reine d'Angleterre voulant le dire en François, profera : 'Mon dame ie prendre congelé' » (I, 110).

The interlocutor Donat slips in telling his story and says, « Copeau qui l'auisa ainsi merde en vos lipes, ie dy melancholique, vint à elle & luy dit, 'Ça ma cousine allons dancer' » (I, 135).

Although many examples of *lapsis linguae* can be found in *Le Moyen de Parvenir,* the following will be the last we shall cite: « — Vous ne parlez que fariboles, ie cuidois dire paraboles... » (II, 220).

Hence, by attributing special speech habits to the interlocutors, such as a portrayal of laughter, tics and exclamations, oaths and interjections, interruptions and commentary on one another's stories, claims to veracity, *lapsis linguae,* etc., the tone, already naturalistic by its eroticism to the point of the grotesque, attains a new level of realism. One of the major contrasts of *Le Moyen de Parvenir* is achieved through this use

4. Charles H. Livingston, « The *Heptaméron des Nouvelles* of Marguerite de Navarre: A Study of Nouvelles 28, 34, 52, and 62 », *Romanic Review,* XIV (April-September, 1923), pp. 105-107.

of natural dialogue, for it would be ultimately quite out of place in the mouths of persons inhabiting the *au-delà*. Not only is this phenomenon comic, but it is also, by the contrast it presents, baroque in character. Buffum's categories of horror and incarnation are not very far removed from the presence in *Le Moyen de Parvenir* of the grotesque, otherworldly, irrational, opposed to and at the same time complemented by an extreme naturalism both in tone and in style.

We are now prepared to explore *Le Moyen de Parvenir* for the possible presence of theatricality and illusion, and we soon find that our efforts are not in vain, at least as far as the style is concerned. We do not find our novel lacking in either quality.

For theatricality, we need only and above all to remember that *Le Moyen de Parvenir* is in the main in dialogue form to see that a consciousness of the stage is present. This is not to say that the dialogues in *Le Moyen de Parvenir* are any more stageable than those of Lucian, or of the *Celestina*. Nevertheless the fact that most exposition is dispensed with in favor of a vivid *tête-à-tête* situation is for all intents and purposes theatrical. We can add to this the argument that the dialogues are not stiff and rhetorical, but, as we have already seen, emanate from natural speech. True enough, our stage is heavily peopled, but this is due to the baroque world view of Béroalde as much as any other one thing. The canvases of the baroque artists are similarly crowded with figures on the various levels.

But what in the style as such may we consider to be theatrical? We have, as an example, the many aphorisms or proverbs scattered throughout the novel, and of which we have as yet seen but a few: « ...il ne se faut facher qu'à bon escient » (I, 94); « Fou enragé qui ne l'escoute... » (I, 12); « Et plus fou est il qui s'y amuse » (I, 12). To this we may add: « O gens de qualité, si vous ne mordez à ces intelligences faictes vous bien aiguiser les dens » (I, 91); « Il ne se faut point estonner que l'on ne voye sa teste à bas ses pieds » (I, 100); « Il ne faut pas dire les secrets de peur qu'estans publiez on n'en recognoisse la vanité... » (I, 131); « ...tout est libre & bon en son temps, lieu & endroit... » (I, 138-139); « ...il ne faut qu'estre effronté pour obtenir faueurs... » (I, 152); « ...pour estre grand & gaigner, il faut ruiner la vertu & le prochain... » (I, 152); « ...le monde est beaucoup de fois plus grand que l'homme qui est le petit monde, & le monde le grand animal corporel... » (I, 159); « ...& s'en faut raporter aux exemples, ainsi qu'vne truye qui auorte » (I, 168); « '...on ne peut seruir à deux maistres, à Dieu & au diable' » (I, 190); « ...les belles se font prier, & les laides prient, chacun fait ce qu'il peut pour viure » (I, 224); « C'est vne belle chose de sçauoir tout; c'est que nostre langue françoise est la plus ample de toutes... » (I, 227); « ...ceux qui parlent tant des friponneries d'vn estat, douient en estre, en auoir esté, ou les auoir trop frequentez... » (I, 253); « ...c'est vn grand merite que de se souuenir de ses fautes, dont par ainsi la retribution est grande en pardons, abondans sur l'iniquité » (I, 258); « Celui qui aura fait le fou tout le long des iours gras, n'assagira pas Mercredi par la cendre... » (I, 267); « ...qui n'aime point l'animal de societé, qui ne fait point de cas des femmes, est sot & meschant ou sodomite » (I, 288); « vn homme qui honnestement aime vne douce femme, est humble et gracieux : mais cettui-là qui les reiette est de qualité d'vsurier... » (I, 288); « Là où il y a tant d'ordre pour disner, il y a du desordre pour faire ses affaires » (I, 310); « ...tousiours le four est chaud, mais la paste n'est pas leuee » (I, 313); « ...femmes sont Anges à l'Église, diables en la maison, & singes au lict » (II, 2); « Iamais fourmage mou ne gasta gorge... » (II, 22); « ...on mange bien en Grece d'vne truye dont on aura mangé le cochon » (II, 37); « ...la Fortune a du poil au front... » (II, 77); « ...il faut estre sergent pour aller en Paradis... » (II, 82); « ...l'on ne meurt que de faute de boire & manger... » (II, 120); « ...qui a bon esprit il boit & mange bien... » (I, 120); « ...il y a desia tant de damnez en Enfer, que les pauures diables couchent dehors... » (II, 130); « ...que l'argent est fascheux & difficile à faire » (II, 147); « ...il faut que chacun viue de son estat... » (II, 147); « ...il ne faut iamais passer ce qui s'offre... » (II, 185); « ...faut que les chouses destinees soient accomplies » (II, 192); « ...les noms sont pour les mortels... » (II, 198); « Les esperances sont plus belles que les effects » (II, 212); « ...c'est vn grand mal-heur que des affaires du monde... » (II, 218); « Il n'y a personne qui ne tasches à faire son profit... » (II, 238); « Quand maistre coust & putain file, Petite practique est en ville » (II, 242); « Iouer au ieu qu'aux cailles on appelle, Aux filles est chose plaisante & belle » (II, 242); « ...malheureux sont ceux qui mentent en vin quels qu'ils soient » (II, 248).

This long, but even so only partial list of statements shows the extent to which aphorism in integral in the style of *Le Moyen de Parvenir,* and to what an extent, too, Béroalde's somewhat cynical world view is couched in the aphorism. As a stylistic device, the sententia is widespread in Renaissance and baroque literature, and is unquestionably a part of dramatic rhetoric, as an examination of, say, the plays of Montchrestien will prove. The maxim, essentially the same thing as aphorism or proverb, is precious; it is a genre created, so to speak, by the salon, and it is likely, as I have already indicated, that this whole movement is being satirized in *Le Moyen de Parvenir.* The frequent recourse of the interlocutors to aphorism is, then, not only theatrical, but also satirical. A similar procedure may be observed in Adrien de Montluc's « La Comédie des Proverbes ».

Another stylistic device which can be considered theatrical is the use of something very akin to the aside. It is a parenthetical comment of the interlocutor, and while it is dramatic, it is also a part of natural speech. In addition, it contributes to the overall tone or world view of the particular interlocutor, and, by extension, of Béroalde. For example, the misogyny of *Le Moyen de Parvenir,* already pointed out in another context, is thus confirmed in two separate places by the use of the « aside ». Thus, Xilander, in the midst of his tale about the Chanoine de St. Martin de Tours says, « ...il faut tout dire, de peur des garces qui nous escoutent, pource que la frequence de telles femelles abondoit iadis auant nostre reformation ainsi qu'aux autres lieux » (I, 232). An even better example of this is the parenthetical remark attributed by Paul Lacroix to L'Autre: « C'est vne bonne personne pour vne femme, elle trouue tout bon, afin de ne se marir point » (II, 199). Such a remark, like the aside in theater, does not contribute to the progress of the action so much as it permits the spectator to catch a glimpse into the character's point of view. Such is the effect of this device in *Le Moyen de Parvenir.*

In the tales told, as in the exchange between the interlocutors, Béroalde sometimes makes use of rapid, choppy dialogue comparable to stichomythia. This device is, like the parenthetical « aside », at once natural to speech and theatrical or dramatic. One can find many examples of this phenomenon, as the following, in which the speech tics, the oaths, the claims to truth which we have already noted also occur: « ' Ie vous asseure veritablement, ainsi que de dire quand tout est dit. — Rien, rien, pour neant. — Ainsi veritablement, comme dit l'autre. — A a. — Laissez moy dire. — Basta, basta, passez reuerend. — Ainsi petits diablotins. Veritablement vous m'interrompez. — Rrraaa. — Ie crie; ie le dis ainsi que de dire, son ouurier auoit nom maistre Nicolas, ce fut lui veritablement, ainsi qu'il fut, ouy certe, ou cent mille petits diablotins, sec & au dela, qui fut cause veritablement qu'elle dit ce mot, & Ferchaudiere y estoit' » (I, 127).

In the following passage the interlocutor Miclot reproduces a short clipped dialogue: « Il n'en est pas tousiours si ardant, il en est feru comme vn chien d'vn baston; si on lui dit, 'Allez à l'Église. — Qui y est ? — Ils y sont tous. — Ils sont donc assez'. Vne autre fois, 'Qui y est ? — Il n'y a personne. Ie n'i ferois rien tout seul' » (I, 208). It is again an interlocutor, this time Magdelaine, who imitates rapid fire speech in the following passage, which contains in addition, examples of rhyme and cadence, which we have already examined: « 'D'où viens-tu ?' fit-il. 'Du four', fit-elle. 'Que faire ?' fit-il. 'Vn tourteau', fit-elle. 'Est-il bon ?' fit-il. 'Tastez-y', fit-elle. 'Est-il chaud ?' fit-il. 'Soufflez', fit-elle. 'Et où ?' fit-il. 'A mon cul', fit-elle. 'Ha putain', fit-il. 'Ha coquu', fit-elle » (I, 256). Like the passage just cited, the following dialogue given by the interlocutor Renee contains the question-response formula: « A la fin ie m'esueillé, & demanday : 'Qui est là ?' il m'entrouït & dit, 'C'est moy. — Et qui ? Moy pauure Ministre. — Et où estes vous ? — Ici. — Et où ? — Ie ne sçay' » (II, 32). And here is an exchange between a confessor and one of the faithful recounted by an interlocutor: « — Respondez comme le bon homme de Vanures qui estoit charron, lequel s'estant confessé, son Curé lui dit, 'Dites vostre confiteor. — Ie ne le sçay pas. — Dites vostre aue. — Ie ne le sçai pas. — Dites la patinostre. — Ie ne la sçai pas. — Que sçais tu donc ? — Ie sçai faire de belles ciuieres roulcresses, ie vous en ferai vne quand il vous plaira, & à bon marché' » (II, 111).

Although most of the dialogue between the interlocutors is lengthy, since each is involved in telling a story, occasionally the exchange between them manifests this same stichomythic character. Here is a short passage in which several interlocutors are involved: « L'Avtre : Ie suis bien aise que vous estes venus sur ces differences; dictes vn peu quelle difference il y a d'vne femme à vn Prestre, ce sont gens de robe longue ? — Ie n'en sçay rien. — Ny moi aussi. — Ne moi etout » (II, 103). The same situation prevails in the following: « — Voila qui est bon, tout sert en mesnage. — Ouy da, mais quelles sont les plus grandes necessitez ou pauuretez de mesnage ? — Ie ne sçay. — Ni moy aussi. — Ni moy. — Ie vous les diray, & les retenez... » (II, 118).

Finally, that Béroalde has the theater proper in mind is evidenced by scattered references to it in the text. Notable among these are reference to allegorical personages in older morality plays, as in the tale of Alciat: « Il y auoit lors une dame qui durant les jeux auoit joué Conscience, qui pour cela en eut le nom tout le temps de sa vie... » (II, 206), and to a morality play of the sixteenth century, « Le Monde, la Chair, le Diable », humorously translated into an aphoristic pronouncement by one of the interlocutors as follows: « Et là là, Mundus caro daemonia, le monde n'a cure de Moines » (I, 79). In a book of such farcical tone as *Le Moyen de Parvenir* we are not surprised, either, to find a reference to the *confrérie* of Les Pois Pilez, a group of actors who presented farces. Of them Paul Lacroix says in his note: « La confrérie des *Pois pilés,* comme celles des *Enfants sans souci* et de la *Bazoche,* donnait des représentations scéniques ou plutôt des parades composées de coq-à-l'âne, de *rencontres,* de rébus, etc. Elle avait aussi un chef qu'elle appelait roi, et celui-ci choisissait une reine, selon la hiérarchie de la pluspart des confréries de métier au moyen âge. C'était aux Halles que l'on faisait le *Jeu des Pois pilés.* »[5]

As is frequently the case, the presence of a given interlocutor at our banquet corroborates an impression given by some other aspect of the text. Such is the case when it comes to the theatrical focus we find from time to time in *Le Moyen de Parvenir;* for among the guests present is a certain Alais or Pont-Alais (II, 94), an actor of whom Paul Lacroix writes: « ALAIS (Jean), ou plutôt Jean du Pontalais, auteur et acteur de moralités, farces et soties au commencement du seizième siècle, tirait probablement son nom d'un égoût appelé le *Pont-Alais,* voisin de l'église de Saint-Eustache, où il avait posé ses tréteaux. Bonaventure des Periers, dans sa Nouvelle XXXII, nous représente Jean du Pontalais comme un esprit-fort qui osait tenir tête au curé de Saint-Eustache, au point de le coiffer avec le tambourin que ce curé avait défoncé. »[6]

Hence, by the very fact that the novel is in dialogue form,

5. Paul Lacroix, p. 80.
6. *Ibid.*, p. 430.

and also through use of such devices as aphorism, the « aside », stichomythic effects, etc., a kind of theatricality which is peculiarly baroque in character is posed. We have the illusion of the stage at many points in *Le Moyen de Parvenir*. This is one of the ways in which Béroalde manages to deceive the spectator. But in what other ways is illusion — the contrast between appearance and reality — present in *Le Moyen de Parvenir?* We have already suggested an essential contrast between naturalism and otherworldliness, a major illusion or prism, and highly baroque. We might add in the realm of form that complexity of genre which makes us agree that *Le Moyen de Parvenir* is « faict comme ces peinctures, qui monstrent d'vn, & puis d'autre » (II, 259). Indeed, that complexity of form, the presence of a story within a story, of a character within a character, and that complexity of genre — the book is at once a traditional collection of *novelle* with a frame; it is *picaresque;* it is a series of dialogues in the Lucianic vein; it is a satire; it is a masterpiece of nonsense literature or *fatras,* etc. — give those prismatic effects which constitute one of the best reasons for calling the book baroque and the view of the world reflected by such complexity baroque, or, in this instance, satirical baroque. We have seen, too, the time upheavals which give us the illusion of timelessness. To this let us add the manner in which the interlocutors move from tale to tale by a process of association or almost stream of consciousness which gives to the novel a dream-like, unreal quality. Yet, I repeat, all this is accomplished within the context of utterly natural speech.

What, however, in the style of the book can be called prismatic, the prism being considered by Hatzfeld to be an essential ingredient of baroque technique[7], and one which surely relates to Buffum's category of illusion?

It seems to me that recurrent reference in *Le Moyen de Parvenir* to eyeglasses is one of the ways in which a minor prism is established. We have already discussed in detail the appearance on the title page of the phrase, « *Et adviēdra que ceux qui auront nez à porter lunettes s'en seruirōt : ainsi qu'il est escrit au Dictionnaire à dormir en toutes langues. S.* ». From the outset, then, an optical illusion is facetiously advocated.

7. Helmut Hatzfeld, « A Clarification of the Baroque Problem in the Romance Literatures », *Comparative Literature,* I (1949), p. 119.

In the text proper, the use of anything producing distortion seems to be criticized, thus bearing out the idea that *Le Moyen de Parvenir* has recourse to baroque techniques for the purposes of satirizing or criticizing the same, thus giving us a satirical baroque style: « Or mes chers amis que i'ayme de toute ma fressure, si vous auez affaire de quelque suiet, cherchez le icy, & ne vous chaille des autres, viuons & boiuons selon nos merites, il ne nous faudra point de besicles sur les aureilles pour en destourner le rhume, ny de cotton dans le nez pour l'empecher » (I, 84-85).

The use of eyeglasses for anachronistic burlesque is pointed out by Bar[8], and the fact that the word *anteojos* appears in *La Pícara Justina* is worthy of mention. But for an external example, let us take the following passage from Sterne's *A Sentimental Journey,* a work not unrelated to the type of literature we are investigating in these pages:

> The old officer was reading attentively a small pamphlet (it might be the book of the opera) with a large pair of spectacles. As soon as I sat down, he took his spectacles off, and, putting them into a shagreen case, returned them and the book into his pocket together. I half rose up, and made him a bow.
>
> Translate this into any civilized language in the world, the sense is this: —
>
> « Here's a poor stranger come into the box; he seems as if he knew nobody: and is never likely, was he to be seven years in Paris, if every man he comes near keeps his spectacles upon his nose: — 'tis shutting the door of conversation absolutely in his face, and using him worse than a German'. »
>
> The French officer might as well have said it all aloud: and if he had, I should in course have put the bow I made him into French too, and told him, « I was sensible of this attention, and returned him a thousand thanks for it ».[9]

Illusion or prism is also achieved in *Le Moyen de Parvenir* by frequent allusion to games, a device often used by Rabelais,

8. Francis Bar, *Le Genre burlesque en France au XVIIe siècle* (Paris, 1960), p. 12.

9. Laurence Sterne, *A Sentimental Journey through France and Italy* (New York, n.d.), p. 100.

but having in our novel the effect of a game within a game, or of some such truism as « Life is grim; let us view it as a game ». We shall have reason to refer to this again in the final stages of our discussion of style, the organic unity and acceptance of life, but in the meanwhile, let us collect at this point come of the references to games. We have already noted that one of the spurious titles of *Le Moyen de Parvenir* was *Le Coupecu de la melancolie, ou Venus en belle humeur.* The word *coupecu,* over and above its erotic implications, is the name of a game, and it is over and over again referred to in *Le Moyen de Parvenir,* which is understandable, given the ready-made pun which it affords. We have already seen, too, how the novel opens with allusion to the change in the rules of the « game », making reference to the substitution of the « molles balles » since the « esteufs deschurent de credit » (I, 3), and anathematizing those who perpetrate such changes: « Confus soient ces inuenteurs de nouueautez, qui gastent la jeunesse, & contre les bonnes coustumes troublent nos jeux » (I, 4).

Within the text, however, allusion is also made to various games, usually with an erotic implication. From falconery comes, for example, the use of the word *tiercelet* (I, 30, 302) for *petit,* which Paul Lacroix assures us takes on this meaning from the fact that the *tiercelet,* the male bird, was smaller than the female.[10] Also from falconery is the term *sacre,* a bird of prey: « ...i'estois esmerillonné comme vn sacre... » (I, 304).

We may find references, also, to the game *main chaude,* in our text called *frapemain* or *fausse compagnie:* « ...adonc il fit baisser le Curé, comme quand on ioüé au frapemain ou à la fausse compagnie : puis, ' Ça enfans, à l'ofrande ! ' » (II, 157). Another child's game twice appearing in *Le Moyen de Parvenir* is *gripeminaut* (I, 317; II, 249). This is a game in which the mother tickles the child and says « gripeminaut » to make the child laugh, but as it is used in Rabelais and perhaps by implication here, a certain personality is involved. Of this question Paul Lacroix writes: « Rabelais, dans son cinquième livre de *Pantagruel,* chapitre XI et XII, nous fait connaître *Grippeminaud, archiduc des chats fourrés,* c'est-à-dire, président de la Tournelle criminelle au Parlement de Paris. Ce Grippeminaud, qui fut sans doute un juge inique et vénal, avait laissé une réputation de mauvaise foi et de sottise. »[11]

10. Paul Lacroix, p. 207.
11. *Ibid.,* p. 218.

Other games referred to in *Le Moyen de Parvenir* include *le franc du quarreau (marelle)* (I, 17), *le pois en vessie* (I, 59), *la petenguele* (II, 175), *la vèze* (cornemuse) (II, 224, 225). We could cite the passages in which these games occur, but it would not substantially further our cause, for what interests us is not so much the particular game as the reference to it as a focal point, or a prism.

To conclude our discussion of theatricality and illusion in *Le Moyen de Parvenir* let us recapitulate by saying that many of the devices of the theater, especially in the handling of dialogue, are present, but that actual reference to the theater is not lacking, while alongside the major prisms brought about through time dislocation, through an erotic telescoping of almost all human institutions, through a great mixture of genres, and so forth, there are also minor prisms of a stylistic order which come from the references to eyeglasses, to the « game », and even to the dance, which I shall, however, deal with more properly in my discussion of movement and metamorphosis in *Le Moyen de Parvenir.* I might add that these prisms, which give an aura of illusion to the novel, relate to the principles of the microcosm-macrocosm, and more closely to the centrifugal-centripetal forces which I have discussed elsewhere. Let us recall in this light Béroalde's statement from *Les Cognoissances nécessaires,* « Je recherche de tout la forme intérieure ». [12]

In Buffum's category of contrast and surprise *Le Moyen de Parvenir* proves to be especially qualified. I have already pointed out that essential contrast between naturalism and other-worldliness which is to be found in the novel. Another broad contrast in the book is the division between the sexes. One of the principal stylistic devices of *Le Moyen de Parvenir* is antithesis, so that we have again in this category the broad tendency corroborated by the stylistic tendency. In other words, the antitheses in this work, as in other baroque works, « correspond to a basic exigency of the author's spirit », to quote Buffum. [13] The use of antithesis is an integral part of Béroalde's world view, and for him, as for Montaigne, paradox

12. V.-L. Saulnier, « Étude sur Béroalde de Verville », *Revue d'Humanisme et Renaissance,* V (1944), p. 253.

13. Imbrie Buffum, *Studies in the Baroque from Montaigne to Rotrou* (New Haven, 1957), p. 42.

is a way of arriving at truth.[14] Once again we cite the statement of the author that *Le Moyen de Parvenir* is « fait comme ces peinctures qui monstrent d'vn, & puis d'autre » (II, 259) to show the degree to which the use of paradox is self-conscious.

So abundant are antitheses in *Le Moyen de Parvenir* that it is difficult to choose illustrations, and I will take only a cross sampling, trying to tie them to the broad currents of the novel.

It is obvious, first of all, that antitheses are present in the tense and time shifts so common to the novel, as can be seen from the following passage containing contrasts built on *devant* and *derriere,* on *boire* and *manger,* on *excellence* and *sottise,* on *l'vn* and *l'autre,* and so forth, as well as on the tense shifts of the verb *prendre:*

> Ie suis tout esmeu d'esprit prophetique, & cognois deuant & derriere qu'ici se resoudront toutes les questions du monde; ainsi qu'il est ordinaire, que sans le boire & le manger, on prend, on a pris & prendra occasion d'enseigner cela qui est tout parfait; & comme la verité & la vanité, l'excellence & la sottise s'affrontent, l'vn & l'autre se pratiqueront en ce lieu, & on verra souuent la gloire proposer à son client l'honneur du premier lieu à la mangeoire, comme aux priuez publics on s'entrefait place honorable pour fianter, & glorieusement; & mesmes à Geneue l'assiette pour poser le fondement est aussi nette que le tranchoir sur lequel vous mangez (I, 216-217).

Another passage shows us time paradoxes in the nouns *present, passé,* and *futur,* as well as in the tense shift from *furent faits* to *seront faits* and has, in addition, antitheses in the words *hommes* and *femmes, filles* and *garçons* (and *neutres*): « Receuvez donc ce present, ce passé, ce futur, beaux & fidelles esprits, vous y trouuerez vn insigne profit, attendu que tous les liures qui furent iamais faits, ou seront faits par hommes ou femmes, filles ou garçons, ou neutres, sont signez, ou marquez, ou paraphrasez, ou predictions de cestuy-cy tant naïf, clair & euident, lequel est la fin finale & intelligible de tous... » (I, 54).

The time theme is equally manifested in the frequent antitheses between the ancient and the modern, no doubt also reflecting the quarrel between the ancients and the moderns,

14. Buffum, *ibid.*

and suggesting the Old and New Testaments. The reader is told, for example, that the dining hall was « paree, comme dit l'autre, autant à l'antique qu'à la moderne » (I, 10). In another passage an antithesis between old and new is given, as well as an explanation of the difference between *antique, ancien* and *vieux:* « Quelle antiquité ? cest ordre est tout nouveau, ie l'ay veu naistre, il n'est donc pas antique, ioint que pour estre antique il faudroit qu'il y eut mille ans, ancien deux cens, vieil plus de cent ans » (I, 189). It is, of course, to be remembered that the pointing out of differences involves contrast just as much as does an antithesis.

Again the ancients and moderns are contrasted in the following passage, in which we learn that the ancients were inferior to the moderns in their mode of dress, assumedly a facetious extollment of the codpiece:

> Ie n'ay garde d'oublier nostre grand Bodin qui premier des mortels, & contre tout ordre naturel, par artifice delectable, & grands reuers d'entendement, en plain jour, en la presence de ceux qui s'y trouuerent, prit la mesure au diable, & luy fit vn habillement, dont depuis il s'est vestu comme on le void aujourd'huy habillé; chose, & ne leur desplaise, qu'ainsi que beaucoup d'autres, les anciens ne sceurent oncques, & jamais ne sçauront, & si vous ne me croyez, allez en Enfer m'en querir vn vestu à la nouuelle mode, & me le monstrez tout vif & habillé, & puis me dementez (I, 19).

The tense shift of the verb *savoir* is drawn to the reader's attention.

It should be noted, too, that related to the contrast of the ancients and the moderns are the antitheses and anachronisms in the names of the interlocutors. This is especially well illustrated by the list of guests who go into another room to prepare a comedy in the Italian style (theatricality !): « Quelques vns de la compagnie, pour faire vne pause recreatiue, se donnerent le petit mot du guet; c'estoit la fleur des plus sages, qui firent vn complot de gayeté pour faire rire la compagnie, & allerent en vne autre chambre inuenter vne comedie à l'Italienne. Ie vous diray qui furent ceux-là, à la charge que si vous le dites, & qu'il m'en soit fait quelque reproche, que le Diable vous emportera : c'estoient Socrates, Plutarque, Rablais, Guaguin, Luther, Ronsard, Pindare, Marot

& quelques autres de mesme farine & pareil bran, & assez sages & fous pour contenter le monde » (I, 218-219).

Theological satire also comes by way of antithesis. Petronius, for example, counsels *joie de vivre* by opposing to the abstinence laws of the church an epicurean approach to life: « Ie vous veux apprendre vn autre secret que m'a enseigné Hilaret; mes amis ne mangez point de chair les iours deffendus, mais ieunez, & puis toute nuict faites bonne chere, auec de bonne chair morte & viue, les nuits ne sont point des iours, partant point deffendus. Vn Consul estoit de mesme opinion, quand durant les tresues il faisoit la guerre de nuit » (I, 138).

Here is an antithetical definition of a papist: « ...Papiste peut signifier pere de la foy ou suivant la foy paternelle... » (I, 61). On the other hand, contrast and surprise both enter into this discussion of the Council of Trent and the « Ecclesiastiques »: « Vrament ie vous escoutois, mais puis que i'y suis remis sachez s'il vous plaist, qu'apres ou aussi tost, ou enuiron le temps, ce fut quand ce fut que le Concile de Trente fut publié, ie ne dis pas celui de Monsieur le Granger, qui est intitulé le Concile de XXX. — Ie vous prie ne parlons ny en bien ny en mal des Ecclesiastiques... » (I, 110).

In the battle of the sexes, contrasts are used that bear evidence of the superiority of man (even over God!) and reveal the same suggestion of misogyny we have observed elsewhere: « Dieu fit la fille, & l'homme l'a faite femme. He bien, voila pas les hommes qui sont bien choses plus accomplies ? » (I, 164).

In that same realm we have a merging of the two sexes in the following passage: « ...& certes ceci est proprement ce qui est & n'est point, & qui s'acheue sans estre commencé, comme dit est, que l'homme & la femme ne sont qu'vn corps, parquoy vn ministre & sa femme ne sont qu'vn : Ergo vn ministre est masle & femelle. » The fusion of the sexes, which is echoed by the intentional shifting of the genders of nouns, is particularly baroque, and might easily fall into the category of metamorphosis, which I shall shortly discuss.

Commentary on war also comes by way of an antithesis which bears the stamp of the irrational: « Par mon serment, si iamais la paix est faite j'iray à la guerre aussi bien que les autres... » (I, 167).

The paradoxes of human nature are frequently expressed in *Le Moyen de Parvenir* by an antithesis between wisdom and folly. Hence, « Tu es tant sçauant en tes speculations que tu en es fou » (I, 198), and, « Vous estes si sage que vous en estes fou » (I, 208). But an even more thoroughgoing picture of the paradoxes of fortune and of human nature is contained in the following passage, which is tinged with cynicism:

> A la verité, quand ie m'en souuiens, n'est-ce pas vne grande misere pour preuue de ceste diableté, qu'il ne se trouuera homme, tant venteur de la pieté soit il, qui vueille acheter vn estat de secret rechercheur des actions humaines pour auertir les autres, à ce qu'ils soient garentis du danger, affin qu'ils se destournent de leurs mauuaises voyes, & que s'ils sont enclins à mal faire, ils s'en corrigent dés le commencement ou s'en abstiennent à l'aduenir de peur qu'ils ne tombent en peril; plustost la plus grand part des hommes sont comme chats guettans les souris, & le plus homme de bien en apparence, sera en perpetuelle sentinelle pour espier si quelqu'vn bronche; non pour l'aduertir & bien & charitablement ,ains pour le ruïner. Et pour faire preuue de plus d'impieté preuostable, on contrainct iniquement les autres, & incite à dire s'ils sçauvent quelque mauuais deportement de leur prochain, afin que l'on l'accable, pour s'engraisser à ses despens, s'il a moyen de payer les ouuriers. Ainsi plusieurs sont riches du malheur des autres, desquels iamais la faute n'est cachee ou diminuee ou destournee, ains multipliee abondamment. Or nous ne sommes plus au temps qu'on estoit sauué par sa faute, ie pense que les bonnes gens qui gemissent sous la tirannie des gros, seront esmeus par charité à bien estimer, & verront en nos discours comme nous decouurons le tombeau de la verité (I, 153-154).

The theme of death is couched in a life-death antithesis which belongs in the domain of the irrational or nonsensical: « Cela me fait souuenir de la fortune de frere Ian de Laillee nostre amy defunct; il sera possible tanstost icy » (I, 247).

This comment on the part of the interlocutor Petronius leads us to another role which antithesis plays in *Le Moyen de Parvenir*. We have noticed already to what an extent efforts towards naturalistic dialogue and the semblance of truth are present in the tales of the interlocutors. It is pertinent to point out here that antithesis is also part and parcel of the comic effects and procedures of their dialogue. Thus we find one of them using such an adverb as « amérodoucement » (I, 69), another describing the intellects of the *beaux esprits* as being « pleins de concupiscences celestes » (I, 226), another fortifying his description with an antithetical analogy: « ...il estoit si engressé que la gresse luy sortoit par les yeux comme les puces sautent dans vn four qui sue de froid » (I, 241).

Comic effects are produced by the interlocutors' use of false antithesis, such as the following, in which the words *minimes* and *maxime* are only etymologically opposed: « He pauures Medecins qui cherchez des causes estrangeres és minimes, que ie vous plains, sçachez ceste maxime, c'est pource que l'on n'en peut auoir sans vent » (I, 188).

A favorite device of the interlocutors is to elaborate upon the *difference* between one thing or another. Thus the listeners are told the difference between *seruantes* & *chambrieres:* « ...notate verba : seruantes sont celles qui seruent chez les gens de bien, dautant qu'à ce qu'elles disent chambrieres sont celles qui demeurent auec les Prestres ou Chanoines pour suruenir à toutes leurs necessitez » (I, 40-41). Similarly, the difference between *le petit volume* and *le gros volume* is presented: « Verre & volume sont equiuoques, le verre est vn volume, il est vray que c'est le petit, c'est l'epitome, d'autant que le gros volume est le poinçon bien-heureux : qui ont belles & amples bibliotheques remplies de tels volumes, ils sont capables de rendre victus tout le monde tant docte soit-il » (I, 44).

The interlocutor who knows the art of engaging his listener's attention has recourse to an antithetical riddle or puzzle. This formula is frequently found in *Le Moyen de Parvenir.* Thus Erasme queries, « ...quel est l'outil de mesnage que iamais on ne prette ny emprunte, & si il n'y a guere de maisons où il n'y en ait ? » (I, 146). And in like manner Sapho asks, « Quelle difference y a-t-il entre vostre nez & le cul du chien ? » (I, 206). The interlocutor l'Autre likewise says, « Ie suis bien aise que vous estes venus sur ces differences; dictes vn peu quelle difference il y a d'vne femme à vn Prestre, ce sont gens de robe longue ? » (II, 103).

Finally, no discussion of the use of contrast in *Le Moyen de Parvenir* would be complete if one did not quote the following passage, in which the contrasting means of « arriving » are recorded: « Ce fut vn moyen de paruenir. Voila, il y en a qui paruiennent diuersement, les vns sans y penser, les autres par artifice, aucuns par danger, quelques vns rencontrans d'vn cherchant d'autre, aucuns courans comme ils attrapent, quelques autres en despit d'eux, & s'en faut raporter aux exemples, ainsi qu'vne truye qui auorte » (I, 168).

Unexpected turns of thought, then, are largely produced by antithesis in *Le Moyen de Parvenir,* antithesis being the preferred device of the baroque artist, since it produces surprise, as Buffum explains.[15] On the other hand, the principal source of simultaneous shock and amusement, or the chief source of surprise in *Le Moyen de Parvenir* is the crude vocabulary coupled with the prolific amount of eroticism, always expressed by verbal play and unexpected turns of thought. Quoting of an example would, in fact, be superfluous; these traits are present on every page of the novel, almost in every paragraph, in every line. Still, I am inclined to say, as Buffum has said of Montaigne, though possibly with more cause, that it is not just *polissonnerie,* but, rather, that « the basic idea is that all human beings, however exalted, distinguished or refined, are alike subject to physical contingencies ».[16] Such an idea is not, in the final analysis, very far removed from the theme of the Dance of Death which, at least in part, underlies *Le Moyen de Parvenir.*

In the next category, movement and metamorphosis, we again find sufficient evidence to justify our calling *Le Moyen de Parvenir* baroque. The over three hundred guests, plus all the persons of whom they speak, give us the crowded canvas of a baroque painter, teeming and swarming with life. Awareness of movement and of change is explicit, through the abundant use of verbs, through references to the dance and other types of motion, and through transformations of various sorts, including true metamorphosis.

Le Moyen de Parvenir is not a static work. Far from it. All is in constant motion, in eruption and agitation. Frequently we have the impression of chaotic activity on the part of the interlocutors and in the stories they tell. We need only quote once again the list of activities of the members of our symposium to see that action, translated directly into verbs, is frantic and somewhat chaotic, even though, as we have seen, there is some stratification in the list:

> Et que faisoient tant de bonnes gens de loisir ? voire, mais que fit-on là ? On parla, on mangea, on beut, on fit st,

15. Imbrie Buffum, p. 43.
16. *Ibid.*

> on se teut, on fit du bruit, on protesta, on rencontra, on rit, on baailla, on entendit, on disputa, on cracha, on moucha, on s'estonna, on s'esbahit, on admira, on gaussa, on raporta, on entendit, on broüilla, on s'esclaircit, on debattit, on s'accorda, on trinca l'vn à l'autre, on fit carroux, on remarqua, on tremoussa, on s'accouda, on cria tout bas, on se teut tout haut, on se mocqua, on murmura, on s'auisa, on se reprit, on se contenta, on passa le temps, on douta, on redouta, on s'assagit, on deuint, on paruint (I, 43).

It will be noticed that the activities are of both a physical and a mental order and, incidentally, are sometimes arranged antithetically.

Of course, the sexual act itself, so vividly described on page after page, gives to the novel a special kind of motion, as can be seen in the following passage, in which verbs showing motion and activity are in the ascendancy:

> La pauure fille qui ne sçauoit où la prendre [her mother, who has just sent her to look for her lost sheep], s'en alla pleurant & se mit sous vn arbre; ainsi qu'elle musoit trop, sa mere dit au valet, « Iean va t'en querir ceste fille va ». Il y alla & la trouua, luy dit : « Michelle reuiens à la maison, ta mere le dit. — Non feray. — Vien vien aga. — Non feray, ie n'iray pas quand tu me deurois tuer. — Si tu ne viens ie te tueray. — Ie ne m'en soucie pas. » Adonc il la prent, la renuerse sur l'eschine, luy escarquille les iambes, se iette sur elle, & luy fiche au bas du ventre son cousteau naturel, & la tue de la douce mort. « Or ça, dit-il, ie le disois bien, o vien à ceste heure. — Non feray. — Et vien Michelle vien. — Tuc moy donc encores vn coup » (I, 88).

Coupled with this sexual debauchery, we have the spinning effects of the banquet's festivity, the general bustle of eating, drinking, story-telling, etc. The pages virtually dance, and indeed we have references to the dance, properly speaking, sometimes fused with the sexual act, as in the ending of a tale recounted by Donat:

> Il luy dit tout bas & elle l'entendit bien clair, pource qu'elle auoit enuie de dancer : parquoy elle le creut & le suiuit, il la poussa contre vn coffre, & luy enseigna la dance du

> loup la queuë entre les iambes, & luy recousit son honneur de la sorte qu'on attache le chose aux nouuelles mariees, & l'asseura que iamais son honneur ne tomberoit par cette fante là. Quand ce fut fait, elle vint dancer, & n'y auoit que pour elle estant affriandee : elle trouua quelque chose à dire à la cousture, parquoy elle en demanda encore, si qu'elle en eut iusques à trois fois, c'estoit assez (I, 135-136).

At another point Xilander says to Cassiodore, « Vrament vous estes un beau danceur » (I, 231); and reference to a dance called the *volte* gives the following passage, also containing aphorism and antithesis, the same *double-entendre* and the same agitated character seen in the passages above:

> — Boiuez vous des coups ?
> — Ouy, d'autant que cela, c'est à dire boire, va à coup & se serre delicieusement : ie diray vne volte si vous voulez; aussi ie la boy mieux que ie ne la dance, & les audaces fortuna iuuat, cela veut dire que qui chapon mange, chapons lui viennent. Ceux qui sont vn peu malades, & se renforcent à boire & à manger guarissent; aussi l'on ne meurt que de faute de boire & manger, & bref de s'abstenir de faire les vertus Cardinales (II, 120).

The story of La Belle Marciole, too long to quote here, is so full of movement that it gives the illusion of a dance, with its minute description of the motions the young maiden goes through to pick up the scattered cherries while the old men watch on, delirious in their voyeurism (I, 27-32). It is one of the best examples of a story set spinning in *Le Moyen de Parvenir*.

Even the two references to the Dance of Death found in *Le Moyen de Parvenir* belong in a discussion of its animated character. The frenzy of these dances is well known, and their presence in the novel seems to give an additional breathlessness. The underlying comment appears to be that there is as much agitation in dying as there is in living. We shall see shortly, too, that death plays a role in the metamorphic aspects of the book, as well as in its movement.

But what is more remarkable is that even the mental states of the people take on this swarming effect. Alain Chartier tells a story about his cousin in which her mental processes « peripatetize » (a verb very suited to describe the mental processes of all the people in *Le Moyen de Parvenir,* interlocutors and their subjects alike); she is « melancolifiee » (an adjective strongly reminiscent of a verb) to such an extent that she must *draw back* when *approached.* In this passage all is in a state of movement and change:

> Ma pauure cousine ayant veu cet inconuenient se signa fort deuotieusement & deuint toute troublee de son sautier, son entendement peripatetisa tout du long, de la culmination de son intelligence curialle; si que depuis elle fut si melancolifiee, que c'estoit vne deplorable imaginoison que la sienne : si les autres s'approchoient d'elle, elle par vne humeur saupoudree de tristification s'en reculoit : à la fin elles l'araisonnerent du dedans, qu'elle auoit au flus & reflus de conflit compagnable; & elle leur fit responce, qu'elle n'estoit pas digne de conuerser meritoirement parmi l'honorifique bande de leur societé doucette (II, 8-9).

Accompanying the copious motion to be found in *Le Moyen de Parvenir* is a strong awareness of change, transformation and metamorphosis. The reader is reminded of the second sentence of the novel, in which the narrator expresses irritation over the change made in the rules of the game, an accusation charged with reference to the protestant religion: « Confus soient ces inuenteurs de nouueautez, qui gastent la jeunesse, & contre les bonnes coustumes troublent nos jeux » (I, 4). Customs are diametrically opposed to these novelties, being something entrenched and unchanging, and the changes that have been introduced result in agitation; they « troublent nos jeux ».

However, there is another kind of transformation that comes about gradually and seemingly without this agitation. Its genesis is described in detail in *Le Moyen de Parvenir.* This is the metamorphosis of a man into a special kind of bird, a cuckold. With or without « movement » the process is accomplished, until the man is thoroughly changed:

> Or pour estre coquu il en faut estre capable, & pour cet effect il faut auoir vne femme espousee, & ne faut pas seulement auoir esgard à la mine, ou encolure mistique qu'vn homme en peut auoir, à cause de l'influence sous laquelle il est né, selon son idee naturelle & predestinee : mais il faut considerer le vouloir & pouuoir des parties interuenantes en ceste metamorphose, qui agit exactement autant de loin que de pres; il n'y a rien en tout de semblable,

> & disent les alchemistes ce qu'ils voudront de leur poudre de proiection, ou cendre à faire des muances : cela n'est rien au prix, dautant qu'il faut qu'il y ait de la presence, ce qui est le contraire en ceci. Celui qui aura fait le fou tout le long des iours gras, n'assagira pas le Mercredi par la cendre, si elle ne lui est posee en propre personne presente, & tel sera ioyeusement coquu quand il seroit à l'autre bout de la terre, & ce en vn instant, ceste forme court plus viste que l'esclair. On dit, selon le conte des bonnes femmes, que les tortues couuent leurs œufs auec les yeux; aussi sont tous animaux, parce qu'ils ne les laissent pas, si de fortune ils ne les ont perdus, comme la borgne, à laquelle nous sauonnames tant les fauxbourgs du derriere l'annee passee. Et bien, les œufs des tortues ausquels elles ne touchent point escloent à la fin, & il se fait vne mutation formelle, comme il conuient és transformations naturelles, si elles ne sont chymicomentales. Ces changemens se voyent en ce qui est commun, mais en ces oiseaux rien n'i paroit de changé, ni en la forme, ni és accidens, ni en la naturelle, ni en espece intrinseque, és formes qui se reçoiuent sans mutation de substance; encor y a-t'il du mouuement au sujet de muance : mais en cestui-ci, soit qu'il s'esmeuue, ou ne se meuue point, & quelque absent qu'il soit, il est penetré, transpercé, outrepercé, surpris, enduit, enueloppé, & tellement organisé en specifique & disposee formation, que subitement, subtilement, tout d'vn coup, voila vn homme coquu, comme il sera demonstré tantost (I, 267-268).

Sexual metamorphosis is a typically baroque characteristic, and it is to be found in *Le Moyen de Parvenir* under several guises. One of the devices of Béroalde is to shift the gender of nouns for certain effects; thus, in reference to Christ in one place we find « ...dautant que son fils represente sa personne... » (I, 65), while in another place we find « A a bien, ie vous diray : sa fils represente son personne » (II, 255). Similarly, the gender of a noun is discussed and an explanation reached as follows, « Mais pourquoy le con d'vne femme est il masle ? Omne viro soli quod conuenit esto virile... » (I, 141).

The sexual act is frequently described as a type of sexual metamorphosis, in which the two persons become one. Thus, « ...comme dit est que l'homme & la femme ne sont qu'vn corps, parquoy vn ministre & sa femme ne sont qu'vn : Ergo vn ministre est masle & femelle » (I, 270). In this connection, the quadruped and the androgyne are evoked. In the following passage, for example, the two sexes are pictured as undergoing various sexual transformations:

> Le spectacle d'immortalité, les effects de concupiscence, le progrez de generation, quatre iambons pendus à vne cheuille, deux animaux encruchez & sousleuez, faisant le quadrupede raisonnable, la beste à double ventre ou à deux testes, l'animal à quatre yeux, l'homme-femelle, la femelle-masle, le protype de l'engeance anagogique, vne femme en proche disposition d'estre chastree, vn homme prest d'estre decoché (I, 313).

In another place an allusion is made to both the quadrupede and the androgyne specifically: « Quadrupes facit pauperiem. Venez vn peu icy, hé coüiluacier de Papinian : l'animal à quatre pieds fait la pauureté, c'est que faisant la pauureté on a quatre pieds, on pratique le doux Androgine, on fait la beste à deux dos, on fait le destin d'homme à femme, c'est faire la cause pourquoi, c'est exercer les bons membres, c'est estre bonne personne, parce que nul n'est bon, & n'y a bonne personne que celle qui se faisant du bien en fait à vne autre : il y a, Fac bene, & bene tibi erit » (I, 62-63). The amusing use of the Latin « proverb » attributed to Plautus and repeated on the following page is noteworthy.

We are not, in fact, wanting for the story of the creation of the androgyne, so that our symposium is complete with the proper Platonic appointments. This is the story as it is told by Sapho: « C'est vn descousture au bas du corps; ce qui auint quand Iupiter eut coupé l'Androgine : il commanda à Mercure de recoudre le ventre à l'vn & à l'autre; cela est cause que le ventre est si delicat. Il cousit l'homme auec vn lacet trop long, tellement qu'à la fin de la cousture il en resta vn bout; & cousant la femme, il prit le lacet trop court, si qu'il y en eut faute, & il y demeura vne fente, faute de points » (I, 205).

In *Le Moyen de Parvenir* death itself sometimes has the quality of a transformation, so much so that « to die » is in one place rendered by the expression « changer d'air »: « Voila comme la pauure Laurence a changé d'air, & auoit à sa mort vne merueille notable, vne chose esmerueilleuse : C'est que son ame sortit de son corps par l'endroit proportionnel & semblable à celuy par lequel toutes les autres ames s'en vont » (I, 67).

The soul of a sergeant, on the other hand, « va droit entre les mains de Proserpine Reine d'Enfer » (II, 213).

In our novel, however, there is one marked omission of change in relation to death. Contrary to our expectations, the interlocutors, who are apparently dead, nevertheless are engaged in all the activities of the living. Thus we find Petronius saying: « Cela me fait souuenir de la fortune de frere Ian de Laillee nostre amy defunct; il sera possible tantost icy » (I, 247). The omission of this expected change belongs to the irrational side of the novel and is, of course, meant to surprise us.

In short, the whole of *Le Moyen de Parvenir* is a study in movement and metamorphosis of every kind and description, and it should by no means be forgotten that in the very title of the novel transformation is implied, even though we are never absolutely certain what the end result is to be. And these devices again show the baroque outlook of Béroalde, the sweeping view, the chaotic activity of the crowded banquet room, and, by extension, of life, the everchanging, ever-fusing, ever-mutable, which does not seem to cease, even after death.

We must now explore *Le Moyen de Parvenir* for evidence of organic unity and acceptance of life, the final category designated by Buffum. There is no question that the novel, despite its chaotic and eruptive nature, has a central unity, and even stylistic ones. Further, it has thematic unity, for in several ways it suggests the acceptance of life.

Unity, which Hatzfeld, like Buffum, insists is present in baroque art[17], can be found in *Le Moyen de Parvenir* first of all stylistically in the use of what in Chapter V have been called ligatures, or sentences at the end of a chapter which are bound to the opening sentences of the next chapter. An example of this jointing effect occurs between the chapters entitled « Canon » and « Théorème ». The chapter entitled « Canon » ends with Margot's saying « Demandez le à monsieur Robin qui a esté à Lubec; pour l'amour de ce qu'il m'en a dit, ie voudrois faire de mesme », whereupon the other interlocutors participating in this dialogue exclaim, « Nous vous le demandons, monsieur. Nous ne luy auons pas fait dire ». Robin obligingly responds, « Escoutez donc ma ratelee » (I, 279). The next chapter, « Théorème », begins with Robin's saying, « Lubec est

17. Hatzfeld, p. 123. « Now, despite all the baroque *fregi, decoros,* and *ornements,* the fusion of the elements into a unity becomes the supreme law. »

une ville fort bien policee, & ou il n'y a point de pauures... » (I, 280), seemingly a utopian state, were it not for the reasons thereafter given for the lack of poor people in Lubec.

Another example of ligature can be found between the chapters entitled « Original » and « Sentence ». The former ends with Baronius' pronouncement that « Ordinairement ceux qui mesdisent de Prestres ou de Ministres, en ont esté, & ce qu'ils en disent de mal, est pour faire croire qu'ils en sont esloignez; comme putains qui s'exercent loin du bordeau » (II, 189). The first sentence of the next chapter is: « Mais à propos de putains, il faut que ie vous fasse vn conte de ma femme qui estoit vn peu putain : elle n'estoit pas de ces enormes putains qui en font mestier, mais de ces femmes de bien qui ont vn ami d'honneur » (II, 190).

Many examples of this device could be cited, but the above two along with those quoted in Chapter V will serve adequately as illustrations. Of course, more of a case for the ligatures in the novel could be made, were it not for the fact that, as we have already noted, the chapter titles of *Le Moyen de Parvenir* are with respect to the chapter they accompany not only in and of themselves arbitrary, but they are more or less arbitrarily dispersed. But the ligatures are reinforced by the fact that the chapter title itself generally has some bearing on the preceding chapter. Of this phenomenon Paul Lacroix says in a footnote to the title of the second chapter, « Poinct », « Nous remarquerons ici, une fois pour toutes, que le titre de chaque chapitre a toujours plus ou moins rapport à la fin du chapitre précédent et renferme quelque jeu de mots, ou bien une équivoque, etc., qu'il est plus facile d'entendre que d'expliquer ». [18]

But aside from this stylistic unity, and aside from the unifying force that comes from the recurrent vocabulary and the recurrent themes, such as time, mutability, death, the paradoxes of the ancients and moderns, etc., there is a unity which comes out of the concept of laughter and the general acceptance of life found in *Le Moyen de Parvenir*. The role of laughter, the place of comedy in the novel is all important. We have seen how the actual laughter of the interlocutors is stylistically represented all through the dialogues. Let us observe, too, that at the times when the theater is mentioned, it is usually the farce or some form of comedy. For example,

18. Paul Lacroix, p. 3.

Alais, it will be remembered, was an author of and actor in « moralités, farces et sotties », and the *confrérie* of the Pois Pilez performed farces. It is worthwhile to recall, too, that a group of the guests go out of the banquet hall at one point to prepare a comedy, *à l'Italienne,* and that the unique purpose of this undertaking is « pour faire rire la compagnie » (I, 218). Similarly, Pausanius, in recounting a tale, says, « Ie pense que ce iour-là estoit fait pour rire » (I, 23). Indeed, one might well conclude that *Le Moyen de Parvenir,* one of whose chapter titles is « Risée », another « Satyre », and still another « Fantaisie », preaches the value of laughter, of a good-humored acceptance of life, which is hardly pictured here as being ideal. To this end, the proverb of Solomon is cited: « Le Sage dit qu'il y a temps de rire & temps de pleurer » (I, 53), and the therapeutic values of laughter are lauded by our mysterious Bonhomme who says, « ...rire c'est ce qui contente le plus, & qui couste le moins; s'il en estoit ainsi de boire, le bon vin ne cousteroit gueres » (I, 140).

We might at first be tempted to think that an Epicurean, even libertine approach to life is advocated on these pages, but when we note that our « sages » are in reality and to a man « fous » engaged in a never-ending tower of Babel in which egomania prevails, and no one interlocutor bears much respect for any other, so anxious is he to get on with his own drinking, his own eating, his own story-telling, we are instead tempted to conclude that the grotesque exaggerations constitute a sort of inverse criticism of this manner of conduct. We cannot know to what extent we have a realistic portrayal of manners here, but everything leads us to a belief that the portrait is certainly highly charged. Yet laughter prevails in all corners of the book. And does not this doctrine of laughter explain, too, the frequent reference to game, the constant punning, the other kinds of verbal play, the sexual imbroglios, the sport made of the clergy, the various forms of satire, in short, the entire form and content of *Le Moyen de Parvenir?* I think it does, and in the end we cannot help but say resignedly of our author, just as he himself suggests, « Il est bon homme, il taxe les vices d'vne belle façon... » (II, 260).

Thus it is that the principal categories of the baroque as set forth by Buffum — comments on style by the author himself, emphasis and exaggeration, horror and incarnation (for which we have substituted the related categories, the grotesque and realism), theatricality and illusion, contrast and surprise, movement and metamorphosis, and organic unity and the acceptance of life — are highly applicable both to the style and to the general world view of *Le Moyen de Parvenir*. As it has been the chief interest of this chapter to concentrate on the style, one or two comments of a general nature remain to be made on that subject.

In questioning the authorship of *Le Moyen de Parvenir*, which I have dealt with in Chapter I, critics have sometimes argued that since *Le Moyen de Parvenir* bears little stylistic resemblance to the other works of Béroalde there is reason not to attribute it to him. In Chapter I, I attempted to point out parallels in the world view between *Le Moyen de Parvenir* and the known works of Béroalde. But to the question of style, I can do no better than to echo Saulnier when he writes, « Béroalde n'est pas l'homme d'un style... » and even more pointedly, « Qui change de genre change de style ».[19]

Be that as it may, *Le Moyen de Parvenir* is a masterpiece in baroque style, and as I have tried to point out from time to time, goes beyond the baroque into a domain I have called *baroque satyrique* (grotesque, erotic) and even *baroque satirique*, perhaps a separate genre which has not as yet been adequately studied. I do not know that I would go so far as Reiche, but it is surely of interest to note that for him the burden of the novel's greatness rests in its style. He says, « Auch unser betrachtetes Werk ist vor allem durch seine sprachliche Form und durch seinen Stil verdienstlich. Erst dem grossen Jahrhundert sollten dann reine, grosse, klassiche Werke voller Ordnung und Selbst-zucht gelingen ».[20] And as we know, it is this very Classical period which in large measure eclipsed the baroque masterpieces of the age which preceded it, works which today are diligently being recovered. Among them, both for its style and for its content, let us rank *Le Moyen de Parvenir*.

19. Saulnier, p. 288.
20. Reiche, p. 69.

CONCLUSION

To recapitulate, the world view of Béroalde de Verville as it is reflected in *Le Moyen de Parvenir* can be arrived at from a number of approaches. First of all, it can be glimpsed in other works known to be Béroalde's. It can to some extent be inferred from a historical and critical examination of the title page. Both of these approaches will, furthermore, assist us in establishing Béroalde as the author of *Le Moyen de Parvenir,* about whose authorship there has been some doubt. In addition, by a careful analysis of the title's meaning, leaning on passages from the text, we gain still further knowledge of Béroalde's world view, while an examination of the first and last chapters of the book supports, deepens and augments this knowledge. Considerations on the chapter titles serve to supplement these insights and to introduce us to reflections on the style, which, in turn, reconfirm our impressions of the book's *Weltanschauung.*

As world view is the thing under inspection, it is of great interest to note that clues of the authorship of *Le Moyen de Parvenir* can be found in the world view held in works known to be Béroalde's. Not only can one find in the known works reflections of the elements of the title and title page of *Le Moyen de Parvenir,* not only can one see in other works that Béroalde is indeed a *raconteur,* but what is more important, one can find in other works, for example in the *Dialogue de la Vertu* and in the *Cabinet de Minerve* the urbanity and wittiness which characterize *Le Moyen de Parvenir.* Even more striking is the raciness to be detected in other works, especially in three poems at the end of the *Soupirs amoureux,* « Le Pallemail », « Le May », and « L'Alchémiste ». This raciness is at the very core of *Le Moyen de Parvenir.* In addition, these three poems, especially the last, show Béroalde's preoccupation with alchemy and the play on images, language and substance which are ubiquitous in *Le Moyen de Parvenir.* Thus there is not so immense a discrepancy between the world view reflected in Béroalde's known works and that of *Le Moyen de Parvenir* as might on the surface be suspected.

Now, further examination of the mere titles of other works, giving hints at the title of *Le Moyen de Parvenir,* leads to additional conjectures about the authorship, while different titles under which the work has appeared give insights into the character of the book. However, and more importantly, if we analyze in detail the title and the title page as they are given to us in the Royer edition, and especially if we set the elements of this page over and against certain internal passages of *Le Moyen de Parvenir,* we find that much of Béroalde's world view is already present on the title page, before the novel even begins. For example, clues as to the meaning of the word « Vertu » are given in the quotation from the *Æneid.* Furthermore, this quotation announces the time motifs — baroque in nature — of *Le Moyen de Parvenir,* and, to some extent, its eroticism. Indeed the quotation « Hac iter est », echoes the title and thus shows the kind of elaborate piling we are to find everywhere in the novel. Likewise, the presence of the phrase « Dictionnaire à dormir en toutes langues » evokes the polyglot editions of the time and so suggests the Bible. Thus, we again have an echo of the title, and, more significantly, we begin to surmise that our book is a « moral » handbook of some kind. Consequently, the religious intent of the satire begins to show itself. The use of the phrase « dictionnaire à dormir » will also be seen to foreshadow the hermetic qualities of *Le Moyen de Parvenir.* Finally, in respect to the title page, although theories on the meaning of the letter « S. » are not conclusive, speculations on « Œuure contenant la raison de tout ce qui a esté, est, & sera » are fruitful; for we may conclude that the baroque themes of time and mutability are here announced, and that these words, along with the phrase « ab A, ad Z. » reinforce our impression that religious satire is present. In short, parody of religious and erudite formulae is clearly at hand.

Furthermore, insight into Béroalde's intentions and into his world view can be gained by a thorough-going analysis of the title, and one can, moreover, arrive at the probable meaning of the title by bringing to bear passages in the novel in which the title is evoked in one way or another. From such an analysis we may conclude that *Le Moyen de Parvenir* is a « moral » handbook of sorts which will lead one to the « perfection » of *bienséance,* but is, by the author's own admission, ambiguous and chaotically composed, as well as hermetic. Thus we are informed of the baroque character of the composition. But we may also conclude from such an examination of the meaning of the title that, in fact, *Le Moyen de Parvenir* at many points claims to be a breviary or religious tome containing « saincts memoires » and « precieuses reliques », and, furthermore, is said to be « le Livre » or the Bible. We may further observe that the time motif introduced in the tense shifts of the subtitle recur throughout the book, and that *Le Moyen de Parvenir* contains many secrets or deep mysteries which the reader is invited to guard, once he has penetrated their meaning. We may gather, too, that Béroalde claims Biblical status for *Le Moyen de Parvenir* in saying « CE LIVRE EST LE CENTRE DE TOVS LES LIVRES ». We can also observe that the phrase « Le moyen de parvenir » repeatedly occurs in the novel and is related to the time themes. This phrase, explained in not very lucid terms by the interlocutor Paracelsus, at certain points in the work appears to mean the way to attain paradise. Under these circumstances, the very title must be construed as one of the most far-reaching ironies of the novel.

Now although *Le Moyen de Parvenir* is obviously burlesque and satirical, one may, after all, argue without too much difficulty the serious substructure, the profound side of a piece of comic or nonsense literature. Analogies can be found, for example, in the medieval *fatrasie* and *fatras*. Thus, the idea that a serious consideration of death and the afterworld lies at the bottom of *Le Moyen de Parvenir* is not unreasonable. Moreover, the very treatment of death in *Le Moyen de Parvenir* bears out the idea that other-worldly considerations are at stake. We see, in fact, that death is sometimes treated in a grotesque and macabre fashion, sometimes with burlesque obscenity, that it is sometimes presented in violent and shocking terms, and that it is even perhaps personified in one of the interlocutors. But, above all, we find that references to death are almost ever-present and ever on the increase. Hence, analysis of the title's meaning in relation to various texts permits us to conclude that time, mutability and death, together with profound religious satire — factors we are able to collect in abundance from the first and last chapters of the novel — are major motifs in *Le Moyen de Parvenir*.

A thorough study of the opening quatrain and of the first

and the last chapters of *Le Moyen de Parvenir* only further strengthens these conclusions. We find that the opening quatrain, which sets the tone of the novel, suggests also a peculiar time setting, and, in fact, states the themes of time and death which recur throughout the book. Turning to the first chapter, we at once notice in the first sentence that the book is held in suspense by the opening conjunction *car,* a resultant conjunction having temporal implications. By its use, the book begins, so to speak, in mid-stream, and considerable dramatic and psychological effects are thereby gained. In the opening sentence we also have, significantly enough, as the very first noun of the novel the word *temps,* followed by a series of terms having to do with time, most of them reflecting religious calendars, so that theological reference is immediately introduced. We can see from these terms, however, that the forms of religion evoked are varied and evidently arbitrary.

At the beginning of the second sentence the theme of mutability is introduced, for the narrator here expresses hostility toward change and comments on the evils brought about by change. In this sentence, as in the next few sentences, we detect, too, a burlesque of Renaissance style and possible satire of baroque traits such as overstatement, exaggeration, obsession with time, and obscurity. A baroque current, as such, though, can be seen in the desire to mystify and to advance manifold themes of time and mutability.

Not only are themes of time and mutability readily apparent in the first several sentences of *Le Moyen de Parvenir,* but very early the juxtaposition of the ancients and moderns and the antithesis of « les sots » and « les sages » can be detected. Besides, in these early sentences we learn that the gathering of these men is of an obligatory nature, a fact that has not previously been adequately insisted upon. This, too, enlists religious as well as political satire.

Furthermore, early in the book we are made aware that the speech of the narrator is sub-standard. He is, then, disengaged, not a part of the group, and is, perhaps, a type of *pícaro;* he appears to hold learning in scorn; and, indeed, satire of precious manners, court manners, of protocol and ostentation is soon on the horizon. Now, the narrator, by virtue of his status as a picaresque type, would have a natural outlook; he would be critical of affectation and false etiquette. A careful examination of the narrator's attitude and vocabulary shows us that behind such a word as *révérence,* which has great multiplicity, lies a criticism not only of high society, but probably of religious ceremony, the protocol of the papal court, whose hypocrisy is apparently under attack.

As for the final chapter, we find here that the sophisticated and ingenious time dislocations of the opening quatrain and of the first chapter are sustained. In addition, we discover that the title of this chapter, « Argument », shows the same irrationalism hinted at in the title. The « thesis » of the book is, in other words, placed at the end of the book. Thus, we find that the conclusion of the novel is placed at the beginning, while the beginning is at the end.

Moreover, the final chapter can be divided into two sections, one still carrying out the dialogues (« the dialogue continuum »), and the other recovering the frame (« the coda »). But both of these sections explore the themes of time dislocation and death. In the « continuum » Justinian seems to represent the folly of mankind held in the grasp of inefficient government. Thus, he represents an amalgamation of most of the facets of society under attack in *Le Moyen de Parvenir.* The corruption of religion and government is especially underlined as both come together under the temporal power of the madman Justinian. Further, Justinian is a religious figure, in that he was responsible for the construction of the Santa Sophia, and for calling together the Council of Chalcedon. Hence, doubly involved are church and state, which were, it must be remembered, not easily distinguished in the Renaissance. In the « continuum » the death of the father, too, is the result of bad government, and incorporates themes of voyage, of departure and return which reflect the picaresque and baroque traits of *Le Moyen de Parvenir,* while the lover from the Dance of Death symbolizes all persons who participate in the dance, restates the death motifs of the novel and announces the terminal quatrain in which bribery is at stake.

The « coda » of the final chapter transfers us from the specifics of Justinian, the father, and the young man of the Dance of Death to generalizations in which the themes of folly and death are retained. The « author » expresses his fear that he will be called a necromancer because he has caused the dead to speak. More than this, he has caused the « bestes » to speak, and we can detect in this statement a pun which may well explain the presence in *Le Moyen de Parvenir* of the interlocutors

Pacolet and Statius. Moreover, this pun may be seen to contain additional theological satire.

In the final stages of the « coda » we are called to reflections on folly. Folly — the folly of Justinian or another — is, it seems, synonymous with egomania, the celebration of the ego; and the boast of the hermetic character of the book which we find toward the end of *Le Moyen de Parvenir* is one form of egomania. Only the egocentric can indulge in such a game of *cache-cache* with the reader. Lucidity invites the reader to participate, while obscurity defies the reader, excludes him, is self-centered. This, then, is the nature of our « author », who is not, by the way, to be equated with Béroalde himself. On the other hand, our « author » suggests that dissensions will arise over the varying interpretations of the book, each considered to be valid because of the egomania of each respective reader. Still another kind of folly found in the « coda » is name-calling, for the « author » sets a curse upon those who happen to be « dicteurs des folies d'autruy ».

Thus, the first chapter of *Le Moyen de Parvenir* presents themes of time, mutability and death, advances the antithesis between the ancients and the moderns, and foreshadows the religious satire which will be the *leitmotif* of the novel, while the final chapter, divided into « continuum » and « coda », restates themes of death, especially in connection with the corruption of religion and government, and portrays folly as a generalized human trait. If we are to conclude that the group of theologians, philosophers and « sages » gathered at the banquet of Dame Sagesse are not what we usually think them to be, we must, even so, be on our guard lest we assume we have any advantage over them.

While the title, the title page and the first and last chapters of *Le Moyen de Parvenir* afford major insights into the purposes and the world view of its author, a study of the chapter titles gives us miniature statements of the same things, and leads us, furthermore, to reflections on the book's style. From such a study we may conclude that the chapter titles reveal satirical intentions against political, theological and philosophical institutions and procedures, that they underscore themes of time, mutability and death, and that while they serve as ornament, it is ornament which is organically related to the motifs of the novel. This, of course, is a principle of baroque art.

The chapter titles, stylistically considered, serve as ligatures.

In other words, the linking of one chapter to another by seemingly arbitrary chapter titles provides a continuance from chapter to chapter which is analogous to the placing of the book's beginning at the end, to the presence of anachronism and to the time dislocations observable throughout the text. The reversal of the beginning and ending of the novel is, in fact, accomplished in part by placing toward the beginning of the book such chapter titles as « Pause derniere » and « Conclusion », while setting at the very end the chapter title « Argument ».

There is, too, a relationship between the chapter titles and the interlocutors, for these titles echo the vain formulae these « savants » indulge in and operate by. Indeed, the pedantic nature of these titles reflects the titles of the works of these theologians and assorted scholars.

Furthermore, simple ironies and antitheses of the kind which characterize *Le Moyen de Parvenir's* style are arrived at by these chapter titles. In a manner of speaking, they say « little » what elsewhere is said « big ».

But, above all, the main currents of the novel are announced in the chapter titles, so much so that a title, subtitle and title page for the novel could be made up from them which would not be a parody, but would really state the contents of the book. The themes spelt out by the chapter titles are the compulsory attendance at the banquet, the apparently religious nature of the banquet, the satire of *préciosité* and pedantry, the various « secret » writings of dissenting professional groups, the ubiquitous motifs of time, mutability and even death.

Then, too, bringing internal evidence to bear, we find that many of these chapter titles are reiterated, often in catalogue fashion, in the text proper. By an examination of these titles and passages from the text, we are able to gather that our book contains no such false, pedantic and valueless scribblings as are to be found in genres suggested by these chapter titles, but that it is the true, the unique, and above all the secret *text* or *breviary* designed for our perfection, and which it is the purpose of this group of convivial scholars, mathematicians, scientists, learned doctors and theologians to compose.

Briefly, the satirical intentions are announced by the chapter titles and again the generalized nature of human folly is hinted at, while clues as to the style of *Le Moyen de Parvenir* are also provided by them.

Turning, then, to the style of *Le Moyen de Parvenir* properly speaking, we find that by applying to *Le Moyen de Parvenir* the categories of the baroque enumerated by Imbrie Buffum in his *Studies in Baroque from Montaigne to Rotrou* we are able to conclude that our book is unquestionably of baroque style, and, more important to our study of world view, of baroque inspiration or mentality. By pushing these considerations a little further, we find that we are in the presence not only of a piece of baroque literature, but more precisely one which is oriented toward the *baroque satyrique* (the erotic, macabre and grotesque) and, even, toward the less restrictive dimension of satirical baroque (all-engulfing satire of human institutions in the baroque style).

The style, then — baroque, eruptive, restless — bears out the themes and tendencies of the novel and reflects rather clearly the world view of Béroalde. Following the procedure of Buffum we may first examine *Le Moyen de Parvenir* to discover leading statements by Béroalde on his style, but because the assumed moral purpose of the book — to satirize the clergy and, more generally, to show the sage to be the fool in this universal satire — is clear in other facets of our study, we may dispense with this category of Buffum in our own considerations on the style. However, we may readily locate, under style, the presence of emphasis and exaggeration, and, substituting the related categories of the macabre and the realistic for horror and incarnation, easily isolate these phenomena also. Likewise, in the categories of theatricality and illusion, of contrast and surprise, of movement and metamorphosis, *Le Moyen de Parvenir* will not be found wanting. Finally, we may examine *Le Moyen de Parvenir* for its organic unity, and see whether it advocates an acceptance of life. Indeed, we discover by the application of each of these categories that *Le Moyen de Parvenir* qualifies for the title of baroque, and, at times, a superabundance of some category, or else certain additional characteristics, lead us to the further classifications just mentioned of *baroque satyrique* and *baroque satirique.*

More specifically, from the comments of the author on his own style, we are permitted to say that the book is baroque, for the very essence of these comments betrays a refusal to compose. The author almost boasts of the pellmell character of his writing, and confesses that the novel is kaleidoscopic.

Furthermore, emphasis and exaggeration are abundantly

manifest in the style and tone of *Le Moyen de Parvenir,* these effects being gained especially through alliteration, assonance, rhyming, puns, repetition, recurrent vocabulary, a great amount of hyperbole, long words, and catalogues. Although these devices are common to almost any piece of baroque literature, it should be noted that here they are also part and parcel of the comic vein proper to good satire.

We find, however, that for Buffum's category of horror and incarnation it is convenient to substitute two not unrelated phenomena, the macabre and efforts toward realism. In so doing, one may ascertain that the macabre or grotesque, plus the far-reaching sensuality of *Le Moyen de Parvenir* give to it the special classification of *baroque satyrique.* Indeed, the whole of the book seems to be permeated with the atmosphere of a battle between Carnival and Lent, or, even more, of a Dance of Death, and to be otherworldly in tone. Yet there are decided efforts toward realism, especially in the speech, which provide a marked contrast with the otherworldly or grotesque exaggerations. Among these efforts toward realism, we can uncover devices such as the portrayal of laughter, speech tics, exclamatory expressions, oaths and interjections, interruption of one interlocutor by another, the claims of the speakers to truth, verbal slips, and so forth, all contributing to a markedly naturalistic kind of ambience.

When we turn to the category of theatricality and illusion, we again find *Le Moyen de Parvenir* qualifying. First of all, we perceive that the dialogue form itself gives to the novel a certain amount of theatricality. But leaving this aside, we can collect from the work innumerable aphorisms or sententia, which, it will be remembered, played a substantial role in the dramatic rhetoric of the period. Moreover, asides (in which, incidentally, the misogynistic slant for the work is reflected), rapid, choppy dialogue akin to stichomythia, and actual references to the theater all serve to bring out the theatricality involved in the author's world outlook. Illusion, on the other hand, is achieved through prisms, both major and minor. Among the major prisms we have genre within genre, character within character, and time upheavals which give to the novel a timeless quality and a dream-like, unreal atmosphere. For minor prisms we may count the optical illusion effected by reference to eyeglasses, and we may also include the frequent reference to game. But what is important is that both the major and the minor prismatic features of the novel contribute to an over-all hallucinatory effect. Thus theatricality and illusion are distinctly present in *Le Moyen de Parvenir*.

In the category of contrast and surprise we may see that the use of antithesis is an integral part of Béroalde's style, as of his world view. There is in *Le Moyen de Parvenir* a self-conscious use of paradox which for the baroque mind constitutes a means of arriving at truth. Moreover, these antitheses reflect the principal themes of the novel. They bear out the time motifs and state the quarrel of the ancients and the moderns. They are used for theological satire, to pinpoint the battle of the sexes (in which the misogynous currents of the novel are again felt) and, furthermore, they are used for comic effects. While surprise issues from this constant use of antithesis, an even more important source of surprise lies in the simultaneous shock and amusement emanating from the book's erotic proclivities.

When we consider the category of movement and metamorphosis we cannot help but observe above all the animated nature of the banquet scene itself. We have before us a crowded canvas, teeming and swarming with life. In addition, the sexuality of thc novel gives it impetus. Stylistically, verbs seem to be predominant, and, among the verbs, those showing motion are in the ascendancy. Frequent references to the dance properly speaking, not to mention the *Danse Macabre,* give the illusion of perpetual motion, while the entire book is characterized by a considerable mental agitation. When we turn from motion to change, we can without difficulty find true metamorphoses in *Le Moyen de Parvenir,* nor should we be surprised to discover that these involve, above all, such things as the metamorphosis of a man into a cuckold, or sexual metamorphoses of one kind or another. We note with special interest here that the androgyne motif is more than once alluded to in our novel, and, in fact, we have in *Le Moyen de Parvenir* the story of the androgyne's creation told by Sapho. But we should above all keep in mind that death in itself is a kind of transformation in the eyes of the author and that the very title of the work implies transformation or change. We need not look further than this for evidence in *Le Moyen de Parvenir* of movement and metamorphosis.

What, finally, constitutes the organic unity of *Le Moyen de Parvenir,* and does its author teach the acceptance of life?

We have seen that the ligatures provided by the chapter titles provide a kind of continuity to the book. We can further see that a certain unifying force comes from the recurrent vocabulary and from recurrent themes such as time, mutability, death, the paradoxes of the ancients and moderns, etc. But the essential unity of *Le Moyen de Parvenir* arises from its doctrine of laughter and its implicit acceptance of life. True, the work attacks and attacks trenchantly human vice and folly, but, nevertheless, it appears to preach the value of laughter and of good-natured acceptance of life. Béroalde does not seek to reform, except, perhaps, through ridicule. Laughter, on the other hand, is frequently alluded to; its importance, its therapeutic values are stated. Indeed, the doctrine of laughter explains away many complex phenomena of form and content in *Le Moyen de Parvenir.*

What, then, remains to be said of *Le Moyen de Parvenir?* In point of fact, a great deal. In this study I have hoped only to establish the baroque slant of the world view therein contained, thus laying the groundwork for serious consideration of a neglected masterpiece. In so doing, I have attempted to point out its artistic merits and to restore it to its rightful domain as baroque satire, a special genre which has not to my knowledge been previously delineated. A great deal of work remains to be done on the novel. As I have said, it would profit greatly from a careful modern edition. In addition, many obscurities of text exist, some of which we may never come to understand, given the intentionally hermetic nature of the book which I have dwelt upon at various points in the course of this exposé. Nevertheless, some of these problems, as well as the identity of some of the interlocutors could be clarified. Furthermore, an interesting case might be made for the contributions of New Greek Comedy, of Latin comedy, of the French farce and of the *commedia dell'arte* to *Le Moyen de Parvenir.* Or, again, the comic vein of the novel might be plumbed for what it has in common with other baroque satire and with the early seventeenth century burlesque genre. One might also make a more complete study of the sources of *Le Moyen de Parvenir* than is Reiche's, avoiding, in the process, a mere pointing out of analogies. Surely a not unimportant contribution to the knowledge of *Le Moyen de Parvenir* would be an investigation into its influence on subsequent comedy and satire, especially on nonsense literature, and even on *livres de haute graisse.* Its influence on Balzac's *Contes drolatiques,* for example, is not to be challenged. Can profit come from a juxtaposition of Béroalde the philosopher-mathematician to Béroalde the writer of nonsense literature? Of this I am not sure, but similar work has been done on Charles Lutwidge Dodgson (Lewis Carroll). Furthermore, some study of Béroalde's other works remains to be done, especially as these works might relate to *Le Moyen de Parvenir.* There is probably, for instance, some relationship between *Le Palais des Curieux* and *Le Moyen de Parvenir.* Also, a study of the genesis of Béroalde's *Idée de la République* and its connections with other Renaissance works on the Republic might prove rewarding. *Le Moyen de Parvenir* might also be studied for its connections with baroque satirical graphic art, with Bonaventure Des Periers' *Cymbalum Mundi,* with Erasmus' *Praise of Folly,* with *La Satyre Ménippée,* with Bouchet's *Les Serées,* etc.

Among the host of studies that are still to be made, I view as of paramount importance the presentation of a well-annotated critical edition of *Le Moyen de Parvenir,* with as complete identification of the innumerable references as possible, and including a comparative study of extant editions in the degree that they prove themselves useful and available. Perhaps of some importance, too, would be the re-publication of the best and most pertinent of Béroalde's other works, for example *Les Soupirs amoureux* [1], *les Appréhensions Spirituelles, l'Idée de la République, Le Palais des Curieux,* etc. This done, the scientific and philosophical discourses as well as the admirable poetry of this all-but-forgotten author might be enjoyed, re-evaluated and brought into focus with their age and the Classical age which is to follow shortly the creation of *Le Moyen de Parvenir.*

Be that as it may, there is still much to be learned about *Le Moyen de Parvenir,* and it is truly unlikely that by exploring the novel thoroughly we run the risk of seeing the French language abolished, as the author facetiously warns us when he says: « ...c'est que ce liure venant à estre gousté, sauouré & digeré, on taschera d'abolir le François & oster de la bouche du peuple ce beau langage, de crainte que ces bonnes & meilleures doctrines ne viennent à tomber entre les mains du populaire,

1. See my study entitled « Bérolde de Verville's *Stances de la Mort* and *Soupirs amoureux :* specimens of baroque poetry » in *Nottingham french Studies,* Volume IX, No. 2 (October, 1970), pp. 55-70.

qui aduenant tel cas feroit aussi aisement la pierre philosophale que les doctes... » (I, 276). Rather, we can only come to a richer appreciation of this masterpiece of baroque literature which, while pointing out the vanity of human nature and human existence (I, 131), while sardonically attacking the vices of all facets of human society, falls back upon the themes of time, mutability and death, always for the primary purpose of laughter. All in all, after this long discussion of the topographical and textual features of *Le Moyen de Parvenir* which spell out the world view of Béroalde de Verville, we can but say in conclusion, « Il est bon homme, il taxe les vices d'vne belle façon » (II, 260).

Appendix A

LE PALLEMAIL[1]

Nous sommes trois passants qui demandons logis,
Au moins pour une nuit, chez vous mesdemoiselles,
Et quand nous nous serons quelque peu rafraîchis,
Du lieu d'où nous venons vous dirons des nouvelles.

Nous venons d'un pays où nous avons appris
Du jeu du Pallemail l'exercice agréable,
Dans les beaux promenoirs de la belle Cypris,
Environnés de fleurs et tout couvers de sable.

Logez-nous s'il vous plaît; nous vous dirons les lois
Qu'on pratique en ce jeu, l'allée et la manière
Comme le mail doit être, et de quel roide bois
La boule peut durer plus longuement entière.

L'allée doit avoir une juste longueur,
Des bords aux deux côtés, pour garder que la boule
Ne se glisse dehors poussée de roideur;
Mais prenne le milieu cependant qu'elle roule.

Qu'elle soit ferme et sèche et dressée unîment;
Car si elle était molle elle serait fâcheuse,
On n'y pourrait mener la boule plaisamment,
Telle incommodité la rendrait ennuyeuse.

Que les bords soient tondus; car si ils s'allongeaient
Lorsque la boule court, ils lui nuiraient à tendre
Au chemin du milieu et si la retiendraient
Si bien qu'on ne pourrait aisément la reprendre.

1. V.-L. Saulnier, *Anthologie poétique de Béoralde de Verville* (Paris, 1945), pp. 125-128.

Il faut pour bien jouer avoir un mail bien fait,
Bien ferme par devant, bien juste à l'emmanchure,
Autrement il serait à défaire sujet
Et donner bien souvent des coups à l'aventure.

Il le faut assez gros et non point trop aussi,
Avant le manche fort et roide de nature,
Le trop long n'est pas bon, ni le trop raccourci;
Mais toujours le moyen fait frapper de mesure.

Pour la boule, il faut prendre un bois ni sec ni vert.
De la racine vive il faut qu'on le choisisse
Et le faire durcir en quelque lieu couvert
Pour être fort et ferme et en tirer service.

Quand on sera fourni de tout également,
D'un mail bien amanché, d'une boule bien forte,
Il faudra se dresser pour frapper justement
Et débuter du haut d'une petite motte.

Si on ne frappe droit, on ne fait guère bien,
Et si l'on sort dehors on a beaucoup de peine
A se remettre en jeu, et si ne fait-on rien
Après qu'on est sorti, si sur l'herbe on se traîne.

Il se faut en touchant tenir ferme en son lieu
Et pousser roide et droit d'une force animée.
En s'exerçant toujours de prendre le milieu
Pour faire sans tourment en moins de coups l'allée.

Quand on a fait devoir de tirer de grands coups,
Il faut prendre la boule en la lève creusée
Et visant à l'archet la mettre droit dessous,
Car on n'achève point qu'elle n'y soit passée.

C'est le plus grand plaisir que, jouant deux à deux,
Joindre le gentilhomme avec la damoiselle;
Mais faut que l'homme soit si adroit et heureux
Que donnant avantage il soit aussi fort qu'elle.

Et faut pour cet effet qu'elle pousse souvent
Conduisant à l'égal toujours son avantage;

Toutefois il est bon qu'elle n'ait le devant
S'elle veut du plaisir à l'heure du passage.

Qui veut à ce beau jeu jouer à son désir
Ne hante lieux publics, mais les maisons honnêtes :
Aux lieux par trop communs n'y a pas grand plaisir;
Car on est empêché des passants ou des bêtes.

Nous vous avons tout dit, s'il vous plaît essayer
Ce que nous en savons, prêtez-nous vos allées,
Nous fournirons du reste, et nous verrez frapper
Assez dispostement dix ou douze passées.

Et cependant sachez qu'ainsi que de vos mains
Le mail chasse à son but cette boule arrondie,
Aussi vos volontés forcent à leurs destins
Les plus heureux désirs qu'ayons en cette vie.

Et vous y exerçant voyez comme en rondeur
La boule se tournant est la certaine image
De cette affection dont l'éternelle ardeur
Fait que nous vous ayons toujours dans le courage.

APPENDIX B

LE MAY[1]

Maintenant que l'Amour renaît heureusement
Et qu'à ce beau printemps il commande qu'on plante
D'un Mai long et dressé la désirable plante
Il faut suivre l'arrêt de son commandement.

J'ai un Mai long et gros et fort également,
Poussant devers le haut une verdeur plaisante,
Qui frisonne sa cime en tout temps verdoyante
Et qui se peut planter assez facilement.

Ma dame, permettez que l'on m'ouvre la porte,
Et je le planterai sur la petite motte
Qui de votre maison remarque le milieu;

Je le mettrai tout droit dessous votre croisée
Où en petits frisons la terre relevée
Fait l'endroit plus plaisant qui soit en tout le lieu.

1. V.-L. Saulnier, *Anthologie poétique de Béroalde de Verville* (Paris, 1945), p. 131.

Appendix C

L'ALCHEMISTE [1]

On dit qu'en ce pays les dames ont envie
D'entendre les secrets de la philosophie,
Et pourtant moi je veux leur être serviteur,
Pour ce que, les sachant, des hommes n'ai que faire,
Aux dames seulement je veux dire l'affaire,
Leur montrant par effet de l'œuvre la douceur.

En infinis endroits la matière peut être
Qu'il faut diligemment en facultés connaître;
Car animale elle est végétant doucement;
Aussi pour subsister sa force est métallique,
Par quoi triple par soi, sa vertu harmonique
Fait une liaison d'un juste assemblement.

Cette matière encore est et mâle et femelle
Et si n'est rien des deux; mais comme naturelle
Aux deux sexes elle est, avecques son vaisseau.
Son alembic aussi est en une partie,
Sa curcurbite en l'autre et le cyment qui lie,
Pour rien n'évaporer, par le col, le vaisseau.

Pour la bien préparer, par une flamme douce
Naturelle de soi il faut qu'elle se pousse,
Les pareils naturels il faut conjoindre ensemble
Par un lien d'amour qui les choses assemble
De nature excitant le formel mouvement.

Il n'en faut rien ôter de peur de la détruire,
Mais faut pour s'en aider par un bons sens l'élire

1. V.-L. Saulnier, *Anthologie poétique de Béroalde de Verville* (Paris, 1945), pp. 128-131.

Et la mûrir en soi sans en rien altérer,
Si ce n'est pour donner vertu à sa substance,
Qui dans soi tient de soi, par égale balance
Ce qui lui faut par elle en soi-même ajouter.

Qu'elle soit animale, il est très-nécessaire
Même de l'animal pour à l'animal plaire,
Qu'elle soit végétable il faut pour la nourrir,
Et métallique aussi, afin que sa durée
Ne puisse en agissant être tôt terminée;
Si elle n'a ces trois, on ne s'en peut servir,

Ce qu'elle a dedans soi qui toujours se végète
Et la force qui rend notre essence parfaite
Et l'esprit de ce corps qui la matière tient,
Cette matière en nous est liée et cachée,
Mais par une sensible elle en est arrachée
Et en se végétant hors du corps l'esprit vient.

Elle n'est pour néant d'animale nature
Car ainsi que vivante en soi-même elle endure
Et montre ses effets par agitation,
Ainsi que le métal elle est ferme et conjointe
Et quand de son semblable elle se sent atteinte
Elle affermit son tout par son émotion.

A part elle se tient existant à part elle,
Mais seule et séparée elle n'est naturelle
Comme quand elle est une en sa conjonction,
Car adonc le secret de nature se montre
Et par leur naturel qui force leur rencontre
Se fait réverbérant la dissolution.

On joint premièrement les qualités ensemble
Et l'esprit attractif également assemble
Pour ne faire qu'un seul ce qui se séparait :
Lors un feu naturel qui la matière excite
Par un doux mouvement les qualités incite
Pour allier en un ce qui se désirait.

Lors pour les calciner les corps on rarifie
Et mettant au plus chaud la plus douce partie

On les fait sublimer au naturel vaisseau;
Puis naturalisant tandis qu'on réverbère
Par inclination l'esprit vient à s'extraire
Duquel au long du filtre il faut distiller l'eau.

Ce faisant il convient resserrer les parties,
Qui en se sublimant se rendraient affaiblies,
Si on ne les pressait en la conjonction,
Qui en les unissant doucement les enflamme
Tant que dessous l'effet de sa dernière flamme
Soit connu le plaisir de la projection.

Pour ces œuvres divers ne faut tant d'artifice
Que pense le commun, mais fortune propice
A ceux qui ont désir d'un tel bien en leurs jours,
Ne faut plusieurs vaisseaux, fourneaux, distillatoires,
Retortes, alembics, enfers, sublimatoires,
Charbon, ni marc, ni bois, mais le doux feu d'amours.

C'est assez, voilà tout, hormis l'expérience;
Mais si par ces raisons on ne sait la science,
Et que quelqu'une veuille en savoir jusqu'au bout,
Lui plaise que traitions ensemble la matière,
Avec un seul vaisseau nous ferons l'œuvre entière
Et par un instrument nous parferons le tout.

SELECTED BIBLIOGRAPHY

ADAM (Antoine). — *Histoire de la littérature française au XVIIe siècle : L'époque de Louis XIII*. Paris : Domat Monchrestien, 1948.

ATHENAEUS. — *The Deipnosophists*, ed. E. Capps, *et al.*, trans. Charles Burton Gulick. 7 vols. London: William Heinemann, Ltd., 1927.

AUERBACH (Erich). — *Mimesis, the Representation of Reality in Western Literature.* New York: Doubleday, 1957.

BACON (Francis). — *Essays, Advancement of Learning, New Atlantis, and Other Pieces*, ed. Richard Foster Jones. New York: Odyssey, 1937.

BALL (George H). — « A Study of Syntax in the *Moyen de Parvenir* ». Unpublished Ph. D. dissertation, The University of California, Berkley, 1938-39.

BALZAC (Honoré de). — *Œuvres complètes*, éd. Marcel Bouteron and Henri Longnon. Vols XXXVI and XXXVII. Paris : Louis Conard, 1932.

— *Les Contes drolatiques, colligez ez abbayes de Touraine et mis en lumière par le Sieur de Balzac.* 2 vols. Paris : Calmann-Lévy, n.d.

BAR (Francis). — *Le Genre burlesque en France au XVIIe siècle.* Paris : Editions d'Artrey, 1960.

BAUDELAIRE (Charles). — *Les Fleurs du Mal*, éd. Yves-Gérard Le Dantec. Paris : Cluny, 1941.

BAYLE (Pierre). *Dictionnaire historique et critique*, 5e éd. Vol. I, pp. 538-9. Amsterdam, 1740.

BÉDIER (Joseph), HAZARD (Paul), MARTINO (Pierre). — *Littérature française.* 2 vols. Paris : Larousse, 1948-49.

BEIJER (Agne). — *Recueil de plusieurs fragments des premières Comédies Italiennes qui ont esté representées en France sous le règne de Henry III.* Paris : Duchartre et Van Buggenhoudt, 1928.

BÉROALDE DE VERVILLE (François). — *Anthologie poétique de Béroalde de Verville*, éd. V.-L. Saulnier. Paris : Hamont, 1945.

— *Le Moyen de Parvenir.* 3 vols. Paris : Delarue, n.d.

— *Le Moyen de Parvenir*, éd. Jean Fort. Paris : Jean Fort, 1921.

— *Le Moyen de Parvenir.* Paris : Garnier, n.d.

— *Le Moyen de Parvenir, œuvre contenant la raison de ce qui a été, est et sera avec démonstration certaine selon la rencontre des effets de la vertu*, éd. Paul Jacob [Paul Lacroix]. Paris : Charpentier, 1889.

— *Le Moyen de Parvenir*, éd. Charles Royer, 2 vols. Paris : Lemerre, 1896.

— *Les Soupirs amoureux, L'Idée de la République, Dialogue de la Vertu*. Paris : Timothée Iouan, 1584.

— *Fantastic Tales or the way to attain — a book full of Pantagruelism*, trans. Arthur Machen. London: Carbonnek [?], 1923.

BLAVIGNAC. — *Le Moyen de Parvenir, étude historique et littéraire*. Genève : Chanard, 1872.

BOASE (Alan M.). — « Then Malherbe Came », *The Criterion*, X (October 1930 - July 1931), pp. 287-306.

BOUCHET (Guillaume). — *Les Serées*, éd. C.-E. Roybet. Paris : Lemerre, 1888.

BOURDIGNÉ (Charles de). — *La Légende joyeuse ou faitz et dictz de Pierre Taifeu, escolier d'Angers*. Paris : Léon Wilhem, 1883.

BUFFUM (Imbrie). — *Agrippa d'Aubigné's « Les Tragiques »*. New Haven: Yale University Press, 1951.

— « The Recognition of the Baroque », *L'Esprit Créateur*, I, 2 (Summer, 1961), pp. 51-55.

— *Studies in the Baroque from Montaigne to Rotrou*. New Haven: Yale University Press, 1957.

Cambridge History of English Literature, ed. A. W. Ward and A. R. Waller. Vol. IV, pp. 292-298. New York: Putnam, 1910.

CHAMPION. — Ed. « Compte rendu », *Revue d'Histoire littéraire de la France*, 31e année (1924), p. 141.

CHAUCER (Geoffrey). — *Complete Works*, ed. F. N. Robinson. New York: Houghton-Mifflin Co., 1933.

CIORANESCO (Alexandre) and SAULNIER (V.-L.). — *Bibliographie de la littérature française du seizième siècle*. Paris : Klincksieck, 1959.

CLOUZOT Henri. — « Béroalde de Verville et la Querelle de 'l'Abstinent', *Revue du Seizième Siècle*, II (1914). Paris : Champion, pp. 322-330.

— « La Date du Moyen de Parvenir », *Revue des Etudes Rabelésiennes*, IX (1911), pp. 141-143.

— « La Sériculture dans Béroalde de Verville », *Revue du Seizième Siècle*, III (1915). Paris : Champion, pp. 281-285.

CONNOLLY (Thomas E.). — *The Personal Library of James Joyce*. Vol. XXII, No. 1 (April, 1955). Buffalo: The University of Buffalo.

CORNEILLE (Pierre). — *Le Cid*. Paris : Larousse, 1941.

COTGRAVE (Randle). — *A Dictionarie of the French and English Tongues*, First Edition. London, 1611. Reprinted Columbia: University of South Carolina Press, 1950.

COUGNY (Edmond). — *Etudes historiques sur le XVIe siècle, théories politiques, Béroalde de Verville, L'Idée de la République — Le Moyen de Parvenir*. (Extrait du Douzième Volume des Mémoires de la Société des Sciences Morales, Lettres et Arts de Seine-et-Oise). Paris : Ernest Thorin, 1880.

CROLL (Morris W.). — « The Baroque Style in Prose », *Studies in English Philology, a miscellany in Honor of Frederick Klaeber* (1929). Minneapolis: University of Minnesota Press, pp. 427-456.

CYRANO DE BERGERAC. — *Lettres - Théâtre : Le Pédant joué - La Mort d'Agrippine - Voyage dans la lune - Histoire des états du soleil,* éd. Charles Simond. Paris : Louis-Michaud, n.d.

The Dance of Death. Paris: Guyot Marchand, 1490. Reprinted Washington, D. C.: Library of Congress, August, 1945.

Danza de la Muerte. Barcelona : Tipografia « L'Avenç », 1547.

DES PERIERS (Bonaventure). — *Contes ou Nouvelles Récréations et joyeux devis suivis du Cymbalum Mundi,* éd. P.-L. Jacob [Paul Lacroix]. Paris : Garnier, 1872.

— *Cymbalum Mundi ou Dialogues satyriques sur differens sujets.* Amsterdam : Prosper Marchand, 1732.

DU BELLAY (Joachim). — *Œuvres choisies.* Paris : Larousse, 1934.

DUCKWORTH (George E). — *The Complete Roman Drama.* 2 vols. *New York:* Random House, 1942.

DUKAS (Jules). — *Etude bibliographique et littéraire sur le Satyricon de Jean Barclay.* Paris : Techener, 1880.

ERASMUS (Desiderius). — *The Praise of Folly,* trans. John Wilson. Ann Arbor: University of Michigan Press, 1958.

FLAUBERT (Gustave). — *Madame Bovary.* Paris : Charpentier, 1929.

FOURNIER (Edouard). — *Le Théâtre français au XVI*[e] *et au XVII*[e] *siècle, ou Choix des comédies les plus curieuses avant Molière.* Paris : Laplace, Sanchez et Cie, n.d.

FURETIÈRE (Antoine). — *Le Roman bourgeois.* Paris : Larousse, 1941.

GIDE (André). — *Le Retour de l'Enfant prodigue, précédé de cinq autres traités : Le Traité du Narcisse, La Tentative amoureuse, El Hadj, Philoctète, Bethsabé.* Paris : Gallimard, 1948.

HAAG (Eugène et Émile). — *La France protestante.* Vol. II. Paris : Sandoz, 1879.

HATZFELD (Helmut). — « A Clarification of the Baroque Problem in the Romance Literatures », *Comparative Literature,* I (1949), pp. 113-139.

HEBEL (J. William) and HOYT (H. Hudson). — *Poetry of the English Renaissance.* New York: F. S. Crofts and Co., 1941.

HIGHET (Gilbert). — *The Classical Tradition.* New York: Oxford University Press, 1949.

HOLBEIN. — *Dance of Death.* New York: The Sylvan Press, 1947.

HOBBES (Thomas). — *Leviathan. New York:* Dutton and Co., 1950.

HUIZINGA (Johan). — *The Waning of the Middle Ages.* New York: Anchor (Doubleday), 1954.

JOYCE (James). — *Finnegan's Wake.* New York: The Viking Press, 1939.

LA FAYETTE (Mme DE). — *La Princesse de Clèves.* Paris : Larousse, 1941.
LA FONTAINE (Jean DE). — *Œuvres diverses.* 2 vols. Paris : Gallimard, 1948.
LANGLOIS (E.-H.). — *Essai historique, philosophique et pittoresque sur les Danses des Morts.* 2 vols. Rouen : Lebrument, 1852.
LEWIS (Wyndham). — *Time and the Western Man.* Boston: Beacon Press, 1957.
LIVINGSTON (Charles H.). — « The *Heptaméron des Nouvelles* of Marguerite de Navarre: A Study of Nouvelles 28, 34, 52 and 62 », *Romanic Review,* XIV (April-September, 1923), pp. 97-118.
LUCAS (Henry S.). — *The Renaissance and the Reformation.* New York: Harper and Brothers, 1934.
LUCIAN. — *Satirical Sketches,* trans. Paul Turner. Baltimore: Penguin Classics, 1961.
LUCIAN of SAMOSATA. — *Works,* trans. H. W. Fowler and F. G. Fowler. 4 vols. Oxford: Clarendon Press, 1905.

MAULNIER (Thierry). — « Les Derniers Renaissants », *La Revue Universelle,* n° 11 (10 juin 1941), pp. 738-748; n° 12 (25 juin 1941), pp. 824-831; n° 13 (10 juillet 1941), pp. 34-35; n° 15 (10 août 1941), pp. 187-193; n° 17 (10 septembre 1941), pp. 325-330.
MILLER (Henry). — *Tropic of Cancer.* Paris: The Obelisk Press, 1959.
— *Tropic of Capricorn.* Paris: The Obelisk Press, 1957.
MOLIÈRE (J.-B.-P.). — *Œuvres complètes.* Vol. III. Paris : Gallimard, 1956.
MOURGUES (Odette DE). — *Metaphysical, Baroque and Précieux Poetry.* Oxford: Clarendon Press, 1953.

NAVARRE (Marguerite DE). — *L'Heptaméron,* éd. Michel François. Paris : Garnier, 1942.
NICERON (R.-P.). — *Mémoires pour servir à l'histoire des Hommes illustres dans la république des lettres.* Vol. XXXIV. Paris : Chez Briasson, 1736.

PALLISTER (Janis L). — « Béroalde de Verville, *Stances de la Mort* and *Soupirs amoureux :* specimens of baroque poetry », *Nottingham French Studies,* Volume IX, n°. 2 (october 1970), pp. 55-70.

PASSERAT (Jean). — *Les Poésies françaises,* éd. Prosper Blanchemain. 2 vols. Paris : Lemerre, 1880.
PLATTARD (Jean). — *La Renaissance des lettres en France.* Paris : Colin, 1925.
POCHMANN (Henry August) and ALLEN (G. W.). — *Masters of American Literature.* New York: Macmillan, 1949.
PORTER, LAMBERT (C.). — *La Fatrasie et le fatras.* Genève : Droz, 1960.

RABELAIS (François). — *Œuvres,* éd. Louis Moland and Henri Clouzot. 2 vols. Paris : Garnier, 1950.
RACINE (Jean). — *Andromaque.* Paris : Larousse, 1941.
— *Œuvres complètes.* Vol. I. Paris : Gallimard, 1951.
Le Recueil Trepperel, éd. E. Droz and H. Lewicka. Genève : Droz, 1961.

RÉGNIER (Mathurin). — Paris : Larousse, 1935.
REICHE (Herbert). — *Le Moyen de parvenir von Béroalde de Verville mit besonderer Berücksichtigung der Quellen-und Verfasserfrage.* Coburg : A. Rossteutscher, 1913.
REYNIER (Gustave). — *Le Roman réaliste au XVII*[e] *siècle.* Paris : Hachette, 1914.
— *Le Roman sentimental avant l'Astrée.* Paris : Collin, 1908.
ROUSSET (Jean). — *La Littérature de l'âge baroque en France.* Paris : Corti, 1954.

SAINÉAN (L.). — « Mélanges du XVIe siècle », *Revue du Seizième Siècle,* III (1915), pp. 18-71.
— *Problèmes littéraires du seizième siècle.* Paris : Boccard, 1927.
La Satire Ménippée, éd. Paul Demey. London : Swan Sonnenschein and Co., Ltd., 1911.
SAULNIER (V.-L.). — Éd. *Anthologie poétique de Béroalde de Verville.* Paris : Hamont, 1945.
— « Etude sur Béroalde de Verville », *Revue d'Humanisme et Renaissance,* V (1944), pp. 209-326.
SCARRON (Paul). — *Le Roman comique.* Paris : Larousse, 1941.
SCHNEEGANS (Heinrich). — *Geschicte der Grotesken Satire.* Strassburg : Karl J. Trübner, 1894.
SCHWARTZ (I. A.). — *The Commedia dell'arte and its influence on French Comedy in the Seventeenth Century.* Paris: H. Samuel, 1933.
SHAKESPEARE (William). — *The Complete Works,* ed. G. B. Harrison. New York: Harcourt, Brace and Company, 1948.
SPIVACK (Charlotte K.). — « Tragedy and Comedy: A Metaphysical Wedding », *Bucknell Review,* IX, 3 (December, 1960), pp. 212-223.
SPONDE (Jean DE). — *Poésies,* éd. Alan Boase. Genève : Cailler, 1949.
[STERNE (Laurence)]. — *A Facsimile Reproduction of a Unique Catalogue of Laurence Sterne's Library.* New York: E. H. Wells and Co., Inc., 1930.
STERNE (Laurence). — *The Life and Opinions of Tristram Shandy, Gent.,* ed. Samuel H. Monk. New York: Rinehart and Company, 1950.
— *A Sentimental Journey through France and Italy.* New York: Brentano's, n.d.
SYPHER (Wylie). — *Four Stages of Renaissance Style.* New York: Doubleday, 1956.

TILLEY (Arthur). — *Studies in the French Renaissance.* Cambridge University Press, 1922.

UBEDA (Francisco López DE). — *La Pícara Justina,* ed. Julio Puyol. 3 vols. Madrid: Sociedad de bibliofilos madrileños, 1912.

VALBUENA Y PRAT (Angel). — *La novela picaresca española.* Madrid : Aguilar, 1946.
VIGNEULLES (Philippe DE). — *Les Cent Nouvelles Nouvelles de...,* éd. Charles Livingston. Paris : Edouard Champion, 1924.

VIRET (Pierre). — *Satyres chrestiênes de la cuisine papale.* Conrad Badius, 1540. Reprinted Genève : Jules-Guillaume Fick, 1857.

VIRGIL. — *The Æneid,* trans. H. Rushton Fairclough. Vol. II. London: Heinemann, 1954.

— *The Æneid,* trans. W. F. Jackson Knight. Baltimore: The Penguin Classics, 1956.

VIOLLET LE DUC (M.). — *Ancien théâtre françois ou collection des ouvrages dramatiques les plus remarquables depuis les mystères jusqu'à Corneille.* Vol. I. Paris : Jannet, 1854.

WARREN (Florence). — *The Dance of Death.* London: Oxford University Press, 1931.

WÖLFFLIN (Heinrich). — *Principles of Art History.* New York: Dover Publications, Inc., 1932.

CONTENTS

IMPRIMERIE A. BONTEMPS

LIMOGES (FRANCE)

Dépôt légal : 1er trimestre 1971